"Dr. Starr has brilliantly articulated why we need a spiritually driven psychology to find the genuine Self. This remarkable book is a synthesis of Western and Eastern thought, taking us though the labyrinth of counseling, psychotherapy, and self help. *Escape Your Own Prison* is a must-read if one is ever to attain inner peace in this anxious, Ego-driven world of materialism." —**Hugh Colmer**, cofounder, Windham Retreat Center, managing director of the Crosscircle Group

"Bernard Starr is a modern Diogenes, who is lighting the way for a nation of aging boomers toward a more honest and effective understanding of themselves. His pathway bridges the analytical framework of psychology with the seeker's desire for a richer sense of life's meaning. In *Escape Your Own Prison* he illuminates the darker reaches of our egos and shows how we can free ourselves from the confines of our limited perceptions of who we are." —**Paul Kleyman**, editor, *Aging Today*, American Society on Aging

"This book is not good news for traditional psychotherapists, but for those of us caught between the demands of the ego and the desire for transcendence, it's a way out and a way up. Thank you Dr. Starr." —**Emily Squires**, cofounder of the Coalition for One Voice, award-winning director and documentary filmmaker

"Beyond the realm of faith and psychology, Dr. Starr's *Escape Your Own Prison* takes the reader on a radical inner journey which challenges preconceived notions about true spiritual consciousness. It offers a refreshing new approach to break free from the illusory prison of the ego and a roadmap to awakening to a powerful state of being with lightening rod focus and limitless potential." —**Judy Martin**, founder of Work/LifeMonitor.com, formerly of American Public Media's Marketplace Morning Report

# Escape Your Own Prison

# Escape Your Own Prison

*Why We Need Spirituality* and *Psychology*
*to be Truly Free*

Bernard Starr

ROWMAN & LITTLEFIELD PUBLISHERS, INC.
Lanham • Boulder • New York • Toronto • Plymouth, UK

ROWMAN & LITTLEFIELD PUBLISHERS, INC.

Published in the United States of America
by Rowman & Littlefield Publishers, Inc.
A wholly owned subsidary of The Rowman & Littlefield Publishing Group, Inc.
4501 Forbes Boulevard, Suite 200, Lanham, Maryland 20706
www.rowmanlittlefield.com

Estover Road
Plymouth PL6 7PY
United Kingdom

British Library Cataloguing in Publication Information Available

**Library of Congress Cataloging-in-Publication Data:**
Starr, Bernard D.
  Escape your own prison : why we need spirituality and psychology to be truly free /
Bernard Starr.
     p. cm.
  ISBN-13: 978-0-7425-5839-7 (pbk. : alk. paper)
  ISBN-10: 0-7425-5839-8 (pbk. : alk. paper)
  1. Spirituality. 2. Psychology, Religious. I. Title.
  BL624.S7265 2007
  204'.4—dc22                                        2007016789

Printed in the United States of America

⊗™ The paper used in this publication meets the minimum requirements of
American National Standard for Information Sciences—Permanence of Paper
for Printed Library Materials, ANSI/NISO Z39.48-1992.

# Contents

# Preface

As I sat cross-legged in the sweltering South Indian heat in the Ashram of Swami Sathya Sai Baba, one of the great sages of India, my mind raced through the spiritual quest that brought me to Putaparthi in this remote part of rural southern India.

It all began over twenty years ago when my doubts about traditional psychology accelerated. I could no longer ignore the gnawing sense that the very principles and techniques that I taught, practiced, and experienced missed the main mark of fundamental change. Yes, traditional approaches to psychological healing were often helpful but were rarely, if ever, transformational.

When I first stumbled into Eastern thinking while browsing in an East-West bookstore in Greenwich Village, a new world opened up, and I knew I was on the path to the right mark. This began a lengthy journey that led me to the teachings of many sages of different Eastern traditions, as well as the writings of gifted Western writers and devotees of Eastern thought. I also directly experienced these traditions at meetings, lectures, workshops, intensives, visits to Ashrams, and audiences with some of the greatest living sages. I learned to sit yogi style, received a mantra, and practiced meditation and chanting. But like many westerners, I was cautious about throwing myself with abandon into these groups; too many of the practices and concepts were alien to my Western sensibility, the kind I associated with cults or quick fixes for everyday stresses. I even questioned my own motives: was I too looking for escape into the exotic and supernatural? Also discouraging was my observation that Eastern spiritual paths were filled with guru groupies and loose thinkers. But I recalled that the same was true for traditional, and many innovative, psychological schools. Psychotherapy and Eastern traditions speak to suffering and healing, which attract seekers who bring their own agendas—often unrealistic ones. Yet there was something so compelling and universal about the teachings of Eastern sages and ancient texts that I began to see the core, not the trappings or motivations of others. Also, I repeatedly met people who had made genuine transformations in their lives by embracing Eastern thought—greater than anything I had witnessed through traditional psychology and psychotherapy.

I continued to focus with increasing clarity on the universal nature of the teachings that rose above any particular culture. More and more it seemed to me that the principles were not Indian, Japanese, Tibetan, or Chinese but rather universal expressions about the nature of reality—the one reality that applied to everyone. The cultural trappings, I concluded, were merely the universal principles absorbed into the various cultures as sages made their way around the world centuries earlier. The passage of time has a funny way of engraving in stone what begins as comfortable assimilation.

All these musings had now come to a dramatic head in the Putaparthi Ashram as I awaited the daily appearance (Darshan) of Swami Sathya Sai Baba, "the man of miracles," as his thirty million followers call him. As I scanned this extraordinary scene, some nagging questions began to surface. The setting and practices were thoroughly Indian. Hindu metaphors and images pervaded most of the discourses and recommended readings. Dress as well was strictly Indian, consisting of *punjabi* suits (loose white shirt and pants) for men and saris for women. Although the thousands of devotees present were from all over the world, everyone appeared to be Indian.

Once the initial excitement of this exotic world wore off, I began to wonder why I had to become Indian, in a sense, to pursue the impressive teachings of Sai Baba or other spiritual masters. All the sages say their teachings have no particular language except the language of the heart and that the true teacher or guru is within each of us. I recalled reading about another inspirational Indian spiritual sage, Nisargadatta Maharaj, who told his followers, "If you understood what I was saying, you would never come back to see me again." Even Sai Baba will tell you that you don't have to come to India or leave your religion to go to the essence of his universal teachings, which he says are at the core of all religions and spiritual traditions. Still, many feel that the only way to embrace spirituality requires adopting the external forms of Hinduism, Buddhism, or other indigenous cultures.

There's an amusing story that I heard at the Ashram about Ram Dass, the American spiritual guru who rose to prominence during the counterculture turmoil of the 1960s. Ram Dass reportedly visited Sai Baba at that time. At the beginning of his interview, Sai Baba asked him his name. "Ram Dass," he replied. Sai Baba responded with "huh?" and repeated the question. He got the same answer, "Ram Dass," and followed it with another "huh?" Again Sai Baba asked the question, and this sparring went on for quite a while until Ram Dass finally said, "Richard Alpert." The interview then proceeded.

Whether apocryphal or legend the message still holds up: It's possible to be authentically on the spiritual path as Bernie Starr originally from Brooklyn. It fueled my determination to resist the temptation of "doing it" the Indian way. I began to think about translating the teachings of Eastern spirituality into basic principles of consciousness, reality, and self that could be fully expressed and practiced in a Western mode. But would something be lost? I asked myself. Would the profound principles be "dumbed down"? The more I thought this question through, the more convinced I became that far from diminishing the teachings, speaking the language of the seeker is essential. Just as Buddhism became Zen in Japan, Theravada in Thailand, and Mahayana in Tibet, Eastern teachings *must* become Western to be fully appreciated by Western audiences.

In the pages that follow, I'll share with you the insights about consciousness, self, and reality that unfolded along my journey and tell how they unveiled a powerful consciousness that we all own but abandon early in life. This book is a guide to reclaiming what I call *omni consciousness*.

CHAPTER ONE

～

# Search for the Genuine Self: From West to East and Back

"Know thyself," the saying goes, but as we're all aware, it's easier said than done. There isn't a more absorbing subject in the world than ourselves, and we all spend a great deal of each day thinking about ourselves and what we need, want, and fear. We pursue countless avenues of experience to help us expand and intensify the feeling of self—lovers, friends, religion, politics, power, money, you name it. Early in the past century, we even developed a science—psychology—designed specifically to help us grapple with the problems of self.

With all this effort, we generally end up with a lot less than we expected and needed. As a psychologist, I can attest to this from professional and personal experience, and so can you, if you stop to think about it for a moment. That's not to say we haven't had some successes, but if the goal is an understood, integrated, productive, healthy, secure, and peaceful self, we've all been doing something very wrong. This book is written to show just where the pursuit of self-knowledge has been derailed and to give a thoroughly practical and effective method for getting it back on the right track.

## Western Psychology and Its Discontents

Most of us are drawn to psychology for self-exploration because we believe it can help us with our conflicts, problems, and sufferings. If we could just unravel the mystery of the forces and events that shaped us into the person we are, we believe we could then alter ourselves into a happier, more effectively

1

functioning human being. For instance, if I have problems relating to other people, don't have the courage to get out of a bad relationship, find myself too dependent on other people, am unable to muster the confidence to make the right career choice or initiate other changes, or just have a gnawing sense of emptiness and yearning for more out of life, a psychological understanding of the dynamics behind these struggles, combined with some form of insightful therapy and a reshaping of my learned patterns of behavior and beliefs, will presumably rescue me and change the direction and quality of my life. Unfortunately, this hope is rarely fulfilled.

Let it be understood that I was once committed to this view as much as anyone, or even more so: I put my professional life where my philosophy was—I taught and practiced these principles. I thoroughly believed in the possibility of personal transformation through traditional psychological principles and techniques. When they didn't deliver their promise to me, those I counseled, or people I observed in treatment with others, like many practitioners I didn't throw in the towel but shifted to the emerging fads that renewed the promise. Isn't that what many of us do—become growth and transformation junkies? In all of these approaches, the key to change seemed clearly lodged in our past experiences, many of them now tucked away in our unconscious, and what we needed to do was bring them to the surface and openly confront them and deal with them. Or, following another strategy, we could discover the false or distorted beliefs that our personal histories led us to and then challenge, change, or drop them.

Even when, as not infrequently happened, progress was painfully slow or totally stalled, the hope and promise still remained. It was just a matter of digging deeper, overcoming resistances, or spending more time and money on it. Thus, if I woke up feeling lousy in the morning, I'd immediately think about the early events and people in my life to explain these feelings. This was the prevailing mood within traditional psychology.

In the 1960s and 1970s, new techniques exploded onto the scene that promised to break through some of the logjams that impeded probing our inner life and allowed us to get to the personal past much more quickly and dramatically to uproot the demons. Confrontational groups emerged, as well as many other expressive feeling techniques like gestalt and primal therapies, to achieve these goals. There was no more coddling or gingerly tiptoeing around presumed fragile defenses. These new approaches were no-nonsense, direct interactions that brought patients off the couch for face-to-face—if not touchy-feely—confrontations that promised to explode resistances and uproot even preverbal and intrauterine traumas.

Now you could lie on the floor and reexperience the pain of the psychologically hurt child, or you could talk directly to mommy as the little child (role playing) to "work out" hidden crippling feelings or reshape the beliefs generated by these early traumas. The drama and energy of these techniques were exciting. The goal of transformation seemed to be no further than finding still better techniques and methods—and perhaps a more charismatic therapist.

As these new therapies played themselves out and the sought-after quick path to nirvana remained as elusive as ever, a new literature of despair began to appear. Quietly the term "cure" vanished, and we started hearing about "lifelong treatments" or many-stepped programs on ladders that led nowhere or back to step one. But at national meetings and in closed-door seminars, counselors and therapists increasingly talked about their own frustration and burnout. The theory was still not questioned—the patients and society were blamed. We argued that the "me" generation was so narcissistic that treatment was difficult if not impossible. Events and technology were moving too fast for traditional or even nontraditional therapy to work. Finally, patients were simply not ready for "real" therapy; we would have to modify our goals to a holding operation, perhaps one lasting a lifetime. Today, many practitioners call themselves coaches rather than healers, dodging some of the responsibility for delivering transformation and eliminating the dirty word *cure*: "I'll give you some tips and guidance, but it's your job to run with them."

## Looking for Mr. Goodbar

I make no bones about it. Frustration with traditional psychology made me receptive to new ideas, and one day over twenty years ago I stumbled onto some writings on Eastern psychology that knocked me over. At this point, many readers may be tempted to lay the book down with the awful feeling that they've been through the Eastern mysticism bit before. I well understand such feelings; I went through them myself.

It's not that I'd been totally unaware of Eastern thought. In the 1970s and 1980s, swamis, Buddhist monks, and mystics of many ilks were crisscrossing America with testimonials of bliss and nirvana, and the writings of Krishnamurti, Yogananda, Allan Watts, and other sages and teachers were mandatory table pieces. But like many others, I was not persuaded by the psychology embedded in the philosophy, poetry, and inspirational writings of the East. I had never connected it with our day-to-day practical problems of survival, relationships, achievement, and change. My mindset, like that of most of the people of the time, held that Eastern meant exotic. The inscrutable, mysterious, ancient wisdom of the East bore no relation to our own scientific psychology and was not likely to be of much help to the benighted, hard-thinking citizens of the West.

Moreover, during the Vietnam War era, Eastern thought was crassly appropriated by the counterculture. It had to do with strange practices and dress, alien religious notions, and arcane deities, all invoked to challenge conventional sensibilities and scandalize conservative politicians and squeamish relatives. Eastern meant Hare Krishnas on the streets and airports, dropping out and assaulting our Western materialism. Eastern also meant Allen Ginsberg chanting "om" for twenty-four hours at the famed Chicago Democratic Convention in 1968. In literature, Eastern practices found seductive expression in Jack Kerouac's *Dharma Bums*, a depiction of clearly self-absorbed, reclusive dropouts seeking to detach themselves from the accelerating materialism and technologies of modern society.

As if all this were not unpromising enough, it also occurred to me that I reflexively steered away from Eastern thinking because I associated it with a nonrational approach, much inferior to Western psychology, which rested on the solid footing of "science." Indeed, in the early part of the last century, psychologists like John Watson were so determined to place psychology on a par with other "hard sciences" that they wrenched it away from its historic nest in university philosophy departments to set up their scientific departments of psychology. Psychology henceforth would no longer be associated with the casual speculative musings of armchair philosophy; it was to be solidly and firmly grounded in modern science—lab coats and all.

This simplistic dichotomy of mystic Eastern thought and scientific Western thought exploded into pieces as I delved into the emerging concepts of our recent "new science" and its vision of the nature of reality. It is now increasingly clear that the science on which psychology was modeling itself (and still is today) was already in the process of unraveling. In fact, scientific psychology was from its inception out of step with what was happening in science as a whole. In the 1920s and 1930s, physicists were discovering that there was nothing solid or absolute in the universe as they explored more and more subtle levels of reality.

It is ironic that just as scientists were discarding the notion of fixed space and mass, absolute time, cause and effect, and certainty, psychology was placing all its bets on just those things: the fixed ego or self separate from the world, the fixed habit, or the fixed cognitive structure—all bound by time and projected along a lock-step, linear path of past, present, and future. Yet this flawed science has shaped the way we think about self and reality.

For example, personality, as I learned in all my psychology courses and taught for many years, is formed early in life—by age five or six according to Freud—and pretty much remains the same. While nothing of such a static and stable nature could be found anyplace else in the universe, psychologists continue to embrace this model. In a flip-flop, it is now the hard-nosed physical scientists who are throwing their hands up in the air and in the spirit of uncertainty are acknowledging what Shakespeare noted long ago: "There are more things in heaven and earth, Horatio, than are dreamt of in your philosophy."

Despite the march of science in new directions, Western psychology has not moved very much from its original mechanistic, cause-and-effect, reductionistic stance. At best, as disquieting news arrives from the front lines of science—neutrinos that shift between waves and particles, subatomic particles that seem to communicate at speeds faster than the speed of light, or the notion that much of the universe may exist in a dimension that is beyond our comprehension—psychologists frantically reshuffle the deck to create the illusion of change. It's no wonder that physics is friendlier to the ideas of spiritual traditions than contemporary Western psychology is. Brian O'Leary, in his book *The Second Coming of Science*, likens the current state of our understanding of human existence to living in a box: "According to the box model, our scientists act as the high priests of our culture, zealously guarding the boundaries. Like billiard balls making endless cushion shots against the inner walls of the box, we seem to follow, in our daily lives, the mechanistic, deterministic assumptions of our present-day science. . . . Meanwhile, leakage outside the box becomes possible only in secrecy or at the risk of ridicule and threats to one's career."

Notions consistent with the new quantum physics existed within many religious, mystical, and philosophical traditions and remained largely ignored by scientific psychology because they were outside "the box." Now, however, the Buddhist concept of the interrelatedness of everything in the universe suddenly doesn't seem so crazy and has scientific credence. Similarly, the Eastern idea that consciousness can create reality, once considered otherworldly, also has plausibility in the light of physicists' findings that certain subatomic particles can be manifested either as waves or as particles and that it may be the act of observing that makes the wave a particle. This interpretation obliterates the fundamental tenet of science that insists on the objectivity and independence of the observer from what is observed. The two appear intertwined. If we and what we observe are related, or perhaps one, then who are we? There was no Mr. Goodbar in sight.

## Out of the Cul-de-sac

Emboldened by the flux in current physics and by my disenchantment with present-day psychological theory, I found I could now study Eastern thought without embarrassment or condescension. I was rewarded by discovering the exciting psychology of mind, consciousness, and reality that lay behind the philosophy and behind the metaphors and images that had initially put me off because they were couched in such alien traditions. Yet, as I peeled away the fancy trappings, I saw at the core principles that addressed the same issues as Western psychology, but with radically different conclusions and techniques. Eastern psychology now struck me as possessing a realistic way out of the dead end that hems in Western psychology.

What really stunned me as I read, studied, and communicated with Eastern scholars was the realization that many of the cherished concepts at the heart of Western psychology were considered and rejected by Eastern thinkers thousands of years ago. Many of our so-called discoveries, such as the ego, the unconscious, and internal conflict, were known throughout the ages and regarded as lower aspects of a more inclusive higher consciousness— a higher consciousness that played no role in Western thinking. The more I uncovered, the clearer it became that the Eastern path comprised a unique approach to human psychology, and that our Western psychologies were by comparison extremely limited.

Eastern psychology talked about a *pure consciousness* that is beyond personal experience or the personal identity "me." This consciousness is what the "me" arises out of. It is the source of identity, and it is not shaped, dictated to, or controlled in any way by the happenstance "me" experience that is but one small projection of this larger consciousness. It's not that we are one consciousness or the other. We are both. But pure consciousness is the ground and personal consciousness is a figure within the ground. Identifying strictly with the personal consciousness reverses figure and ground, resulting in limitation and suffering. Conflict, as the Indian sage Nisargadatta Maharaj put it, "is simply a case of mistaken identity. If you knew who you really were, you would see that who you think you are is a colossal joke."

As the various pieces of the puzzle of psychological existence began to fit more comfortably together, I saw how necessary it was to present Eastern thought to a Western audience as a psychology of consciousness outside of its usual religious and mystical contexts. By doing this, I could prevent westerners from being turned off by the exoticism and setting of the ideas and also help them perceive how clearly Eastern thought relates to Western psychology and familiar topics of psychological theory and personal transformation.

It also occurred to me that Western psychology's rich traditions, tools, and concepts for exploring mind, consciousness, and human development could enrich and broaden our understanding of the personal self in its struggle for spiritual transcendence. Eastern philosophy has opened important doors, but it doesn't have all the answers. In fact, in-depth knowledge of individual psychological development may provide the key to opening the prison of the self. This intriguing conclusion will unfold when we look at the impact of psychological birth and development on spiritual consciousness.

Toward my goal of synthesizing East and West, I have selected the term *omni consciousness* to name the pure, higher consciousness of Eastern thought. It may seem gratuitous to add yet another name to so many others that capture the essence of Eastern thinking—Krishna consciousness, Buddha mind, egolessness, and so forth—but each of these has so many jarring or alienating associations to the Western ear that discussions get confusing and bogged down in semantics. A new term that starts out fresh and is clearly defined jettisons all that previous contaminating cultural baggage. Omni consciousness as the ground of all consciousness transcends culture. At the same time, I want to honor its origin.

"Omni" includes the sound "om," which is considered sacred and primordial in Eastern traditions. Some believe that om is the sound energy that produced the universe, not unlike the notion of the big bang. *Omni* also signifies the inclusive nature of omni consciousness. Thus omni consciousness pays tribute to its Eastern origin but places itself on the Western path of scientific validation in the context of a universal psychology of consciousness.

## The West and "Me"

How does the Eastern concept of omni consciousness really touch our Western sensibilities? What can it possibly tell us? The rest of this book is devoted to answering those questions as completely as possible. For the moment though, let's look at the most basic way we have been accustomed to thinking about ourselves.

Most of us know human existence only through the entity called the self (I/me/ego). Because this self is our sole conduit for knowing the world, we take great care to defend it, expand it, develop it, and procure all kinds of things for it. The fact is, most of our waking energy is spent on servicing this self. For us, self-absorption appears to be not only correct but the *only* meaningful basis for navigating in the world. After all, everyone else is doing the same thing. What else is there?

When we are unaware of another firmer ground of being, any efforts to question or challenge the primacy of what we call I/me are met with fierce resistance. It's like the ferocious response we find in an abused child who defends and clings to the very parents who are his torturers. Knowing no other source of self-validation, the child feels even an abuser is better than the void of the black hole of nonexistence. And nonexistence is exactly what we imagine lies outside this I/me identity.

Omni psychology, on the other hand, considers the self we know, cherish, believe in, and defend as our ally in our struggles through life to be a prison that confines, limits, and imposes punishments on our existence. This may be the hardest concept to grasp in this book because it threatens everything we hold most dear—mainly, our sense of self. Like the clinging of the abused child, we insist on embracing this self, blinding ourselves to any message of a vast and limitless universe beyond the confines of our prison. The self and the prison are one. Any assault on the prison or attempt at liberation will be construed an attack on our very self. Thus, potential liberators appear to us as the most threatening of enemies.

## With Friends Like This . . .

Could the illusion of the separate little self against the world be the basic source of our conflicts and suffering? All the evidence staring us directly in the face says that this self doesn't work. For example, the world based on this self seems to be in no better shape than it ever has been and, perhaps, considerably worse shape. So what else is new?

Yet on the face of it, the self has more than it ever had before. More people than ever before, especially in those societies that glorify the individual self, have more than ever before in history. Yes, there is poverty and famine and very real suffering throughout the world. But the paradox is that the kind of psychological suffering that we are addressing in this book is greater than ever before—and rampant among those who are most affluent and successful. What is the evidence for the suffering self? Just look at all the efforts to anesthetize and obliterate the self—the addictions and escapes that face us at every turn. Sometimes the statistics seem to exceed the total population with people divided into alcoholics, sexual deviants, drug addicts, wife bashers, husband beaters, child and elder abusers, sexaholics, pedophiles, smokers, overeaters, undereaters, compulsive gamblers, and compulsive shoppers, and the list goes on and on. Oh, and we haven't even mentioned the rampage of serious crimes—murder, rape, terrorism, and the like.

Some think that addictions and escapes are exclusive to big, alienating cities like New York, Chicago, and Los Angeles. Yet I once noticed in the newspaper of a relatively small rural town—population of 45,000—no less than twenty-eight anonymous self-help groups advertised (makes you wonder about the meaning of anonymous). The fresh air and open spaces did not seem to quiet the internal suffering of the self.

Articles abound sounding the alarm of a drug epidemic—often in suburban communities and among highly educated and successful professionals. According to a 2005 report by the Substance Abuse and Mental Health Services Administration (SAMHSA), 19.1 million Americans age twelve and older were current illicit drug users—meaning that they had used an illicit drug in the past month. The report also showed extensive nonmedical use of prescription drugs among young adults. People are routinely becoming their own "Dr. Feelgoods," self-medicating with antidepressants, antianxiety drugs, and a host of other mood-altering drugs. The line between medication and recreation has blurred. With the stigma of taking drugs gone, business meetings and social gatherings sometimes become confessionals with sharing about who is on what and which drugs of choice have done most to help with sleep, feeling less anxious (few even speak of being more relaxed), or just getting up physically and emotionally on demand. Trading and sharing pills has also become commonplace. Sadly, many have abandoned any hope for feeling good from within.

Not even young people, who would seem to have the greatest potential for self-fulfillment, are immune from the discontent and violence that sweeps modern society. The self is not only unhappy but feels the need to defend itself from real or imagined assaults. A U.S. government survey found that 20 percent of high school students carried a weapon within the previous month "for protection or because they might need it in a fight." About 32 percent of male students say they carried a weapon at some time. An eyebrow-raising development, although not all that surprising in the face of the rising tide of gun violence in the schools, many school systems, such as in Massachusetts, are installing metal detectors and surveillance cameras. More alarming, on the heels of a fifteen-year-old student's killing of a principal (September 2006), state representative Frank Lasse in Wisconsin introduced legislation that would allow school personnel to carry guns. And in the aftermath of the tragic shootings and deaths of children at an Amish school in Pennsylvania, Greenleaf, Idaho, invoked an ordinance requiring every household to own a weapon and ammunition. At the same time, schools in Nebraska, Nevada, Oklahoma, and Oregon closed down briefly over threats of violence or guns. At one time, "school shootout" referred to debating teams and spelling bees.

Other young people, particularly teenage and young adult women, are looking at their reflections in the mirror with great dissatisfaction, prompting a worldwide epidemic of anorexia and bulimia. The situation has gotten so out of hand, as women strive for the idolized fashion-magazine model image, that a number of countries, like Brazil, have banned girls fifteen years old and younger from beauty contests. That came on the heels of the death of an eighty-eight-pound contestant.

Additional findings show a high incidence of teenage and young adult drinking and drug consumption, and a report indicates that an alarming number have seriously considered suicide. The fact that the suicide rate among young people is spiraling upward says that discontent with the self is real.

## Gimme Gimme Gimme and I'll Be Happy—or Will I?

This unhappy, frightened, angry, and defensive self follows an old, familiar strategy of the self: to get more for itself. The desperate quest for "more" of something, anything (among rich and poor), represents the desperate desire to achieve fulfillment of the self. Sadly, as most addicts find out, "more" does not satisfy (except briefly) but rather intensifies the need for even greater levels of more. As the intensity escalates, we can see more clearly the scope of people poisoning *themselves*, debilitating *themselves*, debasing and denigrating *themselves*, or, out of rage and frustration, turning these processes outward. What we are producing are selves that do not love *themselves*. In fact, they seem to hate themselves and do whatever they can to hurt themselves. When not directly hurting themselves, they are trying to obliterate, escape from, or anesthetize themselves—all oddly in the quest for self-fulfillment and feeling good about themselves.

## End of the Line?

Let's face it, this self with its operating system has reached its limits—perhaps a dead end with nowhere to go. Yet it persists in its familiar grooves. Doesn't this suggest that it's time to take a fresh look at this self and its quest? If the self is generating so much pain and suffering, maybe it's not a useful self. If so, the logical conclusion would be to drastically change it or get rid of it. Here we encounter a paralyzing dilemma that we will be coming back to over and over. If I am not going to be "my self," who am I going to be? Put another way, if I give up the only self that I know, how will I survive? Therefore, I will insist that the self must be what I want—and if it doesn't, I will get very angry. As absurd as this credo is, it is the one that drives the world of the self.

Then, even if you agree that the self should be abandoned, liberated, or transcended, who will do it? Surely the self will not get rid of itself given that its existence centers on preserving and defending itself to the death. So you can see that omni consciousness psychology has a rough row to hoe.

## Over the Wall

But there is a way out. Omni psychology posits that the familiar self or "me" that you totally identify with is a *false* identity. What you really are is omni consciousness, a pure consciousness that is whole, complete, conflict free, and unbound by any particular identity—our original, factory-delivered condition, guaranteed for life. Why we abandon this potent core nature for the prison of the limited self is what this book is all about. As you grasp the nature of omni consciousness, you will see how omni consciousness becomes contracted into the small "me" self—how forces from birth onward conspire to glorify and protect the self, locking you into the prison of the self. All efforts to escape from the imprisonment of this little self in its encapsulated world will fail if the attempts are made *within* the self system. Only a return to omni consciousness will liberate us from the narrowly conceived personal self.

Omni consciousness is based on a solid understanding of the nature of consciousness and the nature of human development. Once you see the distinction between your familiar "me" consciousness and omni consciousness, a number of changes will begin to unfold. For example, once free of your prison cell (even temporarily on parole), or even getting a taste of omni consciousness, you will feel a great burden lifted. You will also find that because omni consciousness lies outside the realm of personal experiences, your experiences, and the narrow identity they have framed, can no longer limit or define you. You are not what you eat, think, experience, or love. You are more. Remember, only when you accept the boundaries of the prison of the self that welcomes, endorses, and embraces the "me" experiences can those experiences *become* you. Whether we are talking about the hurt inner child, or what mommy and daddy did in the early years, omni consciousness observes and knows but is not devastated and doesn't get hijacked, nor is it aloof. Far from being unfeeling, omni consciousness offers you the opportunity to experience genuine feelings that stem from a broader awareness.

## New Age or Old Age?

Although omni consciousness is revolutionary, it is not new. It is actually contained, as I have indicated, within many Eastern spiritual and philosophical traditions, and even in some Western religious teachings. The message, however, is rarely heard because the ears that hear it are the ears of the little self, which stands ever ready to protect its fragile fortress. To reclaim omni consciousness, it is necessary to shift the *locus of consciousness* to a different place within yourself. As simple as this path may seem on the surface, there are many formidable obstacles to reclaiming omni consciousness—mostly self-created, as we shall see. But it can be done. This book will point the way.

## Truth and Consequences

And now I'm faced with another dilemma—call it *truth in advertising*. If I tell the truth about omni consciousness, it's likely to turn you off. Pursuing omni consciousness is not like getting a quick fix. You can't make the leap into omni consciousness with a warm fuzzy feeling of spirituality. It's hard work requiring letting go of the illusions that your sense of security is moored to—and that have defined you all of your life. The ego will not take lightly any attempt to loosen its stranglehold on your sensibilities. To profit from this book, you'll have to make a number of hard decisions. If it can be shown that you truly are living in a self-imposed prison, that you are being guided by irrational forces, that you cannot make real progress toward freedom within your unexamined psychological system, and that freedom does exist and is within your grasp, will you spring for it? How much is it worth to you? Can you accept imprisonment once the truth is revealed? These are hard questions that deserve real thought and honest answers. Finally, ask what the self has actually done for us individually and collectively that we should take such good care of it. If you're not sure, the rest of this book is for you.

# CHAPTER TWO

# Who Am I?

The most important concept in this book—and the one most difficult to grasp—is one that deals with something we all feel we know the most about—our sense of ourselves. We may not know everything, but we *do* believe, or like to believe, that we know who we are and what we need to be secure, successful, and happy, which isn't so surprising. After all, we've been with ourselves for as long as we can remember, and we're pretty familiar with us by now—or so we think. So why do we need to learn an entirely new and rather strange way of thinking about ourselves?

The premise of this book is that the self—the I/me/ ego—that we have come to know and love (or loathe) so well is in fact not our true self at all. It is, if not an outright imposter, at least the usurper of an identity that far surpasses anything it is or can be on its own. Behind this I/me/ego of personal identity and personal experience is another, truer self that is pure consciousness—omni consciousness. The everyday ideas of self so familiar to us comprise only a tiny fraction of omni consciousness.

It's as if we had a full-length mirror that gave us a total reflection of ourselves, and we broke that mirror into hundreds of tiny shards. Then, of the many small slivers available, we chose only a handful and determined that the minuscule segments of us that each reflected was in fact our complete self. What a strange and distorted picture we'd have of ourselves! True, each tiny fragment would reflect a piece, however small, of what we look like, but could we begin to recognize ourselves from four or five such slivers? How about one? Hardly likely.

This book is about seeing the powerful unity behind the fragmented pieces. Certain concepts from the Eastern psychology and spiritual traditions are absolutely indispensable here because they posit the concept of *pure consciousness*, which represents the full self. Eastern thought uses many terms for the idea of pure consciousness, but most of them are either confusing, alien, or off-putting for westerners. Therefore, I use the more neutral term *omni consciousness* to identify the concept of pure consciousness throughout the book. The ego self, or the I/me, represents the tiny shards that generally define for us the identities we shall play out in life.

## The Great Divide

There's no greater divide between Eastern and Western conceptions of existence than their differing views on the nature of consciousness and the status of the ego. The most influential Western psychologies, which we will take a close look at in chapter 5, glorify the ego, giving it center stage in human existence. Not so for Eastern spiritual traditions, which say the ego is a hindrance to attaining the highest state of consciousness.

Esther and William Menaker, early influential writers on psychoanalysis and psychological development, spell out in their book *Ego in Evolution* the traditional Western conception that casts a unity of ego and consciousness that stubbornly persists. In this view, there is no consciousness outside the ego: "The miracle of man is consciousness; but consciousness can only be experienced and implemented by means of the ego. There is for man, then, no awareness without ego. Thus mind and its ultimate expression in conscious awareness and the symbols appropriate to this become a vehicle for a new way of dealing with the reality of the external and internal environment. Interposed between this world and man is a whole new world of his symbolic creation. It is over this world that ego presides" (pp. 2–3).

Compare the reverence for the ego that permeates Western thinking with the irreverent Indian Vedic conception expressed by Swami Muktananda: "The Ego destroys humility, eliminates the heart, exterminates affection, and slaughters a relationship between two people. It makes you slight others instead of respecting them. It is a most dreadful murderer, a vicious plunderer. Don't keep company with it. It creates disharmony. So you'd better get rid of it."

Sathya Sai Baba says the ego precludes peace, the very goal sought by ego worshipers: "When desires are ego-oriented, time and effort are wasted; duty is neglected; the body and its skills are misused. In order to restore peace to the individual and in society, the mind has to be purged of its attachment to the self {ego}."

Tibetan Buddhist Sogyal Rimpoche gives a similar evaluation of the ego but focuses more on the ego's destructive role in generating suffering and delusion:

> Frantically, and in real dread, we cast around and improvise another identity, one we clutch on to with all the desperation of someone falling continuously into an abyss. This false and ignorantly assumed identity is "ego." . . . ego is then defined as incessant movements of grasping at a delusory notion of "I" and "mine," self and other, and all the concepts, ideas, desires, and activity that will sustain that false construction. . . . So long as we haven't unmasked the ego, it continues to hoodwink us. . . . ego and its grasping are at the root of all our suffring. . . . And even if we were to see through ego's lies, we're just too scared to abandon it; for without any true knowledge of the nature of our mind, or true identity, we simply have no other alternative.

For Sogyal Rimposhe, the ego is an invention of mind much like the creation of a character in a play—in this case, a character in a play of consciousness.

## On Roles and Role-Playing

Imagine actually waking up and finding yourself a character in a play. Now let's say you believe not only that that character is you, but that it is the *only* you. So like a real trouper, you dutifully repeat your lines over and over. That's what a good actor in a play does: follows the given script and performs the directed actions. Underneath, however, you have the uneasy feeling that you're limited. You have a persistent urge to be more and a sense that you *can* be more. But you don't know how.

Perhaps you suspect you can be other characters in other plays. You might even yearn to write your own script to express more fully who you are. But you're stuck. And when you do at times slip out of your character, you feel anxious and alienated and rush back into character for the security of the familiar—the comforting sense, no matter how limiting, that you know your lines and who you are.

As the wish to be liberated persists, you try to achieve it through this character—the only one you know as you. You strive to be better as that character—more forceful and convincing. You tune in attentively to the responses of the audiences and the other actors for signs that you are making progress toward your goal of liberation. Yet no matter what happens, what you achieve, or how well you perform that character, you are still the same character with all its limitations and constraints. You can't get outside the character from within the character. You feel frustrated and don't know where to turn.

Does the dilemma of the actor in a play strike a familiar chord that mirrors your life? But it's not only you. How often have you heard someone talk about the frustrations of his or her limited role in life? "I want to get out of this rut. This is not the real me"; "I know I can achieve much more"; "Will I spend the rest of my life living like this [referring to job, personal relationships, lifestyle, etc.]?" You may well have said some of these things to yourself. Despite the desire to change, most of us find that our efforts simply repeat old patterns that eventually bring us back to the starting point. Along the way, we may enjoy some successes—good income, popularity, personal triumphs, sexual conquests—but when all's said and done, we run head-on into that sense of emptiness that, despite drastic changes on the surface, we're still marching in place. We may be more successful at being the character "me," but it's a limited role at best. "Me" remains imprisoned within itself.

Part of the problem is that we can't envision any meaningful self beyond that fragmentary "me" we have assumed ourselves to be. How could we, if we were raised on the exclusive ego diet that can see nothing other than the limited "me"? We believe we are the character in the play of our own making, a fragment of a more expansive and inclusive self. Despite urges, longings, and even fleeting glimpses of a bigger picture, we feel stuck and without choice. Ultimately you conclude, "I'm Barbara and this is who I am. I've always been this way and probably always will. So I'll just accept it and try to improve on it, become a better character in my play." But Barbara, like many others, will still cling to the goal of transcending her limited self through her defined character in the play of life. So begins a lengthy self-improvement journey of getting deeper into ourselves in an effort to secretly get outside ourselves.

Why do we succumb to a limited definition of ourselves if we are, in fact, so much more? Spiritual seekers throughout the ages have wrestled with this question: "I know that I'm more but just can't seem to make the leap." In chapter 4, I will introduce you to my startling discovery that the very experiences we need for developing our personal skills and identity for managing and successfully navigating the everyday material world have another side that is the enemy of omni consciousness. We will take a close look at the hidden forces that steer us away from omni consciousness and lock us into the prison of the self. When you begin to see how your very own experiences and the narrow conclusions you have drawn from them about yourself and the world have made you your own jailer, you may gain the courage to rebel. Then the grip of I/me/ego will loosen, allowing the more expansive reality of omni consciousness to come into focus.

## Clinging to Life

Holding on to the small self makes lots of sense emotionally. Why should you loosen your tight grasp on the only "me" you know? That would be reckless unless you trust that another self is not only real but a better or, at least, an equally secure ground.

Picture yourself fiercely clinging to a ledge in a life-and-death struggle for survival. A slip of your flesh-worn fingers could mean instant death, so all your energy and attention is mobilized toward that one singular, terrifying task of holding on. Nothing else counts as your entire world contracts into the immediate, desperate struggle, narrowing the focus of your entire being and consciousness. Then a sudden glance down reveals that you are actually only two feet off the ground. You instantly let go and are promptly planted firmly on a secure foundation. Your struggle is over, and the world expands while the limited world of the ledge fades into oblivion. But when it comes to the life-and-death clinging attachments of the ego, seeing the firm foundation of another ground is more formidable and not as easily revealed by a quick glance. Where should you look and, more puzzling, who will do the looking? Will you even recognize another ground of being when you are staring right at it?

## Finding the Ground

You can't beat something with nothing. Your limited self, no matter how limited, is still something. You're not about to give it up for nothing—for smoke and mirrors. Quite right. And this book is *not* about a totally blind leap of faith into the void. It's about the step-by-step, or ledge-by-ledge, if you will, climb to an understanding of the state of being beyond the limited self—a consciousness that constitutes the big something that can replace the little something of the I/me/ego self.

To liberate yourself from your limited self you have to identify the consciousness that underlies *all* the different plays and characters. That omni consciousness is within you. It *is* you. You have lost sight of it, as we all have, because from our earliest years we are channeled into the limited construct we call "me." In the course of psychological development, our identification with a narrow "me" consciousness evolved and became fixed through a misunderstanding and inflated valuation of our personal experiences. When you begin to grasp the self-deception behind this process, you will gain the courage to forgo the "me" and reclaim your true identity along with the freedom that goes with it. You will be ready to embrace omni consciousness.

## Wishing Is Not Doing

Perhaps you resonate with the description of a narrowed and cramped self. You may even sense that your conflicts, problems, and suffering are directly related to imprisonment in a limited image of the self. Good. But agreement is not enough. Prisoners can only free themselves when they truly wish to be free. An escape-proof prison is one in which the inmates don't *want* to escape. Such a prison obviously suffers few breakouts.

Reconnecting with the liberating consciousness requires exposing a long string of experiences from our earliest existence that places a veil over omni consciousness. Even our biology conspires to keep us on a path of distraction that prevents us from finding out who we really are. Our powerful physical needs and early total dependency on others from the moment the umbilical cord is cut keep us seeking identities from sources outside ourselves. We end up spending a lifetime defining ourselves through these external forces. Once the template is set in our early years, recasting becomes a monumental task until you "see" and refuse to be a prisoner any longer.

Emotional hurts and traumas are particularly potent in narrowing our identities. The affronted ego becomes so intent on defending itself that it loses sight of all other possibilities for being. For this reason, emotions, especially intense emotions, are extremely dangerous. They commonly distort reality, locking us into the reactive posture of the ego—like the person clinging to the ledge. The more intense the emotions, the more powerful the reaction to protect the ego. Yet like our embrace of the ego, we love our emotions and are loath to see how destructive they can be. I will have much more to say about this in chapter 3.

Furthermore, we thoroughly immerse ourselves in the struggle to expand and enhance our limited self, in an effort to make it something it cannot be, leaving little energy or desire to turn attention elsewhere where we might discover a firmer ground. The ego self is caught in its constricted definition with its conditioned, habitual responses. It is ruled by remembrances of the past and projections or fantasies about the future. A threat to the ego triggers memories of past assaults, which reinforces the need to defend. The ego then projects soothing, expansive solutions. For example, personal rejection might generate a fantasy of great social success in the future, or projected power and success to offset the assault. The present moment is lost. Creative living becomes almost impossible as the *reactive consciousness* of the limited self constantly promotes the delusional thinking of an expanding experiential self. Thus we enter a lifelong quest to enhance this limited ego self through acquisition and expansion (much like the effort to improve the character in the play). We tolerate no rest or reprieve from this acquisitive drive lest we face the unthinkable—that we *are* this hopelessly limited self. Breaking the pattern requires an understanding of the powerful forces that make the prison of the self seem so natural.

## The Experiential Self: The Only Self You Know

The self that we identify as *I* or *me* is only one limited projection of consciousness. At birth there is only *impersonal consciousness* or awareness—the sense of "I-am-ness." This I-am-ness is devoid of all the attributes that we will later experience as inseparable parts of the "me" feeling. It is this pure consciousness prior to the conditioning of the "me" self that I call omni consciousness.

Promptly, however, a "me," or an ego self, emerges through the interplay of consciousness with personal experience. In other words, things happen to you, you assume possession of those happenings (take them for your own), and then you use them to define who you are.

Each of us is born with a complex biological makeup into a particular environment that exposes us to a unique set of internal and external experiences. Your parents may be loving or rejecting, you may be colicky and irritable, or you may be quite rhythmic and content. The possibilities for individual differences in experiences are enormous. But from the moment consciousness bursts onto the scene, we start identifying the never-ending parade of experiences as *my* experiences. Thereafter, we continuously organize perception around the concepts *me* and *mine*. At first we confine this to a limited scope of experiences mainly tied to the body (e.g., reflexes and bodily sensations in early infancy), but later that widens as our awareness expands. "Me" becomes the focus of all experiences and actions. Eventually "me" and my experiences are one. We then seek out similar experiences to reinforce and validate the sense of "me." Through all this, we are unaware that we have been squeezed into a narrow container. Worse yet, we become the narrow container and stamp a permanent label on it—*me*.

## "Me" and Experience

In principle, consciousness doesn't have to be limited to personal experience. Although the experiential world is compelling and magnetically consumes your entire attention, the fact is, *you do not have to accept delivery of experiences; you and your experiences are not the same.* Unfortunately, though, few can see that liberating alternative, because all pleasure, pain, happiness, and security seems embedded in personal experience—and that's where the "me" gets embedded and imprisoned.

At this point, you might be a bit skeptical, if not outright confused. What does it mean to be me outside of my experiences? What else is there? It's this very puzzlement that punctuates how successful our conditioning is in directing us away from omni consciousness—where the "me" melts into the vast ocean of consciousness and awareness where you are no-thing and everything. There are moments when we all taste that consciousness—moments of joy, ecstasy, creativity, and love, and even when waking in the morning before we dress ourselves in our imagined characters for our daily play of little "me" consciousness. We are so married to the "me" of personal experience that we fail to recognize the ground of being—our ground of being—in the brief encounters with omni consciousness. The guest departs and we promptly slip back into the "real me." You conclude that nothing but that sense of "me" presence with its ownership of experiences can be the real "me"—I must feel my experiential baggage for me to exist.

## The Beat Goes On

We continue to work from within this limited self in a frustrating and hopeless effort to change or develop it. We may try to get outside it, but we can't do that from within. We are trapped in a prison of our own making and aren't aware of our complicity. We embrace experiences, define ourselves by them, and hold on to them while at the same time trying to get away from them to redefine ourselves. We want to stay in the prison and at the same time be outside the prison. It's a stalemate strategy at best.

This process of self-definition through experience continues relentlessly. Our bodies and our psyches are bombarded with all kinds of persuasive messages from our environment that tell us who we are. We actively tune into them, and very soon they take on the force of conclusions. If I experience much anxiety and tension, then I conclude that I am a frightened person. If I experience frustration and deprivation, I define myself as a needy person. If I experience comfort, success, and support, I conclude that I am a strong, happy, and secure person; I then look for more experiences to gain even greater security. In addition, the people around us—parents, siblings, relatives, friends, teachers, and others—tell us directly or indirectly who we are, and we incorporate these messages too; indeed, we actively look for them.

Psychological theories that we will scrutinize in chapter 5 will beat the same drum, getting you to confidently march in step along your narrowly defined path. The experts will argue over which messages are more important for shaping the self. But most agree that the self is born of both biological and psychological *experiences*, and that these experiences in turn define the self that becomes our lasting guide through life.

## The Rigid Self Takes Charge

Once this self is defined, it becomes a rather fixed contraction of consciousness. First, you firmly believe you are your experiences. Then, the environment that you happen to be born into exposes you to a consistent pattern of experiences that keep reinforcing the messages that lead you to conclude who you are—or who you think you are. If you are the frightened, lonely infant, chances are that you will be exposed to a continuous pattern of parenting that will keep reinforcing the emerging frightened and anxious "me." As a result, you are likely to become hypersensitive to rejection and ready to find it everywhere. You are now "on guard."

The world is a big, complex place, and the desire for the individual little ego self to feel secure is overwhelming. We, therefore, must defend the conceptual "me." Why not? It's our only currency—or so we believe. To accomplish this requires constant reinvention of the self we have defined by repeating experiences that confirm its limited definition. So the frightened self will find frightening experiences, or interpret experiences as such, to feel its familiar at-home self. An angry self will find reasons for anger at every turn. The secure self will find secure experiences to rediscover itself. The very constancy of the self that we defend and promote becomes further proof of the reality of our defined selves. Wherever we look, we find our familiar self—so it must be real. But this need for sameness and continuity becomes another barrier against real change or spontaneous action in the present. Once the initial definitions of self are set, we proceed to elaborate them—we dig deeper and wider grooves for our defined self to stave off feelings of vulnerability. The frightened or needy self seeks strategies to protect and defend itself, and these reactive strategies in turn become part of the self, for example, "I must be cautious and not take too many risks."

So getting beyond or outside the self becomes increasingly challenging, if not impossible. The self as a defined object seals and limits its destiny. The ego self very promptly becomes *reactive* rather than creative or truly responsive to the real moment. While we may want to change—even crave change—we experience change as a *not*-me loss of self. In creating this experiential self, we have traded the power of the subjective consciousness (omni consciousness) for the confines of a prison. Here, in a nutshell, is the dilemma of the personal self: it wants to grow, change and become but can't as long as it's locked into its fixed definition that experiences all else as "not me." It's the ultimate catch-22.

## Self-Consciousness and Becoming

Very early in personal psychological development, the little ego self becomes self-conscious and perceives itself for what it is—a mere speck in a vast universe—and becomes anxious. You may even recall from your childhood the many times you were overwhelmed by the demands of life. As children looking at the world and the future, we seem to need so much in relation to the world around us. "How will I make a safe niche for myself, let alone achieve enduring security, peace, and fulfillment?" Many of these questions and doubts continue throughout our lives.

The lifelong vulnerable ego self persistently translates its feeling of insecurity into needs. Now, I need things—power, sex, money, possessions—anything that will make me feel stronger, more secure than I am. These needs can never be satisfied because they are up against the ego's definition of incompleteness and vulnerability. We are born in need, bred in need, consumed in need, and ultimately imprisoned by need. What deceives us is the belief that we are really seeking the fulfillment of a need when, in fact, we are seeking the state of need. Think about it. No matter what we achieve, we ultimately find ourselves back at square one, needing and seeking all over again—sometimes desperately, while often minimizing the very gains we struggled to achieve. The projected, limited self that is embodied in the ego is so identified with need that if we should experience sustained satisfaction, we sense a diminished or vanishing self. Satisfaction becomes a fleeting moment between driving needs. We must promptly generate new needs to swing into action to feel alive. It is the individual expression of the corporate mentality of expansion—a constant upward growth curve, with so much percent increase required each year. Not achieving the goal is considered failure, and heads must roll. The idea of "enough" or maintaining a level of achievement is as good as failure. Similarly, the individual ego never lets up in its quest to seek and achieve more. That's not to say that we don't meet with some success, or the feeling of success when we believe the delusion that we are getting to the final destination. Winning gives temporary security, even exhilaration and ecstasy. But typically it's short lived, as the gnawing sense of something missing returns from the depths. As in a recurring nightmare, we are staring at the familiar hole that needs to be filled.

## More of What?

Rarely do we consider what "more" means. For fabulously wealthy corporate executives, the thirsty need for more drives them, as we have recently seen, to criminal activity in financially raping their companies, shareholders, and employees that makes no rational sense whatsoever—unless you understand the driving force of the ego's insatiable feeding frenzy. And the legacy of "more" is apt to be anxiety, dissatisfaction, and self-recrimination. If we reach a satisfactory plateau, we can only briefly appreciate it before we must rev up for the next height. Gratification of need satisfies only fleetingly before we again need more and are compelled to move on to the next new, "truly" satisfying more. It's reminiscent of a cartoon picturing an attractive young woman getting into a taxi with a determined, purposeful look. She snaps instructions to the driver: "Get me to my next relationship—and step on it." This is the same posturing of the ego with respect to whatever it has designated as more—"get me there, and do it fast!"

From the depths of its very core, the ego self is driven to becoming (continually expanding or transforming) rather than being. The ego self assumes that it suffers from a "deficit" that must be corrected. Paradoxically, the ego needs the feeling of deficit to glue the system together. The deficit mentality puts the ego on a persistent hunt for fillers. That's why few people can live in the moment. For the ego, the sought-after peacefulness of the "now" moment will remain an illusive mirage. But the pain of becoming and never quite arriving lends a sense of concreteness and reality to our conceptual ego self.

## Testing the Ego

In addition, becoming, with its consequent needing and suffering, prevents the ultimate threatening test of the ego's self-sufficiency. As long as the ego is pointed to the future where it imagines completeness will be achieved, it can avoid the feared test of its wished-for omnipotence—a test that no ego can pass. "If I am complete, then I should be the world and have the world at my disposal"—a remnant of psychological birth, as we will see. A constant stream of becoming keeps this test at a manageable distance. The dreamland of yearning to become must be constantly reborn to keep reality at bay.

For this reason, rarely do people enjoy the fruits of their labors and striving. And almost never does success give people the feeling they thought it would. Typically you may yearn for success and build all sorts of fantasies about how success will transform your life. These fantasies will energetically spur you on and justify the intensity of your single goal. "When I get that promotion, the sought-after perfect relationship, the successful deal, the perfect house, the cosmetic surgery, the ideal weight, then my life will. . . ." Bingo, you're successful, but surprisingly you quickly move on to yearning for something else, forgetting how you were supposed to feel about the earlier success. It's amazing how quickly that happens. "So I have the house. Everybody here has a house. And mine isn't all that great compared to the others. What I really need is a swimming pool and a tennis court—then I'll really feel good. The face lift is fine, but I still don't have a man—that's when I'll really be happy." Sound familiar? Yet we persist in this thinking, rarely realizing that if we achieved the last longed-for goal that didn't have the anticipated sustained euphoria, how will the next one do it? But we want to believe, or, more accurately, we don't know where else to turn to achieve the ego's unrelenting restlessness. We are so absorbed in wanting, needing, and getting that there's no room for any other self to enter. Omni consciousness is nowhere to be found.

Then, there's the ultimate showstopper: "Yes, I've achieved what I wanted, but now I'm old." In chapter 6, we will look at the dilemma of the aging ego. Aging, as we will see, strikes a crippling blow to the very foundation of the ego's assumptions about self and reality that sets the stage for a spiritual emergency. If the wakeup call is heard, the third age of life will provide an exciting last-chance opportunity for embracing omni consciousness.

## Getting It All

We can readily understand the blow to the ego when we fail to achieve our goals and desires. But oddly, sometimes total success—the ego's ultimate dream realized—can be equally painful, even disastrous. Fortunately for the ego, few ever make it. Or the process of achieving success stretches out, giving us time to alter or raise our yearnings before we get "there"—so we never quite arrive and can keep reaching. We trick ourselves to keep the game of deception going. In this process, our lives are lived for us by these yearnings. We are not even the directors of our own play.

A therapist friend who treats many successful people in Hollywood told me that patients often come to him for help when they hit the top, not the bottom. Most revealing of the ego's shackles—and the saddest cases—are those in which success comes so fast and is so complete that there's no time to regroup for new goals. In some instances, hugely successful people—a number in the entertainment field (you've read about them)—have killed themselves, or nearly did so, not because they failed, but because they couldn't "handle the success." What is even more astonishing is that we casually accept this explanation and related ones as rational. Remember, success is beautiful. It is what everyone craves. Most can't even imagine super success but think it would bring super bliss. How, then, can we suddenly shift to believing "it's hard to have everything and be at the top"? Would that really make any sense if the quest were rational? Doesn't that tell you something about the fraud the ego lives by?

Here's a better explanation: the sudden loss of needing leaves the ego stranded, without its modus operandi—it then implodes on itself. Whatever state we are born into is defined as zero so that need can have a long way to travel to keep its juices flowing. A cave man might have considered a bigger cave the ultimate fulfillment of need. For the brooding millionaire, the need to fulfill "more" can carry him to the stratosphere of need. "I am enough" is foreign to the experiential mind—it is akin to death (ego death) for most people. A recent story in the *New York Times* told about the jealousy and frustration of young twenty- and thirtysomething multimillionaires with tens, if not hundreds, of millions from their young startup tech companies who look enviously at the multibillion-dollar success of the startup company YouTube that was less than a year old and sold for 1.65 billion dollars. From the prison of the self, the lament of the ego has no boundary.

Is this state of affairs necessary? Some maintain that reaching for "more" is part of the human condition. If so, are we then doomed to the legacy of unhappiness, lack of fulfillment, grasping, aggression, and despair that endless reaching breeds? But then there are those who have found another ground, challenging that pessimistic view. That ground is the ground of being: omni consciousness. Omni consciousness is beyond need, beyond becoming, and, therefore, beyond conflict. And omni consciousness is attainable because it is within everyone. When you experience omni consciousness, you will know there is a way out.

## Object or Subject?

A source of energy like electricity from a power plant can heat or air-condition a skyscraper, light up a city, power lawn mowers, shavers, hair dryers, computers, and TV sets, even run automobiles, and the list goes on. The power from the plant—electricity—is unchanging and widely available. At the same time, each specific use of electricity is local, fixed, and delimited. A waffle iron will not cool a room, and a reading lamp will not toast muffins. Yet each draws its power from the same source.

Omni consciousness is like the power plant. Its power produces generalized energy that can be used in an infinite variety of ways. In our terminology, this energy is called *subjective* because it has limitless potential and is not confined to a particular use or set of uses. It has not been *objectified* as a washing machine, say, or a city lighting system. When we direct this power system into a specific electric motor, designed to accomplish a certain task, we objectify the energy. We call the motor an *object* because it is discrete, limited, and rigidly defined by its structure, which determines what it can and cannot do. We recognize and accept that fact. We don't confuse the objective use of energy to perform certain tasks like heating and lighting with the subjective, limitless possibilities of the energy itself.

A particular object can be fabulous, even miraculous, in performing its designated functions when energized. But the refrigerator can't fly or play music—for those functions you need other objects. Lodge your identity totally in a particular object self and I assure you it will be limited—the very limitation that you experience as "I want to be more." You can be more but not from within your limited object self; for more, your identity must return to its subjective source—omni consciousness.

In the case of the ego self, we do quite the reverse. We take the objective manifestations of our lives, our particular experiences, and determine they are the subjective "us." It's as if we took the reading lamp for the electric power that makes the lamp work. Or, imagine a toaster self conscious of itself wanting to be a car for greater freedom and mobility. Make no mistake, *when we confine our identity to our objective experiences, we tie ourselves to a mental construct of "me" that is local, fixed, and delimited.* This confusion of limitless subjective potential with immediate specific usage underlies much of our inability to deal with concepts like omni consciousness. More important, it undermines efforts to liberate ourselves from the prison of the self.

## Living or Being Lived?

The ego object that we define ourselves to be *cannot live but can only be lived.* Surely the ego self is alive (or real). But its life comes from the subjective self—omni consciousness—just as the reading lamp is an inert, nonfunctional object without the energy from the electric power plant. Once energized, it can then perform its object functions.

Like any fixed object, the ego self can only live within the boundaries of its given properties, and once defined, these boundaries cannot change any more than the lamp can decide to be an iPod. They may vary a bit within their parameters, giving the impression of change, but such change is strictly narrow and not transformational.

We have trouble grasping the distinction between objective and subjective selves because we experience our limited object, nonsubject self as if it were a subject. Our very experience of awareness, the self-conscious presence of being here, gives us the feeling or illusion of being the subjective force that is in charge. In fact, our conscious presence, when lodged in the ego, is nothing more than a passive witness to the happenings of our programmed ego object. Consciousness has so identified with this ego object that it just stands by, powerless to intervene as a truly subjective force. The dramas projected by the ego, and driven by powerful emotions, are so dazzling and convincingly real that consciousness not only identifies with them but also turns over its potential subjective powers in the service of this programmed object that can only spin in its narrow orbit. There may be yearnings to grow, develop, change, become something else, but a limited object self cannot generate these actions. Can a shadow exercise volition?

The unconfined potential power of omni consciousness can generate real change but has been abandoned in favor of the ego object. The ego has a stranglehold and will not let go. In this state, we can only be lived by the programmed limits of our object self that we have empowered while dreaming we are the subject. In fact, the ego reduces our lives to a dream that unfolds as we the dreamers merely witness the events like spectators in a movie theater.

So here is the programmed object, the ego, trying to get outside itself, wanting to be the subject, the *noumenon* that can transcend any particular manifestation or *phenomenon*. But how can it do that as a mere object? It can't. It's stuck. It can only simulate the subject and its potential transcendence through delusion—distortions of reality that give the ego object the appearance of the subject. Torah scholar and teacher Rabbi Simon Jacobsen calls this distortion "looking at existence from the inside out rather than the outside in"—overvaluing the ego self and not seeing the broader picture. He uses an allegory to persuasively make his point. Imagine, he says, a refrigerator talking to the electricity that powers it. "Where do you go when I'm shut down or the plug is pulled?" The electricity responds: "I go where I have always been. I'm everywhere and have always been here. Who are you? Where did you come from and how long will you be here?"

Like the refrigerator believing it is the ultimate reality and the electricity its temporal, subordinate servant, we have a distorted picture of our egos and assign them undeserved importance and power. Rather than transcending the ego to discover the ground of consciousness, delusion works to exaggerate the power of the ego, thereby simulating (or impersonating) the true subjective power—omni consciousness: "I will become, I will acquire power, I will accumulate, I will achieve, I will expand," and so on. But the ego keeps returning to the same place and same feeling of limitation. It's amazing how everything converges to support the delusions of the ego. We distort, invent, block out, forget, feign ignorance, or follow blind faith in the belief that the ego object can get outside itself to achieve change and omnipotence. We beat up on our shadows in a furiously futile effort to make them come to life.

The key to getting out of this trap is the recognition that *we the subject as omni consciousness have empowered the ego. The power plant has ceded to the reading lamp.* Worse, we have forgotten that we are the subject (the noumenon) rather than the object (the phenomenon). We have the power for limitless possibilities; the ego self is only an objective manifestation of one small aspect of our total subjective self. The refrigerator cannot define the electricity. It can only express it in one form. While the refrigerator is stuck with its singular form and expression, we as omni consciousness can take charge of our state of being. Omni consciousness can make real changes by directing the subjective power of consciousness.

Lodging existence in the subject—omni consciousness—should be a relatively simple matter. All that would seem necessary is to let go of the object (the ego), and the noumenon is then freed to exercise its full subjective power. In principle, it's simple; in practice, incredibly complicated. The first crucial step is to become aware—profoundly aware—that *you* have abandoned *your* powerful subjective consciousness. Once you see that *you* have let the ego object take over, the split between omni self and ego self, between subject and object, will begin to dissolve. Or at least you will understand the nature of the prison of the self.

My pursuit of omni consciousness accelerated when I fully grasped the distinction between subject and object. I realized that I had lived much of my life as an object while investing heavily in improving or developing a better or different object self rather than returning to the source that empowered it.

## Unity of Consciousness

You may have heard the statement that there is no real distinction between subject and object. This is the elusive principle of *nonduality*. Some think that nonduality is just one of those tricky, "talking in tongues," Eastern mystical concepts like "the sound of one hand clapping." But like many insights from a different consciousness, it's very real. Nonduality is difficult to grasp because in our ordinary experience we perceive a distinction between subject and object. For example, I, the observer, experience objects, be they thoughts, feelings, people, or things. When you and I look at each other or interact, we experience each other as separate and independent. How, then, can the observer and the observed be the same? The following example may help.

Imagine a right hand hitting the left hand. Then the head talks to the right hand and says, "Hand, don't do that again or I'll get very angry. I'll just give you one last warning. Don't do that again." The hand hits again. "Well I warned you." With that, the left hand smashes down hard on the right hand a number of times. We could continue this debate among the three players—the two hands and the head—with increased confrontation and violence, but the example is enough to make my point. If you were unfamiliar with hands and heads and were observing this dispute through a close-up camera, the three players—the two hands and the head—would appear as separate entities interacting. But if we pulled the camera back for a panoramic, wide-angle view, you would clearly see that the three players were in fact one—all part of one self. In a flash, you would firmly know that the debate was an absurd fraud: subject and object are one. All the players in the debate are part of the same entity and a single consciousness. The conflict can only exist—or be taken seriously—as long as the split into separate and independent entities of subject and objects is sustained. The consciousness that invented the problem (for whatever reason) is the same consciousness that is trying to resolve the problem ("I warned you"). Yet the conflict cannot be resolved in the context of the split. It's patently ridiculous to deal with this situation therapeutically by talking separately to the hands and the "I" (the head). In chapter 5, I will show that most psychological counseling and treatment does just that. More disturbing, it's the *fragmented* way we have been taught to think about ourselves and our struggles. Yet, as soon as the oneness of subject and object is perceived, conflict cannot be sustained—the fraud is unmasked.

## Splitting Off Conflicts

It's more difficult to see the false split between subject and object when we are talking about some familiar psychological problems. "I'm angry at my dependency and want to get rid of it. I'm mad that I need a woman or man so desperately and therefore make bad choices. I want more out of life and feel frustrated and discouraged." The consciousness that interprets experiences and registers them as dependency, need, yearning, or frustration is the same consciousness that is now taking the subjective position with respect to itself and splitting into subject and object. That's why your conflicts stubbornly persist. The conceptual entity "me" is the *same* thought process or projection as the perceived objects of want, desire, and so forth. The split is all in *your* mind. There is the mental state of "me" the observer and the mental state of the objects registered in the mind. This is the duality that is an illusion. Both subject and object are actually the same consciousness. No amount of dialogue between these split parts will resolve conflicts any more than in my example of the fighting hands. In omni consciousness you can see the unity of the split-off parts and resolve conflicts. Omni consciousness is the panoramic view. Mind tends to register experiences as separate objects. Omni consciousness observes but doesn't register experiences as splits. It sees the unity of all consciousness—it is unity.

## The Natural Mind

If your mind got you into your problems, it's your mind that must get you out of them. How do you go about turning your mind around to serve you? Throughout this book we urge you—exhort, really—to take control of your mind. Controlling the mind is essential to liberating omni consciousness. You may bristle at this urging to tamper with your mind. Popular mythology says the "natural mind" has an inherent wisdom that will take care of itself. A closer examination will show that mind consists of fragments of consciousness that generate more and more fragments that *live* us in the sense I've just mentioned. Often our minds spin out of control just when we have the illusion of being in charge. Let's try a quick experiment to show the extent to which this "natural mind" runs out of control.

## An Experiment in Looking at the "Natural Mind"

In the very place where you are seated right now, find a comfortable position, relax your whole body, and close your eyes. Breathe evenly, concentrating just on the inhalation and exhalation. Eliminate all other thoughts from your mind. Now count in your mind: 1 for the inhalation and 2 for the exhalation; then 3 for the next inhalation and 4 for the exhalation. Continue this for a count of one hundred, thinking of nothing else but the counting of the breath.

GET SET, BEGIN

Other than experienced meditators, most people find they can't do it. Distracting thoughts keep popping up—worries, things you have to do, tasks you forgot to do, sexual thoughts, annoyance over the inability to concentrate, old memories, bills you forgot to pay, phone calls you were supposed to return, complete dialogues and debates, and other thoughts that seem to be random. It's just amazing how much can be crammed into the mind in just one hundred seconds or less, even when you are mobilizing to concentrate on something else.

Few people can do the task flawlessly for even a count of ten without distracting thoughts. For many, counting to one hundred seems like an eternity. Yet we are talking about controlling the mind—*your mind*—for less than two minutes. That should shock you! It's no small matter. Your out-of-control mind should be at the top of your list of self-concerns. If you can't be in charge of your mind for a matter of seconds when you are trying, what's going on when the mind is entirely on its own? What's your mind doing when you're watching television, walking down the street, reading a book, talking to someone, or just "being yourself"? Most people really don't know what their minds are doing—they haven't paid attention. Their minds are on automatic, and automatic in this instance means *out of control*.

The fact is, if you honestly observe your "natural mind," you will see that it is out of control most of the time. Thoughts come and go with great speed. Thoughts trigger other thoughts, some of which set off physiological reactions that pump hormones into your system. These physiological reactions produce other thoughts and more reactions—and the process goes on and on.

For apparently unexplained reasons, you might suddenly feel anxious, agitated, or depressed. You could be spurred into action by one of these thoughts or reactions. Through all of this, your conscious presence convinces you that you are in charge of your mind. In reality, your mind is whipping you around, and you are a passive eyewitness with only the illusion of control.

Yet we resist taking charge to bring order and direction to our minds, calling that artificial and rigid, with the negative connotation of "mind control."

We prefer to be "loose" and to "flow"—all of which provides additional glue to keep us stuck in the prison of the self. Omni consciousness is beyond mind and, therefore, cannot be whipsawed by mind. As you become more centered in the state of pure awareness, mind and thoughts lose their power to control you. The energy of mind and thoughts shift to their source—omni consciousness—placing you in charge.

Taking charge of mind through omni consciousness is not the usual notion of control. We commonly think of control in physical terms—a concrete, "hands-on" manipulation. Nothing could be further from the truth in the case of omni consciousness controlling mind. Omni consciousness controls mind by *not controlling*. It stands back and is the witness to mind. Thoughts come and go while omni consciousness just observes. In witnessing but not reacting, the mind and its thoughts lose their power to live you. You—the ground—are in charge. Then you can use mind when you need it for its *instrumental activities* like problem solving, working, creating, and all the other cognitive skills and powers of mind. Mind is a vital part of our being and functioning in the world.

## Spirituality and Omni Consciousness

Is omni consciousness a form of spirituality? It is in the sense that *spirituality* is a term used loosely to refer to conceptions beyond our familiar ones. But *spirituality* has so many varied usages that it is more likely to confuse than clarify. It frequently suggests something otherworldly, perhaps magic, spirits, or vague indefinable and unknowable forces. Some people use *spirituality* to mean related to God or devotional religion. Others invoke the term in opposition to scientific understanding or knowledge. On a more popular level, spirituality can mean eating vegetarian food, practicing yoga postures, not wearing animal furs, believing in the power of crystals, or recycling wastes and being mindful of the environment. These diverse usages render the term *spirituality* unclear, if not meaningless. Even if you explicitly define spirituality, it still carries the taint of varied personal meanings and associations. That's why I find it useful to call spirituality a state of consciousness—the pure awareness of omni consciousness.

If there is state of consciousness (omni consciousness) beyond our usual or more familiar conscious state that is untainted by personal experience and is conflict free, then it should be demonstrably real and potentially verifiable. You can experience omni consciousness directly (later exercises will guide you), which may be the most convincing proof. Although it may pose problems for our familiar ways of knowing, there is nothing mystical or otherworldly about omni consciousness. It is just a state of consciousness that is difficult to recapture and hold on to because ordinary experience points us away from it. There are other obstacles, too, as we shall see when we continue to track the emergence of the limited self.

## Mystical or Different?

For the person who thinks only concretely, abstract thinking may appear mystical or otherworldly. For those who readily engage in abstract thinking, the process is quite natural and obvious. In chapter 4, I will show that young children have limited mental processes and therefore are unable to see certain relationships that are obvious to older children and adults. For example, when one of two equally sized balls of clay is rolled into a sausage shape, a four-year-old will typically say there is more clay in the sausage shape than in the ball shape, even though he or she has seen it made from an identical lump of clay. For those who cannot see that the amount of clay is the same in both instances, it may appear mystical that others know this with great assurance—and can prove it.

Similarly, we assume that our adult level of perception is the highest possible. Therefore, when a group of people "know" something that we sense is true but beyond our ability, we call it mystical or spiritual. Likewise, if you were able to perceive only two dimensions—length and width but not height—a person who could perceive three dimensions would seem mystical and in possession of strange, magical powers. As a two-dimensional person, you would constantly bump into things since everything would appear flat. You would have to navigate the environment cautiously with guidance or even a navigational map. Three-dimensional viewers, on the other hand, would move seamlessly and effortlessly. That might seem baffling, if not mystical, to those who never experienced three-dimensional perception. Yet these "powers" would be quite natural, commonplace, and easily subject to scientific explanation for a person living in a three-dimensional world.

Also, the term *spiritual* has become associated with people who supposedly have mystical or supernatural powers. These gurus, priests, channels, what have you, then become intermediaries to the "other world." This leads to cultism, which is usually inimical to individual development. There are, of course, true teachers who will point the way for you to reach within yourself to connect with dimensions of yourself that are outside your present awareness or ability to fully grasp them. Finding them, however, may prove difficult. In any case, it's best to be cautious of the term *spiritual*. It carries so much excess baggage that it cannot help to clarify and may only serve to obfuscate an already complex set of understandings. We need these under-standings if we are to take back our minds, rid ourselves of our dependence on the ego-self object, and return to the reality of subjective consciousness—omni consciousness. Yet the term *spiritual* is so widely used that it is at times unavoidable. But let's be clear that in this book, *spiritual* means the realm of omni consciousness. If omni consciousness is the gateway to a divine or other dimension, you will know when you get there! Therefore, for the moment, we will put that question on hold.

## On the Road to Reality

The road back to omni consciousness involves five understandings. The re-mainder of this book is to show you more specifically how to get on the path of these understandings. Each one has its hazards because each challenges and defies your usual way of looking at yourself and the world. Each nudges you to loosen your grip on an illusory reality that you firmly embrace. In ef-fect, each understanding moves you away from the dream state of ordinary consciousness.

1. Omni consciousness is the ground of consciousness, the genuine self. It is a state of consciousness beyond the limited projection that translates personal experiences into a personal identity called I, me, self, or ego; it is the subjective state that generates the "me" object. Both omni consciousness and the "me" object are the same consciousnesses, only omni consciousness is the totality and "me" is a particular limited pro-jection and contraction of omni consciousness. Projected object states can only change in very limited ways. But the subjective state—omni consciousness—can generate change by creating new and varied ob-jects. The self that we know is a limited object that we want to act like a subject. It can't. That's why we feel stuck, frustrated, unhappy, and unfulfilled. To achieve liberation, we must change the locus of the self from the object that we think we are to the subject that is our true na-ture.

2. All is one. Everything that you experience in mind is part of the same consciousness. There are no separate independent fragments. All con-tents of mind are reflections and projections of one source—omni con-sciousness. It is through the illusion of experiencing the contents of mind as separate entities that consciousness gets fragmented. Treating these fragments as real separate entities that can meaningfully interact is what locks us into ego consciousness.

3. The character "me" does not exist as a concrete entity. It is a network of concepts in your mind and exists for only as long as you are willing to maintain it. The problem is that you believe your mind and its contents comprise all of consciousness, so all of your energy is invested in supporting, protecting, and defending your own creation. Mind is a contraction of consciousness. Its contents are interpretations from a particular set of experiences that become rigidly encapsulated. To escape from the prison of the self you must *go out of mind*. As I will explain in greater detail in chapter 5, going out of mind is not losing control or going crazy. On the contrary, only when you are outside of mind can you control and direct mind. Outside of mind there is no little self, only consciousness—omni consciousness.

4. It is *your* mind. You do not have to accept delivery of experiences. This is a fascinating and simple principle that seems almost too good to be true. What makes it difficult and seemingly out of reach is the refusal to believe: "But I had a terrible childhood that made me who I am." How many times have you heard or said things like, "She rejected me—I can't let her do that to me"? We fight tooth and nail to cling to our pains and negative emotions. But the fact is, you *don't* have to lock in to your experiences—if you dare to let go of your identification with experiences and lodge yourself in omni consciousness.

   When you cease to react to, interpret, or embrace experiences, you are free from their control. In our usual state of mind, stored experiences and interpretations create a fixed setting that yields conditioned reactions. Conditioned reactions are robotized; they do not respond to what is happening here and now but rather to the past. Once mind based on past experience is your reality, the present is forever lost. Yet the present is the only true reality. In that sense, the world of the mind is unreal.

   When you are in charge, you can see that consciousness and experiences are separate. Become aware of the space between and you will be liberated from a limited definition of self that is dictated by personal experiences.

5. You will gain great flexibility psychologically when you know who you really are—omni consciousness. Then you can move seamlessly among different roles and identities without fearing the loss of self. When you are no longer imprisoned by personal experience, you will discover the vast energy and possibilities of consciousness.

These understandings, however, like the affirmations in chapter 9, are only useful if there is a place in consciousness that can receive and act on them. Otherwise, they will remain limp sentiments. You will read them, nod your head in agreement, say them over and over to yourself, reach for them in moments of tension or despair, and firmly believe you have embraced them, even recommending them to others. But you will not live them. The problem is that the self that hears the principles and affirmations is the same self that is imprisoned and identified with its imprisonment. Only by locating another place in consciousness that is outside the encapsulation or imprisonment can genuine change take place. The first step is to get a firm grasp on who you really are.

# CHAPTER THREE

◅◦▻

# I/Me/Ego—Personal and Impersonal

Philosopher René Descartes declared, "I think, therefore I am" (Cogito ergo sum). Eastern philosophers and sages dispute this, asserting just the reverse: "I am, therefore I think." Thought is a manifestation of consciousness. There must be an "I-am-ness" prior to thought, insist the sages. Otherwise, who is thinking? Child psychologists might also take issue with Descartes. According to Swiss psychologist Jean Piaget and other child development researchers, thinking as mental representation emerges in rudimentary form at about six months of age. Yet infants, it is believed, have a sense of being prior to thought.

In the Eastern view, pure I-am-ness is the ground of consciousness—what I call omni consciousness. Thought then channels I-am-ness into a narrow personal consciousness called mind that is conditioned by our happenstance and limited experiences. Mind is the breeding ground and playground of the ego. We then confuse this small me-ego consciousness with the whole of consciousness, making it the prison of the self.

Psychologists tell us that very early in life we experience the separate "I" distinct from others and the world around us. The I/me ego that emerges becomes our volitional center. We feel that all action derives from this core; it's where our sense of presence in the world is lodged. When we wake up in the morning, we reach for that self-conscious presence to ground ourselves for the day's onslaught on the world. The emergence of a separate self with its distinction between the "I" and the "not-I" isn't something we think through and then decide to establish. It just seems to happen. That separate "me" feels right and the only way to function in the world. There's no other contender in sight or imaginable. Why question it?

So the I/me/ego self emerges. And because we assume or firmly "know" that this self is the only basis for our survival, pleasure, and power, we throw all our being and energy into protecting and developing it. We slavishly feed and serve the self from the moment we awake and dress ourselves in the I/me/ego identity until the reprieve at night when we collapse into deep sleep. Why not? If this "I" is all I have and it is essentially separate and alone, then it's my only currency for survival. Better clutch and protect it. No wonder that "I" want to possess things. The more "I" can identify things and experiences as mine, the more expansive and solid the feeling of I/me/ego.

The commitment to the growth and ascendancy of my personal self or ego, that separate "I," is no small task. The separate little "I" surely has a long way to go to master the complex world it has differentiated itself from. Think back to the times in early childhood when you perceived yourself as a separate being. Many report a feeling of aloneness, despite how warm, supportive, or encouraging their parents might have been.

There is an existential quality to this feeling of aloneness that has a very realistic basis. Indeed, if you are separate, are alone, and need a great deal now and in the unknown projected future, this little self is justifiably anxious. Mommy and daddy may help (or not), but it will still be a daunting task for this little "me" to find enduring security. And the keener the awareness of itself and the complexity of the not-me world, the more overwhelming the task of survival will seem. So the very asset of awareness is also a source of anxiety by providing us with information that will make the task of the self seeking self-sufficiency more difficult, if not seemingly impossible. But we have no choice. Here is the self, there is the world. The lines are drawn and the course of action clear.

If all this wasn't oppressive enough to lock us into the prison of the self, our most popular psychological theories will weigh in to confirm that I/me/ego self development is the way to go—and they will nudge and guide you along the path. Freudian psychology, ego psychology, self psychology, cognitive psychology, and a bevy of other "-ologies" will exhort you to strengthen the "I" to enhance "mastery" of the world. These conceptions, which have infiltrated and dominated our thinking about ourselves, will be powerful and persuasive reasons for redoubling our efforts to mobilize our energy for the struggle between the "me" and the not-me world. But the "I" warrior will have to fend off threats at every turn that can undermine the ego and destroy its illusions. A tremendous amount of energy must be spent to support and navigate the vulnerable ego through the minefields of life. Small defeats can be the most threatening. "If I fail at small tasks, how will I achieve the sought-after elusive goal of wholeness and mastery?"

Once we perceive the relationship between our delineated ego and the vast not-me world, the nervous system is thrown into a state of anticipation and readiness—even spasm or shock. No wonder that we deny, exaggerate, and glorify the ego in a frenzied orgy of delusion to distort the true picture of the plight of the pathetically vulnerable ego. We will immerse ourselves in fantasies and strivings to help this ego believe that it can master the world and attain security despite all the evidence to the contrary. Much of this will be projected into the future where we can relax the anxieties of the moment by visions of an expansive ego to come. But can this speck of an ego become secure through achievement and growth? Or does its very foundation of separateness forecast ultimate defeat?

## I Am My Emotions

Emotions play a vital role in feeding the ego's need to feel powerful. Intense emotions give illusory validation of a vibrant "me" entity that can stand up to me/world confrontations.

"I am angry, I am happy, I am sad, I need, I have to have, I yearn to become." These are things that we have all said and believe. When we talk to friends, loved ones, or therapists about our discontents, it is usually the triumvirate of "I" plus a need or want plus an emotion. "I want something and am angry or frustrated that I don't have it." Often these perceptions of self are the driving forces of our behavior. If I am angry, I want to do something to get, appease, or rid myself of the anger. I want to push it away, release it, work it out, change my environment—do something to free me from the grips of anger. The triumvirate tells us how to release the negative emotions. The object of want must be delivered to me. All three elements are necessary for the feeling of "me." Take away any of these elements and the chain is broken and the familiar "me" collapses.

For example, you might feel that you desperately need a relationship in order to be happy. The more desperate you feel, the more justified is your anger that you don't have a relationship: "Would I be this angry if I didn't really need something?" This validates and intensifies the need, which generates more anger to hold the package together. It also conveys an intense feeling of "me," the entity that needs. If there is no "me" to want, or if the "me" detaches from the equation, there can be no desperate needs. And without needs, there is nothing to be angry about. So the three—"me," need, and anger—are interrelated and self-propelling.

There must be a force of intensity that gives the ego the feeling of a powerful presence. Emotions, especially anger, accomplish that. We need a trigger for the force—needing and wanting conveniently provide it. Both imply deprivation and an insult to I/me/ego, further validating that there is an "I" that justifies the intense emotions in the service of the needs. Then, of course, we need the coherent concept of an "I" as the center of volition for these activities. That feeling gives further proof that I am here, real and alive. The "I" also becomes identified as the container for receiving the acquisitions of needing and anger. The "I" can then imagine it is expanding to fulfill its fantasy of omnipotence. The very experiences that are embraced to expand the critical mass of the felt ego become the baggage that will weight it down, limiting its range of mobility.

## Splitting the I/Me Self

Ironically, we embrace this drama and at the same time try to stand outside and oppose it. How often have you said you don't like being angry and want to rid yourself of anger? We don't like needing and strive to fulfill our needs so we will not need. If I achieve fulfillment of my needs, I won't have to be angry—there will be nothing to be angry about—until the cycle starts all over, as it inevitably does. Still there's a logical problem. If I am angry, then anger is an integral part of my self. How can I get rid of that which is essentially me? If I and anger are one, then getting rid of the anger is getting rid of part of the "me" self. It will not feel like me any longer without the anger. On the other hand, if I am separate from the anger, then I am not angry because the anger is not a definitional aspect of the self, just something outside of the self that I am experiencing—then there would be a space between me and the emotions. If that's so, then maybe I don't have to do anything but merely not pay attention to that which is not me. That makes sense. But tell an angry person to drop the anger and you're likely to hear: "You can't do that. You can't just ignore your emotions without paying a price." Isn't that just another way of saying I *am* angry—that I and my emotions are one? So we are back where we started.

The fact is that we are so married to the notion that we are our emotions that we can't even think about the self without them. In therapy, patients who even temporarily give up their favorite emotional crutches report a free-floating feeling and the irresistible urge to reclaim their destructive emotions to feel whole: "What a relief—I got my identity back." Other voices will reinforce your identification with emotions. Psychologists and psychiatrists will warn of the dangers of ignoring or rejecting emotions. They will tell you that doing so is a form of pathology, denial, or intellectualization or, worse, the road to self-disintegration. Motivational groups will insist that you must assert yourself, not let yourself be pushed around, or you will be a powerless leaf in the wind. Don't we even teach our children to fight for themselves? These recommendations seem logical if, and only if, we are locked in at the level of believing "I *am* angry," meaning "I am my emotions." If you buy into that, then indeed you will disintegrate if you give up your anger because, as we noted earlier, you will lose what you believe to be an essential part of the "I" feeling—it's like losing a limb. The same dynamic will lock you into other obsessions and psychological conflicts. The very quest to solve your problems is the problem. *You want to free the self, yet you want to do it by getting rid of what you have defined as essential to the self.* Your identity is lodged in those very conflicts. If you give up one set of conflicts, you will have to find new ones to get rid of the anxiety generated by the feeling of loss of self. You will repeatedly return to your self-imposed home as the vulnerable self with conflict and suffering. It is a familiar pattern that rules many lives.

## Case Illustration

Jim was always angry or complaining about something. His boss didn't pay enough attention to his ideas, and he was angry that he wasn't paid more for his technical skills (he was a computer programmer): *"They* are ripping me off." His wife wasn't involved enough in their sex play—he was angry and frustrated. If they went on vacation, somebody always did something to prevent him from having his imagined ultimate pleasure and fulfillment—the room wasn't right, the car wasn't waiting, the good restaurants were too far away, and so on. When one complaint subsided, another was sure to pop up to instantly to fill the gap. When his sex life improved after he and his wife saw a sex therapist (at Jim's insistence), his complaint shifted to his feeling that his wife didn't appreciate how hard he worked and that she didn't do enough for him (even though she worked full time and earned as much as he did). Through all of this, Jim never questioned his need to be angry and his feeling of his self being lost without the anger. Each situation and feeling had its compelling rationale. His feelings seemed so real and justified. Jim's anger may seem transparent, but isn't it the same with most of our so-called needs? We want to satisfy our needs, yet we need to need. No sooner do we satisfy a need than a new one is there to replace it.

So on one level you seek freedom, while on another level you have set conditions that preclude that possibility. As long as "I am my emotions" is the underlying assumption, you can only create momentary illusions of freedom from conflict—in the future. This process makes life tolerable by holding out some promise of freedom from conflict. Yet despite the failure of any so-lutions to ever work or endure, we still never question our underlying as-sumptions about the nature of self. Why? Simply because we have excluded any other concept of self. Yet another self is there and can be embraced. Even better news: nothing needs to be done or sought. One merely has to give up some very tightly guarded assumptions. Why is this task so difficult, espe-cially if it can offer so much? The prison of the self is heavily guarded and de-fended by none other than the ego self.

## Impersonal Consciousness

If I am not my emotions and my experiences, then what am I that is personal and my own? Is it possible that I can be something that is not personal? If so, in what sense is that me? Here we are stuck in the belief that anything gen-uine or authentic must be personal. *Impersonal* is a dirty word. It sounds cold, detached, unfeeling, aloof, perhaps uncaring. On the other side, we assign all the positives to *personal*. Looked at more closely, this false distinction is an-other entrapment of the self.

When experience is personalized, it channels energy and identity into a narrow sphere that excludes all other possibilities. As I have indicated, "I am an angry person," or any other narrow identification, compresses potentially limitless consciousness into a constricted box. By detaching from these nar-row definitions, the I/me retains its limitless expression of "I am" (omni con-sciousness). Omni consciousness is not defined by experiences. Its universal nature is sensitized to all life and all possibilities, broadening rather than lim-iting its connectedness, feelings, and expression. Being completely open, it doesn't have to defend a particular lens setting or fight its limitations. Its openness encompasses all. Contrary to our belief, ownership of experiences limits rather than expands the self. We so eagerly and greedily seek owner-ship of experiences that in the very process we abandon ourselves rather than celebrate ourselves. The impersonal is, therefore, more sensitive, not less.

## Another Look at Subject and Object

In chapter 2, we saw the relationship between energy and a specific object that uses the energy. The energy source—the subject—can animate many different objects. The more we understand about the perceived I/me/ego, the clearer it becomes that it is experienced as a subject but is, in fact, a limited object. A subject is the center of volition and action. The subject can grow, change its appearance, or, in other words, become many different forms. The word *become* is crucial. Becoming means freedom of motivational choice. The subject as center of existence controls energy in the broadest sense—it is the source of energy. Through the person we define ourselves to be, we *feel* we are a subject. In other words, you walk around thinking and feeling that you are in charge of your life and behavior. You feel that you have choices, make decisions, and are moving toward goals that will give you pleasure and fulfillment. But actually this is an illusion if your operating system is the ego object. Your conscious presence (self-consciousness) gives you that feeling. In fact, you are merely a passive witness to the person (object) you have defined and limited yourself to be—an actor in a play of consciousness. A person as a specific personality is only one particular projection and conceptualization of omni consciousness. Like a shadow, which is merely a reflection, a personality is a reflection of consciousness. As such, it is an object, not a subject. Like a shadow, the personality as object is limited. No matter how hard you try, the shadow can't be liberated. The tail can't wag the dog.

We keep returning to the realization that conscious presence lends to the illusion that you can exceed the structural bounds of your self-imposed self-definition. Structure limits and restrains action but can very efficiently execute its program. Because you can observe what is going on (conscious presence), you are fooled into believing that you can act like a subject through the object. The Indian sage Nisargadatta Maharaj, commenting on this charade, described the performance of the ego as "a slapstick comedy." But it's not so funny that we spend our lives and energy in this vaudeville act.

We are stuck with this thing called conscious presence, and we don't know what to do with it. We can see many possibilities, yet we feel limited. Whatever we achieve suddenly shrinks against the great expanse. We want, we need, we want to be, and we look outward for these things hoping that some acquisition or attachment will, somehow, catapult us into our expansive vision. But how can the particular be the whole? We look away from ourselves to find ourselves. We want to become something we are not in order to be ourselves. How can that happen? I will reject myself for the not-me so that I can be me. But being me will only promote the quest for a new not-me because any ego self will be limited and then generate the quest for the whole. But you are looking in the wrong place. One of the aims of this book is to help you locate the genuine subjective self—omni consciousness, the power plant of being.

The first step is to become aware that there is a consciousness beyond the ego that is not limited by the constrictions of self-definition. The next step will be to help you experience this state of consciousness from which vantage point you will know (although not necessarily master) the difference between self as subject and self as object. Once you taste omni consciousness, the ball will be in your court. Will you run with it?

## Case Illustration

Mike at age fifty-five felt that all the pizzazz had gone out of his life. He had achieved all that he strived for in his life and, by his own admission, much more than he had dreamed of when he was younger. He had a comfortable apartment in the city, a country home, two grown children who were successful and on their own, and a stable relationship with his wife, and he was in reasonably good health. Although he went through his daily chores, he described his dominant feeling as "like waiting to die." His thoughts focused on some past regrets. "If I had gone into that partnership years ago, I would have a much bigger and more important law practice today." His worries concentrated on money. Although he had enough to do all the things he and his wife enjoyed, that realization did not diminish his worry. "What if I can't get new clients? My rent keeps going up and I have no assurance that I'll be able to pay it." When it was pointed out to him that even under the worst scenario he wouldn't go under, he acknowledged that fact but continued to obsess. Trying to deal with Mike's problem at the level of the problem is futile or at best can have only limited gain. Mike wants his delusion back. He longs for the excitement of the dream world of his younger days, when he imagined achieving all of the things that he now actually has achieved. The dream, as long as it was in the future, fulfilled the need of the ego to believe in its omnipotence: "If and when I achieve my goals, I will be the invulnerable, omnipotent me." Mike is there, and he is not omnipotent—and he doesn't know where to go anymore to get that powerful feeling. Having achieved, he no longer believes in achievement. But not knowing where to go for his longed-for feeling of omnipotence, the future having disappointed him, he returns to the past. "If I had done this, if I had done that. . . ." Since the past doesn't exist, nor does its hypothetical possibilities, the ego feels somewhat stroked. "I could have been omnipotent, but I just had bad luck or made a wrong decision." So he lodges his energy in the fantasies of the past and allows those fantasies to live him. When even that doesn't do the trick, he tries to reinvoke the delusion of the future. "If I could only get my hands on a lot of money, then I would have the old feeling back." Beating and shaking the same old ego just can't get it going anymore—it has played its games and has nowhere to go. So he halfheartedly thinks about some quick hits—the stock market, a new partnership—but he can't really work up much enthusiasm. Deep down, he senses that the gig of the ego is over.

Added to this is the age factor. We give it a descriptive label—midlife crisis—that we believe explains something, but it doesn't. We look at the content of the expressed "problems" when we should be looking at the structure. I'm reminded of a resident in a nursing home that I met. Annie was seventy-eight years old. A stroke left her confined to a wheelchair, but she was still mentally intact, alert, and articulate. She had been an English professor at a major university before retiring. When I praised some of her accomplishments, she fired back: "A lot of good it did me—look at me now." Annie was expressing the universal ego perspective: "If I grow and become, I will be invulnerable." It's the driving delusional force that makes the ego-based existence tolerable. But under the best of circumstances, the ego reality will break down *in time.*

The ego feasts on time. But time becomes the natural enemy of the ego when feast turns to famine, as we will see in chapter 6. While the ego plots its omnipotence, time chips away. At some point, time gets the upper hand and the ego can no longer ignore its message: "That ego of yours is temporal—no matter what you do, it will vanish." So the problem for the ego is its unreal assumptions, expectations, and demands. "If life will not conform to my demands, I will get mad and not accept life. I will find new delusions to fight reality. And if they don't work, I will shut down." At one point of despair Mike reached the conclusion that he probably had a *slight* genetic deficiency (slight so that his ego would only be slightly slighted) that prevented him from really being at the top. Here we have the final food to protect the ego's delusion. "What this ego would have been if not for that imagined defect." Now he can wallow in the dream world of "what if"—reality doesn't count. It also subtly resurrects the ego's delusion of "more." Real "more" didn't work, but mythical, unattainable "more" would work—"if I could only believe it."

How would psychotherapy or professional counseling address Mike's crisis? Chapter 5 will show that traditional therapeutic approaches typically join the distortions of the ego to help clients construct more workable distortions for stumbling less falteringly through life. But the faulty operating system would not be challenged.

## Personal Narratives

We all have our personal stories "explaining" why we are "compelled" to behave—sometimes irrationally—the way we do. But understand, it is only when "me" is at the center of action that personal narratives and the persuasive explanations that justify compulsions are believable:

"I am angry because she doesn't respond to me," "He doesn't pay enough attention to me—I'm depressed and frustrated," or "I never get the right man—I'm so depressed—what's wrong with me?" We can now parade the items of personal history to explain these current dilemmas and justify the emotional responses. The more wrenching and painful the emotions of the narratives, the less likely we and others will question the logic. While there is an internal logic to these packages, it is all premised on "me." Without a concrete "me" entity, the whole thing falls apart. Conversely, the "me" can only have existence if it is at the center of experiences and exists over time as an entity. So the "me" entity needs experiences to be "me," and experiences need a "me" entity in order to register the experiences and conclusions. Experience and "me" are bonded.

Once the "me" entity is relaxed and the self is lodged primarily in the pure awareness of omni consciousness, there is no "me" to be dominated by experiences and, therefore, no need for the debilitating emotional reactions of anger and depression. You can then observe the happenings, even experience the feelings conditioned by personal history, but there is no need to react. Within the all-inclusive awareness of omni consciousness, there is no enduring, historically fixed "me" to defend or protect. If there is no thing to defend, then the emotions simply do not flow, or, when they do arise, they are temporary and quickly fade. The usual conditioned responses that we readily accept as "normal" then seem unnecessary, if not silly, when we are lodged in omni consciousness. There is no compulsion to act—you are in charge and can *choose* to act.

This discussion leads us back to the troubling point we continually get stuck on. "How can I be me without my personal history? Without the feeling of the 'me' entity that is stable and coherent over time, I will be nothing—at least nothing that is familiar or that will feel like *me*." *It is this inability or unwillingness to let go of personal experience that prevents us from getting to our omni consciousness.* It is the trapdoor of experience that we fall into from birth onward that lands us in the prison of the little ego self. We cannot see a place outside the prison where those bars and limitations cannot confine us. Yet that place—omni consciousness—is within you. It is your ground of being.

## Locus of Self and Consciousness

Where is your center of being and action? Chances are you never asked that question. You know yourself as you are and assume that your self/world posturing is the only "real" one. It's like color-blind people not knowing that there is another way of experiencing the world, or the child who is farsighted seeing things blurred when up close. When given glasses, farsighted children are amazed to learn that others see that way all the time without glasses. But how could they have known?

It is essential to realize that consciousness can be lodged in many places and you have a choice. Is your locus the whole of consciousness (omni consciousness) or a fragment? Much of our existence is pulled to fragments of consciousness that live us when we allow our locus to be confined to a cramped cell. We become an emotion, a striving, a goal, a project, a need, and so on. Think of the times when you have been lived or driven by a fragment. Observe people around you. Can you see the fragments that drive them? Some become a possession like a car, a house, or the clothes they wear. For others it is a role: manager, boss, supervisor, doctor, lawyer, great dancer, and so forth. Some can't function outside these roles. Can you see how their possibilities have been narrowed? Where is the locus of your consciousness?

All of these identifications are concepts that are energized by rays of omni consciousness. When we identify with these fragments, we mistakenly take them for the whole. Once this identification is made, all energy is shifted to that locus. We overinvest in the fragment, forgetting our true identity. When identify is confined to a single projection, you will feel stuck and trapped. How can you know that a fragment as the locus of consciousness can never lead to satisfaction, that it is a lifeless object that is dependent on its source? You will know once it runs its course and its lifelessness becomes apparent—with disappointment, emptiness, and frustration the legacy. You will then be inclined to get angry and strive to force your identification to give you the fulfillment and satisfaction that you feel you deserve. But the lifeless object can't do that for you any more than your shadow can give you a better job, exciting relationships, or anything else. Only by returning to the source of consciousness can you capture the vast possibilities of consciousness and be free to make unencumbered choices. As the source, omni consciousness does not have to get anywhere. Therefore its actions are not for the sake of something else. Its creativity is true creativity. Being is its power. Being is its own end and its own satisfaction. Existence becomes unified and all-inclusive. You are home.

## How We Know the Ego Self Is Here

To know and feel ourselves as real, the self must be conceived of as a coherent, solid entity in space with duration, so the self of our perception consists of mass, time, and space. We have to bear in mind that no such self exists. The self we identified as a child is not the self we see in the mirror today. This self is a mental concept held together by the glue of memory and our desperation to believe that it is a real entity, not just a mental construct. In defiance we continue to think and feel ourselves to be an enduring, continuous entity. To buoy up that belief, we need certain experiences. First we need to feel this self moving as an entity in time. It has to have been somewhere, have arrived in the present, and be heading somewhere in the future. The past, present, and future tracking of the self gives it a feeling of concrete reality. The self must be on the move to reinforce the very sensation of self. That's why the self is busy coming from somewhere and moving on. It can't stand still. In the agitation for forward motion, we can't experience the silence of the "now" moment that would reveal the enduring and unchanging I-am-ness of omni consciousness. When immobile, the self starts losing the feeling of concrete reality.

According to the Tibetan sage Tarthong Tulku, the self must, therefore, "be up to something all the time." Feeding the "up to something" stance are intense feelings. Anger and anxiety are at the center of the self's movement. Anger and anxiety keep the self moving in its self-created time frame and are, therefore, necessary for the "life" of the self. Anger says we are not enough and need more—also that we probably deserve more, thereby justifying the anger. Anxiety is the barometer or dipstick of the self's progress toward maintaining itself as not only a concrete, solid object but one that is growing, expanding, and becoming. When it slips or stalls from this course, anxiety arises to activate the system to do something to prop up the fading illusion. Anger promptly enters to jolt the system into action—almost like cardiac resuscitation. Anger also injects a single-mindedness of purpose and action, which by obliterating all other considerations confirms the righteousness of the course and the action.

This busyness always has a convincing content that engrosses us and distracts from the underlying need just to be busy in the service of the ego. It all seems so real that we need this or that, or that we have to move on, convinced that we are actually getting somewhere, although we are never quite sure what "getting there" means, since when we get "there," we promptly reorient ourselves to need more and get somewhere else. Remember the woman in the cartoon who was racing to her next relationship. Somehow, we don't question that racing even though it almost never delivers the expected or promised peacefulness and self-contentment. Little successes and accomplishments along the way bring feelings of pleasure, which further validate the whole package. But pleasure and fulfillment can only be short lived because the self, to feel itself, must get busy and move on. The present is too short, if it lasts at all. So to reestablish its enduring quality, the self must point its delusions to the future and keep moving. A never-ending pattern emerges. The self arrives in a future which by the very fact of its arrival is no longer the future and therefore must be scrapped for a new future. Through all of this, we believe we are in charge of ourselves and are actually seeking pleasure and fulfillment. But the very needs and assumptions of this conceptually driven ego preclude the goals it seeks.

### Case Illustration

Jane "desperately" wants to get married. She has had an endless succession of relationships. Most go well and are satisfying for a period of time. But despite the "desperation," something always happens to justify ending the relationship and moving on, to get busy all over again to desperately find a new relationship. She has defined her neediness and busyness around relationships. No rational arguments will stop her from moving on. The life of the ego is at stake, and that becomes the only reality.

## The Middle Ground

Most of us function best in the middle ground between failure and success. At the bottom, there is despair and anger that the ego self is nothing. At the top, there is the confusion and despair of having lost the ego by achieving its goal—the illusion is gone and there is no grounding; there is a desperate need for need: "I am at the top and still want and need to become more—but what?" In the middle, there is the driving force of moving ahead or maintaining a position so as not to fall into nothingness. Looking upward, there is the euphoria of moving up to become the ultimate wish of the ego—"I am the world." Fortunately, most of us reside in the middle range or reinvent it when goals are not achieved. But this posturing is limiting and debilitating. It traps energy in the service of delusion. You are not free to be yourself.

## Need for Experiences

As we have just seen, the experiential self needs a constant flow of experiences to feel its existence and foster the delusion of a concrete entity. The experiential self craves experiences and is addicted to them. Positive and negative feelings about the self become tied to whether or not certain experiences are acquired. If the self is experience, then the more experiences, the bigger and better the self will be. Conversely, the fewer and less powerful the experiences, the lower the judgment of that self. Missing out on experiences can evoke devastating feelings of deprivation and craving. Consequently, the self is always on the lookout for new experiences to enhance itself and to feel more expansive and powerful. On the negative side, when the self is deprived of experiences, there is a feeling of disappointment, frustration, and anger—the self does not take lightly barriers to its upward and onward movement.

When the self is lodged in omni consciousness, experience does not define the self. The self is already whole and complete. Therefore, experiences cannot frustrate or control the self. Did you ever wonder why some people desperately need experiences and others do not? There are those who seek experiences, desire them, and enjoy them but are not devastated when they slip away. Their selves are not easily wounded by the absence or loss of experiences. For others, circumstantial events like not having a date or party invitation, not getting a desired promotion, having to postpone a desired trip, and so forth can throw a person into a deep depression or rage. The locus of consciousness makes all the difference.

## Flying High

Added to the magnetism and excitement of experiences is the fact that we live in an instant-gratification society that spews out excitement all around us. Flip on the TV or drop into a movie theater and you are flooded with exciting images. It seems like everyone lives in the vortex of fast action and quick takes. See how fast the images change. Rarely does the camera even pause for sustained reflection. We are conditioned to move fast physically, visually, and verbally. It's all so exciting. No wonder we want it all—and fast. We get up in the morning and start e-mailing, faxing, and express mailing. Even a plane or a car is no haven—we can call from both. We can send e-mail over a cell phone from any location. We don't have to "waste" a moment. Should there be a momentary lull, the music and video iPod is ready to roll. We can be in the throes of excitement and motion from the moment we awake and start being lived by the need for excitement until sleep brings a brief reprieve. Should there be any letup in excitement, we can always fill in with a pill or injection to stay "up." All the instant communicating also feeds and inflates a sense of self-importance—even trivial events can no longer wait, as in the cell phone call to say, "Yes, I'm on the bus and will be home in ten minutes with the pizza." According to psychologist James Hillman, we live in an extroverted society where anything less than mania is considered depression: "Fast food, fast cars, fast photo service and the speed checkouts are only some of the testimony to our desire to make a hyperactive lifestyle the norm." Visit a health club and observe self-improvers working out on a stationary bicycle while reading a magazine or report, bombarded by jarring music over a loudspeaker, and talking on a cell phone—often all at the same time. Compare that to the yoga principle of one-pointedness—being fully present and silently concentrated with a single focus in the unified "now" moment.

Aside from the question of whether or not our bodies and nervous systems are built for this barrage of stimulation, there is the bigger question of what it is doing for us, if anything. We still don't know who we are, why we are here, what we are doing, where we are going, or what we will do when we get to the goal of our drivenness. But one thing we know for sure: we want to get there *fast*. Yet when we get "there," we feel little pleasure or relief as we rev up the engines to start all over again. Is this what you want? Are you living or being lived?

## The Ego Lie

The ego is founded on the false belief that it can and must be invulnerable. But with no conception of another secure ground of being, it cannot face the painful truth that it is a mere speck. Enter delusion for renewal of hope. Foremost is the paradox that pain and suffering are embraced for the safety of the ego. Overcome pain and suffering, the ego believes, and invunerability will be the bounty. We are back to the future where delusions flourish—and ultimately collapse when the bounty is not bountiful but empty. New sufferings must then be generated to keep the game going. So truth is forever beyond the ego, and the universal delusional dream state is what we consensually call reality. But true reality resides beyond the ego. At the higher level of omni consciousness, the ego game is transparent, and you cease to get sucked into its debilitating vortex.

## Feeding on Danger

To fuel the sense of threat and danger that jump-starts the ego into perpetual action to achieve "more," very early in its development the ego attaches personal psychology to the sympathetic nervous system. This fatal turn forever dooms the ego to a path of no return from conflict, pain, and suffering.

The parasympathetic and sympathetic nervous systems are parts of the autonomic nervous system that regulate body functions and control organs, the blood system, and hormone secretions among other physiological mechanisms that are largely outside of voluntary control. While parasympathetic responses are designed to conserve energy, lower blood pressure, and maintain homeostasis (balance), sympathetic nervous system responses are nature's way of grabbing our attention in dangerous life-and-death situations by initiating reactions of fear, flight, and fight. The adrenaline and other hormones it pours into the nervous system when we face danger heighten alertness, which gets us to react instantly to threats like fire, attacks, and other life-threatening assaults. This mechanism was vital for day-to-day survival when humans lived in jungles and other natural environments with dangers at every turn. In the modern, industrialized world, the life-and-death response to physical threats should be called on less frequently. But don't tell that to the ego. Once the ego attaches its "me" psychology to the sympathetic nervous system and seals the connection, it establishes the urgency of all desires. Ego quests—including ordinary daily activities—are then placed on a par with life-and-death physical survival. As distressing as they may be, rejection, failed relationships, frustration, losing a promotion, or other assaults on the ego's sense of worth and importance are not life-threatening comparable to facing down a lion or cobra in the jungle.

The linking of the ego and the sympathetic nervous system becomes self-propelling. First the ego generates intense reactions through the sympathetic nervous system. The heightened alertness and tension then convince the ego that there's real danger, thus pumping up further sympathetic reaction. It's a process that sustains and rationalizes the ego's frenzied acquisitiveness. "Look how endangered I am—look how hopped up I am. I must, therefore, act with life-and-death determination and force to get what I want and need."

Breaking the tie between the ego and the sympathetic nervous system will be an important task for escaping from the prison of the self and restoring the primacy of omni consciousness. But that's no small task. It requires loosening the addiction to self-consciousness—a self-consciousness that we falsely believe is the secure foundation and essence of our being. Efforts at dislodging yourself from that conviction will elicit the most ferocious, all-out life-and-death sympathetic nervous system alert. Yet at every turn, self-consciousness will drive you deeper into the prison of the self.

## The Self-Consciousness Trap

Here's an analogy that will give you a graphic picture of how the very self-consciousness that we worship for delivering the feeling of a concrete, separate, and alive "me" is actually limiting.

Blood circulates through the body, nourishing all the organs. Then, when passing through the liver, it gets cleansed—impurities are removed. In a sense, the liver is the blood doctor. While the blood is made up of individual cells, we still think of blood as a system—a totality. Individual blood cells are not crucial. In fact, we can lose blood or donate blood without harming the system. The body will restore the lost or donated blood, reasserting the primacy of the blood system as a whole and its connectedness, interrelationship, and interdependence with the rest of the body.

Now let's imagine an individual blood cell with self-consciousness. The self-consciousness enables that individual blood cell to feel separate, distinct, different, and perhaps unique in relationship to other blood cells—or the entire organism. It feels only itself. Although the blood cell might have an intellectual understanding of its relationship to other blood cells, and the body as a whole, it nevertheless is dominated by the feeling of "me" separate and distinct from other blood cells. "I am me, and they are them."

Moving the scene forward, let's imagine that our self-conscious blood cell is not feeling well. Something isn't right, and because of its self-consciousness it can experience bad feelings. Maybe other blood cells are also feeling distress, but the one blood cell in question doesn't directly experience those other blood cells and isn't interested in their well-being as much as its own. So as it enters the liver, the blood cell complains to the blood doctor, demanding relief. The blood doctor explains that it can't effectively treat the one cell but must look at the whole system for an understanding and effective treatment. In fact, the treatment, the doctor says, might be to minister to other organs or another part of the blood system that might be generating the problem. The doctor is more interested in the integrity of the whole system—and organism—than the individual cell.

The individual cell does not like that evaluation, which steps on its sense of "numero uno." The blood cell demands personal and individual attention as well as relief from the bad feelings generated by its self-consciousness. As the cell turns nasty, making demands and threats to the doctor suggesting incompetence, even malpractice, the liver doctor finally caves in and says, "Take two aspirins and I'll take another look next time you come around." The cell feels relieved and encouraged. It got individual attention and sympathy, and for the moment it feels better, even though the underlying pathology has not changed and the systemic problem still remains. The organism may, in fact, be heading toward disaster. That escapes the attention of the individual cell as it wallows exclusively in preoccupation with itself.

Doesn't this story remind you of our own self-consciousness that elevates individuality while obliterating expansive awareness and connectedness to a wider cosmic order? The moral of this allegory: you must transcend self-consciousness to restore wholeness, wellness, and universal awareness—omni consciousness. But addiction to self-consciousness has deeply entrenched roots reaching back to the onset of psychological birth.

# CHAPTER FOUR

# Psychological Birth
# and the Spiritual Self

## Part 1: Delivery of the Limited Experiential Self

"That damn ego keeps tripping me up. Why can't I just drop it?" is the frustrating question voiced in every spiritual group I've ever attended. This question is understandable since the ego guards the door to higher consciousness, confining us to the prison of the self. This conundrum is not new or exclusive to initiates on the spiritual path.

Getting beyond the ego or "me" consciousness has eluded spiritual seekers throughout the ages. I once asked a Hindu pandit (scholar) why it's so difficult to let go of the ego, especially once you taste transcendent consciousness—call it God, divinity, Buddha mind, higher consciousness, creative energy, bliss consciousness, or other terms for the expansive egoless state. I was hoping for a simple magic answer. No such luck. He rattled off the standard script that I had heard many times: "The grip of the ego is so tight and its deceptions so varied that it's a lifelong (or over many lifetimes) struggle to defeat it." In practice, we know the pandit is correct—just count the casualties that stumble on the path and the few who make it to the mountaintop. Still, his descriptive "explanation" bothered me. It struck me much like the same cop-out that therapists use for their failure to cure by calling every emotional problem an addictive disorder and their clients victims requiring lifelong treatments on ladders of varying and often increasing steps.

But then I recalled that sometimes significant, even sudden, dramatic change does occur. Could those instances provide a clue to solving the puzzle of ego consciousness dominating its source (omni consciousness)—the object reversing figure and ground and leading the subject?

For example, I recall five-year-old Nora surprising everyone by unexpectedly giving up her favorite pastime—thumb sucking. Nora's habit seemed so pleasurable and soothing that her parents envisioned it continuing into her first job interview. Indeed, why shouldn't it be almost impossible to break or let go of a strong habit that is reinforced over long periods of time, even years? Behavioral psychologists in the 1930s and 1940s thought so, prompting them to warn parents to swiftly put a stop to "pernicious" habits by whatever means. So zealous were they in their war on the objectionable habits that they invented restraining devices and other draconian deterrents. But then, outfoxing their neat theory, children were observed to give up thumb sucking—and other habits—as abruptly as Nora, with no special intervention. You and your children may have done so as well. How does this happen?

Psychologists now offer a simple explanation: the child decides not to be the baby any more or strives to emulate other children in his or her school or playgroup, or some other powerful motive enters the picture. Psychological dynamics—especially motivation—can instantaneously override almost any habit. If that's the case, then dropping the ego should be a cakewalk since the rewards and motivation seem so great. What's the problem?

In pondering this question I asked myself, "Is there some overlooked aspect of psychological development that could provide the key to the mystery?" As I mentally played and replayed the sequence of normal psychological development, my attention kept returning to the very beginning of psychological birth when the I/me/ego first appears. I began to suspect that events surrounding psychological birth that we assume are strictly positive have a negative downside. Could that explain the vicelike grip of the ego that clouds our ability to see omni consciousness? I wondered. Then it suddenly hit me and seemed so obvious. Of course, "normal" psychological development encases us in a wall of personal experiences that become the *prison of the self*. I then asked, "Could fully understanding the nature of the prison point to an escape hatch?" I held that hope in mind as I took a fresh look at psychological birth and development armed with my newly discovered insight.

## What Is Psychological Birth?

*Psychological birth* is the moment when the infant perceives itself separate from the surrounding world of other people and things. It's when the I/me emerges, establishing the foundation for the ego self. Some experts say it's not a moment at all but a process that begins between four and six months of age. Psychiatrist Dan Stern observed infants and concluded that it begins even earlier—between birth and two months. Other investigators suggest that a primitive rudimentary sense of self may be present at the very beginning of life, or even in the womb. But most agree that the process accelerates between six months and two years of age, and by age two the structure of the separate "me" is firmly established.

Understanding the process of psychological birth is crucial for grasping the predicament of the imprisoned self and the daily struggles we all face in our effort to achieve liberation from conflict and suffering. Surprisingly, I discovered that the creation of this unique, separate self, so necessary for effective functioning in the world, sets in motion processes that undermine our efforts at liberation.

We celebrate psychological birth as a landmark event because it begins the journey of the individual self on its quest to acquire the skills and attributes necessary for fulfilling its needs and desires. The physical world is an endless, complex maze that we must understand and navigate for effective day-to-day living. In focusing strictly on the positive, though, we fail to see that psychological birth is a double-edged sword. On the one hand, it's a vital process in the individual ego's quest for mastery of the world; there's little need for acquiring skills until a separate self is identified. Just notice the joy of the infant with a growing sense of "me" when discovering that he or she can make something happen by pressing a button on a toy, or suddenly finding himself or herself walking. Other acquisitions will set the stage for learning to manipulate and control the immediate environment that will later extend to managing the intellectual and social worlds of work, interpersonal relations, and play throughout the life span. So psychological birth should not be taken lightly or dismissed. On the other hand, psychological birth administers a shock from which we never recover—a shock that will propel the imprisonment of the self into a narrow identification with personal experience.

## Psychological Birth: No Gain Without Pain

The pluses of psychological birth are clear: to grow, to become independent and separate, to acquire skills and develop talents and abilities, to create, and to evolve into a unique person. That all sounds desirable and positive. Why, then, is it a shock?

Separation and individuation create the sense of a stand-alone "me" that wrests the infant from the attachment security it previously owned that must now be replaced by independent achievements. With psychological birth, security is no longer a given—it's conditional. "Free lunch" begins to fade as doing and achieving replace passive getting. There is, however, a much more profound sense of loss. The feeling of oneness with the world evaporates as psychological birth delivers the separate, individual self.

Separate also means alone, disconnected, and dependent. The trauma of this loss is undoubtedly intensified and encapsulated by the inability of the infant to understand what has happened. On a feeling level, something is gone. But how can the infant know the source of this loss? He or she can't. Could this be the basis for the common feeling that most of us have of something missing—an elusive state that we seek to recapture in a lifelong journey that takes many forms? Can this goal even be achieved if it derives from a primitive state of consciousness that has vanished from our grasp?

### Before "Me," the World Is One

Prior to psychological birth, the infant exists in a state of oneness. Psychologists believe that the newborn experiences a unity of self and world with little distinct awareness of a separate "me." There are many terms used to describe this state. Famed psychiatrist Sandor Ferenczi called the first few weeks of life a state of "absolute unconditioned hallucinatory omnipotence." That's a technical mouthful. Expressed more simply, perhaps *cosmic unity* captures its tone.

In stark contrast to the feeling of omnipotent unity or oneness is the infant's actual helplessness and total dependence on caretakers for survival. When psychological birth occurs with the emergence of the separate "me," the infant begins to experience a "me" that is relatively helpless and dependent juxtaposed against the vast not-me world. A loving, protective, and supportive environment can cushion this perception; a physically or emotionally pernicious one can intensify the sense of alienation.

How does the shift in self/world perception feel to the vulnerable infant? We can only speculate since we have no way of getting inside the infant's psyche. But from what we know about the limited capacity of infants for processing information, it's likely that the infant perceives this transition as one in which the world has changed rather than one in which he or she has changed.

In other words, infants in the early, precognitive phase of existence (before mental concepts, ideas, and representation) not only experience a unity of self and world, they simply do not know that the world is separate from them. What a terrific feel-good and powerful sensation the self/world merger must provide. "I am the world" defines the infantile precognitive state of omnipotence that protects the child from perceiving his or her vulnerability in a vast "out there" not-me world. This *cognitive narcotic* or *cognitive anesthesia* enables the child to grow and develop in a relatively anxiety-free zone. Perhaps it is an evolutionary shield or protection that provides "breathing space" for human development to unfold and flourish during the long incubation period that humans require.

Imagine the consequences if the infant were able to accurately perceive the complexity of the world and his or her state in it. An analogy might be the experience of standing at the foot of Mount Everest believing that you had to climb to the top never having seen a mountain before and possessing no mountain-climbing skills or tools. Fortunately, information is only gradually revealed as personal development unfolds over a period of years. Otherwise, awareness of its true powerless and vulnerable state might overwhelm the undeveloped nervous system, severely impairing further development.

## The Power of Powerlessness
It's paradoxical that the child feels most powerful when in fact he or she is the least powerful and feels powerless when in fact he or she has achieved psychological birth and has begun to acquire considerable skills as well as the potential for effectively navigating much of the physical and social environment.

Let's be clear on this point. Here is the infant, eyes closed, sucking a finger or nipple, warmly wrapped in snug clothing, pressing close to the mother's breast, feeling the soothing rhythmic heartbeat of the mother. The infant is in bliss consciousness. This bliss, however, has nothing to do with external reality. There are no achievements, acquisitions, or attributes connected to generating it. It's just a given feeling that's wired in. In fact, the infant is helpless, dependent, vulnerable, incapable of survival on his or her own, and without any skills for effectively interacting, manipulating, or navigating the physical world. In contrast to the feeling state of omnipotent bliss, the infant is totally impotent and in grave danger of annihilation without protective custody and support.

Yet it's this precognitive, blissful state that is welded into our organismic memory—a state that we strive for, are driven by, and perhaps organize our lives around. Many of our fantasies and insatiable quests for good feelings (including drug addiction and other addictions) may be symbolic efforts to recapture the omnipotent bliss consciousness of infancy prior to psychological birth. Quite funny, if not tragic, when you think about our drivenness in these terms.

## Psychological Birth Trauma
Child psychologist Margaret Mahler, in her pioneering studies of the crisis confronting the child during psychological birth, concluded that separation

and individuation are "a kind of second birth experience . . . a hatching from the symbiotic mother-child common membrane." In plain language, psychological birth rips the child away from a snug attachment. This is a time of great stress for the fragile defenses of the infant. When there is a lag in readiness for this individuation and separation, there is "organismic panic." Mahler gives the example of a toddler who has precocious motor ability enabling her to physically move away from the mother but is not emotionally ready to handle separation. This distress, she says, can produce severe disturbances.

In "normal" development, the panic that Mahler graphically describes is toned down by more effective mother-child interaction. For the disturbed child, "the physical fact of separation can lead to ever more panic-stricken disavowal of the fact of separation and to the delusion of symbiotic union." Thus, the child might refuse to walk or talk to maintain the belief in non-separateness or fusion with the mother.

I believe that *all* responses to the panic of individuation and separation involve delusion. But the "normal" delusions are universally shared, making them acceptable and unquestioned. One example is the "transitional object" described by psychiatrist D. W. Winnicott half a century ago. It's something almost every child and parent is familiar with. You may recall your transitional object from childhood. The transitional object is typically a blanket, doll, or other object to hold, rub, or snuggle with to bridge the separation/individuation panic. Parents know the magical power of these objects to soothe the young child. The magic is essentially delusional in that the objects symbolically restore the symbiotic relationship or feeling. Clearly, a piece of cloth or other object can't protect against real dangers. Yet this magic gets imbedded in our psychological baggage, as Mahler notes: "Vestiges of this stage remain with us throughout the life cycle." A humorous example of the enduring power of the transitional object is in the original film version of *The Producers* when accountant Leo Bloom (played by Gene Wilder) in a stressful moment pulls out a piece of cloth from his childhood blanket that he keeps close by for soothing self-medication—the transitional object lives on.

More important, the transitional object endorses and validates delusion as a response to loss—that is, the need in some fashion to restore the symbiotic relationship. This will forever point the child, and later the adult, to experiences "out there" to rescue the self and restore security and wholeness. These strategies will take many forms: sex, money, possessions, accumulating academic degrees, personal power, submission, self-denial, conformity, and sadism, among numerous others. Ultimately, these maneuvers will fail because delusions cannot be fulfilled. The only real solution is to turn inward to find the complete self of pure consciousness—omni consciousness.

Unfortunately, the course of psychological birth and development will obliterate the path to omni consciousness as the frenzy to drown in experience to save, preserve, and empower the separate "me" self gains momentum. This strategy takes hold in the belief that an expanded or grandiose ego can become omni consciousness. It can't.

## Attachment

Fueling the focus on experience for survival and expansion of the self is the process of attachment to a caregiving figure, usually the mother, that intensifies at about six months of age. Psychiatrist and child development expert John Bowlby saw bonding of attachment behavior as a motivational center that is built into human nature. Attachment behavior is so powerful that Bowlby likens it to a physiological system: "The enduring attachments that children and other individuals make to particular others . . . is conceived on the analogy of a physiological system organized homeostatically." In another way of putting it, attachment becomes an entrenched operating system. Any threat of separation from or loss of the attachment object (the caregiver) produces intense fear and anxiety. The security feelings delivered by attachment to the caregiver become a powerful antidote to the panic of separation and individuation of psychological birth.

While attachment to a consistent, caring, and loving person is essential for a secure sense of grounding in the world, it also establishes the template for transferring the process. The success of bonding to a caretaker in providing comfort and security establishes the more pervasive conclusion that security rests on attachment to something "out there." Initially, attachment to the mother or other caregiver may be the most potent and visible form of attachment. Eventually, though, attachment will spread to a widening universe of "out there" objects and experiences like power, neediness for things, clinging behavior, obsessions with accumulating possessions, and sexual and many other obsessions. When fearful or anxious, the child, and later the adult, will reach for a host of experiences believed to soothe and obliterate pain and suffering and provide a secure foundation of power and control. In this manner, attachment becomes the addictive process reinforced by the other side of the attachment coin—the anxiety and terror generated by the loss of attachments.

Since attachment is designed to protect the I/me/ego, it emerges as the glue that explains the ego's fierce grip and the barrier to dropping the ego. It also casts light on the "mystery" of powerful attachment to things out there and the never-ending need for more and more accumulation of things and experiences to construct a false sense of security that can restore a primitive state of being that never had a footing in reality. No wonder that spiritual aspirants have such a tough time in following the dictum of scriptures and sages to detach from desires and possessions as a primary condition for letting go of the ego and ascending to higher consciousness. Spirituality requires letting go of the "out there" and finding security and wholeness in a broader inner reality. But in that quest it hits up against the thick wall of accumulated developmental attachments.

## Psychological Birth Recast

We can now restate psychological birth as the transition from the omnipotent, narcotized state of oneness to the feeling of a separate self and separate physical world. This birth inevitably comes as a shock because, despite its enhancements, it is also experienced as a severe loss of personal power. Even though infants can develop strategies that may be more or less effective in soothing themselves or buffering the blow—and the environment may be more or less loving and supportive—the shock still remains. A transition from "I am the world" to the realization that the self is a mere speck in a complex, confusing, and overwhelming world cannot easily be accepted, nor can the fear and pain it generates be summarily canceled. The perception of the self as a speck is instantaneous and irrevocable when the cognitive ability to see self and world as separate entities is attained. As I have emphasized, infants have no way of knowing that they were previously in a narcotized, dreamlike state in which feelings dominated reality. In that precognitive, affective, and egocentric mode, *feeling* powerful is the same as *being* powerful, with power not having any concrete basis in the physical world.

To summarize: In the omnipotent state, no achievements, abilities, or skills were needed to generate the feeling of power—it comes with the territory of the first stage of life. Enter psychological birth. The narcotic is gone. Unable to know that he or she has moved from one level of consciousness to another, the child can only intuitively or reflexively conclude that the world has changed—and changed for the worse. It's as if a vital limb has been lost and the child wants it back.

Now awakened from the dream by cognitive growth and the emergence of a demanding ego, the infant seeks in the physical world what he or she previously had in its affective (feeling state) egocentric mode. But the conclusion that the child reaches about the nature of the world and what has happened to him or her will lead to pursuits that cannot achieve their intended purpose. The quest to achieve things in the physical world that will restore the earlier feeling state of oneness or omnipotence will not work. The child is pitting cognition against affect, reality against a nonexistent feeling state. This is like speaking Chinese to someone who only understands French, or worse, someone who speaks no language at all. This interpretation of psychological birth explains many of the lifelong strivings for elusive goals that all spiritual traditions speak about with frustration.

## Loss of Connection

Once cognitive transition unfolds, there is a loss of connection with the earlier state and its language. The earlier state is now viewed through the principles that govern the present, more advanced state. And there are no achievements possible in the relative world that can recover the earlier affective state with its sense of power and oneness. That state has no correspondence in the real, cognitive world. But the persistent and unyielding effort to achieve that impossible goal will forever enslave the child and encapsulate him or her in a delusional world that seeks to regain the affective goal of omnipotence. This strategy will provide a powerful obstacle to later efforts to give up or transcend the ego in favor of a broader, more complete consciousness that is at peace and one with the world. In other words, the primitive oneness of the infant and child, and the faulty efforts to restore that state, become the major impediment to achieving a higher-order spiritual oneness in adulthood. This analysis may in part explain why the evolution of consciousness or "enlightenment" remains elusive. Many understand what needs to be done. Few can escape the prison of the self and its attachments to accomplish the task.

Furthermore, one of the major problems that prevents us from entrapment in this developmental dilemma lies in its universality. The impediment is inherent in shared human experience, and thus consensual delusion becomes consensual reality. If everyone shares the same delusions, it is a monumental task to see through them and identify them as delusions.

Throughout childhood and later, we become increasingly aware, or at least strongly suspect, that the desired feeling of omnipotent oneness is irretrievable and that no one can give it to us—not even mommy or daddy. This may explain the profound despair and hopelessness that some people, especially adolescents, experience. All our efforts to console them seem ineffective, and we can't, no matter what we do, mobilize them toward a more positive or hopeful outlook. Many feelings of desperation may, in part, derive from this state.

## Part 2: The Pangs of Psychological Afterbirth

As dire as some of the consequences of psychological birth may be, the newly discovered separate self is not about to throw in the towel and expire. And development itself provides tools for protection against the shock of psychological birth.

### The Self Fights Back: Stages of Psychological Development
Me, me, me, and more me.

The egocentric nature of the young child is one powerful, protective narcotic. You can readily see that when young children overvalue the self and experience themselves as the center of the universe. Egocentrism processes the world through the lens of "me." But there are differences. For example, in infancy and early childhood, only "me" may count. Later on, others may also count, but "me" just counts more. So while egocentrism manifests itself in many forms throughout life, it has a special character in early childhood (two to seven years of age).

Early childhood egocentrism defines the world more by feelings than by formal external rules. This extreme form of egocentrism can be observed in many behavior patterns. I've always found children's drawings particularly revealing. Young children in this egocentric stage will typically produce nonrepresentative or incomplete drawings. For example, when asked to draw a person, a three-year-old might scribble (also called a kinesthetic drawing) or draw loops like in drawing 1. The four- or five-year-old is likely to draw a variation of the "potato head," a head with limbs and fingers—sometimes a plethora of fingers (drawings 2, 3, and 4).

A number of interesting observations leap out of these drawings. There is a consistent pattern in the thousands of such drawings I've obtained over the past twenty-five years. First, we must understand that whatever these drawings may mean, the children did *not* give me what I asked for. This is not judgment, so don't jump to their defense—it's factual. The instructions clearly say: "Draw a picture of a person, of a girl or a boy, or a man, or a woman. Draw the whole person, draw all of the person."

### Observations
Keeping these instructions and the illustrations of the drawings in mind, we can make the following observations.

1. Drawings 1 to 4 are *not* of the whole person. Parts are often missing or in the wrong place, or there may be too many parts, like many fingers. In drawing 1, there is no representation of a person at all.

Drawing 1

Drawing 2

**Drawing 3**

2. The children, regardless of what they produce, are typically proud of their drawings. "Will you hang it on the wall? Can I show it to my mother?" and so on.

3. The drawings are executed quickly, usually in one take. Rarely are there erasures, and the children almost never ask if the drawing is correct.

4. These children almost never copy. They may look at someone else's work, but they do their own thing.

5. They are likely to get angry or annoyed, rather than defensive, if you question them about their drawings: "What is . . . ?" "Where is . . . ?" "Who . . . ?"

When we stand back and observe objectively without defending or rationalizing the drawings, the children's responses seem quite odd in light of the fact

**Drawing 4**

that they did not give me what I asked for—a drawing of a complete person. They can't, you might be tempted to say. Still, even if that were the case, when children—or adults—do something that they clearly know is wrong or inadequate, they exhibit predictable defensive strategies: "Oh, this is stupid." "I'm tired." "I don't feel like doing it." "Can I do it over?" "I can do this better." "I'm not in the mood." Yet none of these reactions appear with the incomplete and nonrepresentational drawings. And surely these children know what a person looks like.

Even more curious, when children begin to produce more complete and detailed drawings like drawings 5 and 6 (usually by age seven and eight), all the above-mentioned defensive strategies surface, including copying, erasing, and self-critical remarks. Isn't that just the opposite of what we would expect? They are proud of the incomplete drawings and critical of the more complete and accurate ones. What accounts for this apparent contradiction? Are these children possibly revealing something significant about their differing perceptions and concepts of reality?

## Defining Reality

The drawing task in effect asks children to define what makes a thing a thing. In this case, what constitutes a whole person? The younger children are saying through their proud, incomplete drawings that for a thing to be a thing (or, in this case, for a person to be a person), it doesn't have to have all the parts, as in drawings 1 to 4. If it has one part, several parts, or any part, that's enough to make it that thing. More important—and this is the case with the nonrepresentational scribbling, loops, or circles—they are saying that if I *feel*

**Drawing 5**

Drawing 6

it's that thing, then it is that thing. In this system of "logic," all the behaviors described above make sense. If the child makes his or her own rules, then everything he or she produces is perfect or, at least, okay. In the case of the older children, who produce more complete drawings (5 and 6), for a thing to be a thing it has to have all of the parts, and those parts have to be in their correct places. These children are clearly following an implicit *external rule* that provides a reference standard for everyone—a logic that is more familiar to us. They have developed to a higher cognitive level. Swiss psychologist Jean Piaget called the two-to-seven-year-old stage *pre-operational thinking* and the seven-to-eleven-year-old stage *concrete operational thinking.*

The difference between egocentric and rule-oriented logic also explains other typical behaviors of children. For instance, three-year-olds do not socialize effectively without close supervision. Leave a group of three-year-olds alone expecting them to play cooperatively and pandemonium is likely to break out with each "me" trying to take center stage. In a world where each person makes his or her own rules, real socialization is short-circuited. In contrast, older children, with more developed cognitive skills that internalize the world of rules, tend to do overkill with their newly acquired perception. For them, rules become absolute. You can overhear these eight-, nine-, and ten-year-olds arguing about rules like Supreme Court justices.

The same understanding applies to the acquisition of academic skills, such as reading, which can prove difficult for the very young child. Learning these skills involves accepting externally given rules at every step. For older children, formal learning is more natural, as it resonates with their newly acquired language of rules. These children search for rules and compare their own ideas with external rules.

Imagine the power of egocentrism: the absence of anxiety about the accuracy of productions. As I noted, the young children show virtually no anxiety or self-criticism of their drawings no matter how incomplete. If "I feel it's that thing" makes it that thing, then there is no need for anxiety or sense of failure. "Whatever it is, I'm right." In other words, the world is defined by my feelings, not rules.

We've all passed through this stage. It's a powerful form of omnipotence that we lose by about age seven, when the world of external rules becomes part of our cognition. As this unfolds, we also lose more of the feeling of owning and ruling the world that began to fade with psychological birth. The world becomes foreign terrain that we must learn about to survive. We and the world become increasingly separated. At the same time, we don't forget the powerful narcotic that we all once owned, and we can't understand how or why we lost it. We want it back, but it is beyond or outside our advanced logic. We have lost the connection to the language of the egocentric feeling state. The natural defense against the revelation of psychological birth—extreme egocentrism—has come to an end.

## The Spiritual Connection

At this point, you might be wondering what this detailed exposition on child development has to do with spirituality. Everything! Personal psychology and spirituality are intimately intertwined. Eastern spiritual and other religious traditions cannot address the connection because they lack developmental psychology. Western psychology has a lot to say about development that can enrich spirituality—and has the tools to investigate it. Ignore personal psychological development and you leave a big gap in understanding obstacles on the spiritual path. It's the missing piece of the puzzle. Many aspects of personal psychology are essential for effective functioning in the world. Yet they can also be barriers to spiritual consciousness, until you fully understand the connection between the two dimensions as part of a more inclusive reality.

As we progress through psychological development, we face a two-pronged attack. First, our consciousness is channeled into a limited ego object called "me." I've already noted that this object is limited in its growth and transformation possibilities by its very nature as an object rather than a subject. Second, this limited "me" object then not only wants to grow, expand, and improve itself, but it also seeks an unattainable affective state (omnipotence), which it feels it once owned.

Here, then, is the dilemma of the experiential self in a nutshell. Psychological birth sets the individual on a path of personal development that will result in great strides, while at the same time guaranteeing struggle, conflict, alienation, and anxiety. Making matters worse, as the experiential self seeks restoration of its lost sense of omnipotence, it devalues actual achievements; they pale in comparison with the lost feeling of egocentric power. Remember how confident the three-year-old was with his incomplete sketch that he felt was perfect, and how apologetic the seven-year-old was about his much more complete effort. Repeated failures to recapture a sense of wholeness and perfection produce frustration, disappointment, constant quests, and, ultimately for many, resignation or even a sense of hopelessness.

Thus the developing person, dependent on the experiential self for definition and fulfillment, gets caught on a never-ending treadmill of needing and wanting. The sought-after feeling of security and power remains always in an elusive future. Even when all goals are achieved, there is disappointment and sometimes shock that the desired feeling is not part of the bounty; it can't be—there's no representation for it in the physical world.

We therefore concoct dreams and delusions to make this quest seem real and attainable. No matter how we try, though, we still run up against the brick wall of using an inadequate tool (the experiential ego self) to achieve an impossible goal (the restoration of our precognitive sense of power and wholeness). This is the story and fate of the ego. With all the frenzied, exclusive attention to seeking "out there" a lost continent of self that never existed in that domain, the true source of oneness—omni consciousness— fades into oblivion. This is exactly what all the spiritual traditions are suggesting when they say that spiritual seekers look in the wrong place. Unfortunately, spiritual traditions don't have the developmental perspective to provide the understanding in terms of the individual evolution of the self. Yet that very understanding is necessary to fully grasp what you are up against—that you have willingly participated in the construction of the prison of the self. You must now break loose. To do so, you will have to let go of false sources of security.

## Defending the Experiential Self: A Dead End

No matter how many positive values we ascribe to psychological birth, the process of psychological differentiation and separation cannot be achieved without pain. The experiential self has suffering built into its very core. As we have seen, the nature of psychological development is such that the trauma of psychological birth cannot be resolved on its own terms; the emerging experiential self is too mired down in distortions. It cannot see beyond "me" and "mine" and its obsessive striving to achieve the grandiose goal of the ego restoring the precognitive sense of omnipotence. The double whammy cripples it; hence, healing, compensation, and treatment can only be *relatively* effective in reducing the pain by making delusions and distortions less intense.

Only by lodging awareness in omni consciousness can the distortions of personal psychological development be resolved. Omni consciousness stands outside personal experiences and therefore is not defined, shaped, or bound by the developmental phases and shifts. In omni consciousness, the self is whole and complete, and one can again experience the power of the subjective self. The limited projected self is then no longer a threat, because the omni consciousness state does not need omnipotence or other intense feeling states. Moreover, the painful conflict between affect and cognition can be witnessed and resolved.

Omni consciousness allows you to be your experiential self for navigating the relative world without being imprisoned by it. Techniques for returning to omni consciousness will be described in later chapters.

**The Pluses and Minuses of Other Landmark Changes**

In response to the trauma of psychological birth, we set out to expand the ego self through experiences. Starting in infancy, the self becomes identified with internal and external experiences. The self is drawn into more and more experiences in every stage. Eventually, omni consciousness contracts into the experiential ego self.

The story of how experiences hijack consciousness brings us back to the beginning of psychological birth.

The reality of the infant (zero to two years old) is largely sensory. That's why Piaget called it the *sensorimotor period*. For a child in this stage of development, nothing exists beyond sensory experiences. All the child "knows" is what he or she sees, hears, touches, smells, or tastes at the moment. So experiences and self are perceived as the same. In the next stage (the *preoperational period*, ages two to seven), the child is able to form mental images and mental representations of the world, enabling him or her to carry the world within. The child now has thoughts and can think about the world through mental representation. It is not surprising, then, that age two is when language development begins to accelerate rapidly. But the child is still drawn to sensory experiences and overestimates their importance. Some experiments conducted by Piaget will give us a clearer picture of how the mind works at this period.

**Conservation**

*Conservation* in Piaget's psychology means the awareness that superficial changes or transformations are not real changes or transformations. You walk into a room and immediately notice that the furniture has been moved around and there are new decorations on the walls. It is a familiar room that has been reshuffled. A young child walking into that room may experience it as a new room he or she has never been in before. You have conservation, the child doesn't. Similarly, a three-year-old seeing a familiar person with unfamiliar clothes and a wig might think the person is a stranger. Without a sense of conservation, we would experience reality as an overwhelming parade of constant flux and change that would keep us off balance, anxious, and confused. And, indeed, this is just the case for young children who can't conserve yet, and they are often confused. Conservation lends stability to our experiences by enabling us to see sameness in the foreground and change in the background, which is one aspect of what is meant by the Eastern concept of the "illusion of experience"—that something we experience can be real and yet not real.

Piaget called our attention to the importance of conservation in psychological development through a number of experiments he performed with his own three children over many years. Jacqueline at age four is presented with two round balls of clay of the same size (figure 1). One of them is then rolled into a long, thin sausage shape. Jacqueline says that the sausage shape has more clay than the ball shape. When the sausage is rolled back into a ball right before her eyes, she says, "Now they are the same."

Try it yourself with a young child. You can keep repeating the task, and each time the child will say, "Now it is more. Now they are the same." An eight-year-old, who typically can conserve, will immediately say that the sausage and the ball have the same amount of clay. He or she knows that the change from ball to sausage is a superficial transformation and that the amount of clay remains the same regardless of the shape. It is an instantaneous process of awareness. The child does not have to think it through; he or she just knows it.

Similarly, Piaget's well-known conservation of volume experiment illustrates the same point. When presented with beakers A and B (figure 2) with equal water levels, a five-year-old and an eight-year-old will say there is the same amount of water in both. When the water in B is poured into the tall narrow vessel C, the five-year-old will say there is more water in C than A while the eight-year-old (if he or she has achieved conservation) will say there is the same amount of water in A and C. Training or trying to teach the principal generally does not work unless the child is close to achieving conservation.

The reason lies in the fact that the five-year-old is still in the preoperational period while the eight-year-old is in the *concrete operational period*.

**Figure 1.    Conservation of Mass**

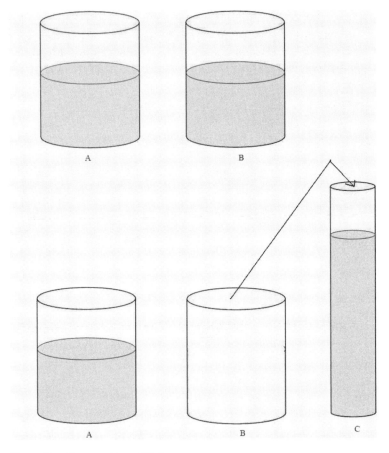

**Figure 2. Conservation of Volume**

Preoperational children are not capable of performing many mental operations that are obvious to the concrete operational child. Their realities are quite different. The preoperational child is dominated by perception, meaning that he or she is overly impressed with the way things appear—the sensory input. In addition, the child can only handle one piece of information at a time and cannot reverse operations mentally, all of which are necessary to perceive conservation. Indeed, if *you* were presented with only A and C and did not see B poured into C, you couldn't be so sure that A and C had the same amount of water. You might make an intelligent guess, but you couldn't be certain.

Because the preoperational child is only able to consider one thing at a time, C looks like more than A. Consequently, preoperational children live in more unstable worlds than concrete operational children, who are not as influenced by superficial changes. This difference in part explains why young children are more emotionally unstable and reactive, are less able to grasp and apply rules and their variations, and have difficulties in social interactions unless supervised by adults. As conservation emerges, children are better able to navigate on a steady course as the world swirls around them.

For Piaget, the achievement of conservation applied to cognition of the physical world is a giant leap in development. But applied to the self, conservation is the underpinning of omni consciousness. Conservation of the self transcends all temporal and superficial transformations of consciousness. With conservation of the self, the ego can be seen for what it is: one manifestation of a higher, all-inclusive consciousness. The unity of conservation of the self is the essence of omni consciousness.

## Part 3: Hungry for Experience

As we have seen, part of the reason that the preoperational child can't solve the conservation of volume task is that the tall, narrower receptacle (figure 2) *looks* like it has more water. This sensory piece of information is so dominating that other information is not recognized. Similarly, when presented with twenty-four wooden beads of which eighteen are red and six are brown, the preoperational child will say there are more red beads than wooden beads. The sensory experience of lots of red beads takes precedence over the more abstract notion of wooden beads.

So, right from the beginning of our existence, we're riveted to appearances. Remnants of this stage will persist throughout our lives. Admittedly, an infant has little choice but to be drawn to the outside. The infant is, after all, totally dependent for survival on the external world. In short, the infant *needs* and must *get*. Because the process of needing, wanting, and getting persists throughout childhood, the self becomes totally encapsulated and defined by needing and getting in response to the pushes and pulls of its own body and the outside world. So even when a person becomes more independent of his or her environment, the self still feels most secure when it is needing, wanting, and getting. More important, the ego self continues to scan the world of experience for acquisitive opportunities to define itself more sharply and fill its hole of incompleteness.

Other factors also reinforce this self that is defined by needing and getting. For example, the infant is pushed and pulled by hormones and other physiological forces that direct him or her to identify the emerging self with these states of excitation. If we fail to pay attention to bodily demands, other processes will be set in motion to force us to act. Hunger, for example, can trigger autonomic nervous system responses that put us in a state of anxiety, fear, or panic; other states of deprivation similarly affect us. So we are led to conclude, "I am my body; I am my needs."

## Will the Real Self Please Step Forward

This conclusion is further reinforced by the lack of knowledge of any other self. There's no reason to look for another self when all the forces are powerfully telling us that we are our bodies and sensations. Our attention is so absorbed in striving to satisfy needs and seek safety and wholeness that there is little time or opportunity to raise the question, "Who am I?" Even when relaxed, we know more needs are coming. This may explain why when reaching a goal of, let's say, wealth, we can't relax and bask in the achievement. Often it's back to the drive gear with new reasons for needing and getting more. Just look at all the super-wealthy people who still need more—even committing ruinous criminal acts to get it. It's as if the self, once defined as embedded in needing and getting, is unable to get outside of the needing-and-getting system. And we never realize that we are enslaved to the process and that the getting is just incidental to keeping the system going.

All the while we're doing this, we feel we're actually acting independently. In fact, the self has become defined by its experiences and cannot easily extricate itself from that definition. As we have noted, experiences become *my* experiences, *my* needs, *my* good and bad feelings—and feelings are crucial. They validate the self. When they are absent, we feel a sense of loss of self. As a result, we actively seek states of activation to reestablish the feeling and presence of "me." So while we think we are seeking good feelings and gratification of needs, we're primarily seeking the feeling states that define "me."

This process puts us on a never-ending trail of seeking the self in intense feeling states and then losing the feeling of self in quiescence. At this point, we're no longer in charge of our experiences but are enslaved by them. We can't see that omni consciousness is separate from experiences. The experiential self may be a useful crutch in the early years of development, but shedding our reliance on experience is essential for getting to the higher self. Remaining defined by our experiences is like leaving the scaffolding up after the building has been completed on the conviction that the building cannot stand without it. Carrying the analogy a step further, it's more like living on the scaffolding and never even entering the building.

But as soon as you taste omni consciousness and know it's you, a different relationship to your experiences develops. You are here and they are there. You can *accept delivery of experiences* or *not accept delivery*. The self is not affected in any basic way by experience. Experiences may be desirable or undesirable, pleasurable or painful, but the self is not transformed by experiences. Once you arrive at this state, you've achieved *conservation of the self*.

## Object Permanence

Another important event in personal psychological development is the arrival of *object permanence*. What this means is that something mental—an image, a thought—comes to represent things in the world. Prior to that, behavior is largely reflexive or sensorimotor and thoughtless, meaning that the world exists only when there is direct sensory contact with it—when you are seeing it, hearing it, touching it, and so forth. In other words, out of sight, out of mind. With object permanence, you can carry the world around with you as thoughts, images, and other mental representations. The stage of pure experience without concepts is difficult for us to imagine, although we have all passed through it. We are so accustomed to lodging our existence in mental activities that we can hardly imagine life without mental processes.

According to Piaget's cognitive developmental theory, object permanence begins in primitive form at about age one and is achieved in more complete form by age two. Attachment to people and objects requires object permanence. You cannot be attached to things that don't exist for you or for which you have no mental representation. It is at this point in development that the emergence of thought catapults development ahead, but at the same time it initiates the lifelong addiction to a concrete ego self that is established in thought and mind. It is no coincidence that Margaret Mahler sees the beginnings of psychological birth at about four to five months of age. This is precisely when Piaget observed the rudimentary signs of object permanence emerging. There must be the mental capability to perceive and record a separate object or person for a panic reaction to occur when mommy isn't present.

Before object permanence is achieved, the infant will not search for an object that is held before his or her eyes and then dropped. At the early stages of object permanence, the infant will follow the trajectory of the dropped object but will not engage in a persistent or systematic search—the object ceases to exist when it falls out of the infant's field of vision. When object permanence is firmly established at about two years of age, the infant will then search for the dropped object and will not give up the search easily. Here we have the beginnings of wanting, needing, and yearning—all parts of attachment.

The problem is that attachment is attachment to mental concepts—the representations of objects. Pure awareness is energy and cannot be attached to anything. Our mental concepts of these objects become associated with feeling tones. These feelings then become triggers or signposts of attachment. Ultimately what we become attached to are feelings. The illusion of these mental concepts is that they are *my* concepts and, therefore, part of *me*. Without *my* feelings of wanting and yearning, there is no sense of reality or, moreover, there is the sense of loss of reality.

Now you can see why we can't let go of our feelings. Also, the more intense the feelings, the greater the sense of a concrete ego self. An enormous amount of energy is required to keep this illusory package going. It's all conceptual and nonsubstantial. We have become encapsulated in a narrow prison of our own creation. What is needed to escape this prison is to recapture the sensorimotor mode but with the capacity of developed awareness without attachment—*omni consciousness*.

## Conservation and Higher Consciousness

Conservation speaks to our immediate world of perceptions and enables functioning by a reversal of the old adage: what you see is not what you get. It helps us transcend the illusion of appearances. To recapture omni consciousness, we must apply conservation to the inner world of the self. I call the highest form of conservation *conservation of the self*. It's the awareness that the higher self (omni consciousness) is greater than ego manifestations and yet is the same as the manifestations. Identifying with the ego is like believing the clay sausage is different from and greater than the ball of clay. Just as conservation of volume lends stability (the tall, narrow glass and the short, wide one have the same amount of water) by cutting through the transformation and not taking the superficial change seriously, conservation of the self lends the greatest stability by maintaining constancy of the self. In this process, you are stabilized in a self that is changeless and permanent. The "I" remains the same in the face of all apparent changes that take place as you navigate through life. You remain firmly grounded. The particular forms that the ego assumes are then experienced as manifestations of omni consciousness. Identification does not get engrossed by or attached to a particular form but remains lodged in the omni self. Conservation of the self allows you to become the sausage but still know its essence—you don't regard it as the only possible self that you must defend. This enables you to take on many roles and forms while maintaining a sense of sameness and constancy within.

With constancy of the self, you remain calm in the face of external changes and turmoil. You are always home, so how can you feel isolated or cut off? Only when you identify with external circumstances that continuously change will you constantly feel pushed and pulled. Your identity is outside yourself, and you appropriately feel lost and anxious. As long as you stay focused on the constancy of the inner self, the outer plays will only be slight ripples against a firmly grounded self.

## Constancy and the Technological World
Constancy of self is especially important today in our complex world of rapid change. There was a time in the preindustrial world when life was more stable. Families lived in the same community, if not the same house, for generations. One's niche in life was determined early. Possibilities for change were few. Nobody even thought very much about radical change. New technologies evolved slowly and filtered down to the populace at a trickle. While this static society was constricting, it did not tax self-constancy. The environment itself provided a large measure of constancy, making inner constancy less crucial for maintaining outer stability. That's not the case in the modern, technological world.

In almost every arena of life, we are confronted with change. Our outer worlds are in a constant whiplash of change. From the basic question of what we should be and the smorgasbord of options open to us to the externally imposed changes, maintaining balance is an arduous task. Neighborhoods change, often compelling us to give up our roots. Jobs and career decisions compel us to relocate and dislocate. Entire technologies and professions may suddenly vanish, replaced by job descriptions we never heard of in our youth—or even a few years earlier. In striving for self-fulfillment, we question all of our relationships and feel that they are tenuous rather than permanent—and certainly statistics on divorce and remarriage speak to these fluxes. Our children grow up and move to faraway places, often with our encouragement—after all, you have to go with the flow. New technologies arrive at such a rapid pace that before we get used to one, a new one arrives, often making skills and careers obsolete. Whether we are talking about a car, a camera, a computer, an iPod, or fashion, what we thought was so advanced is suddenly behind the times. And in many jobs and professions, age, rather than insuring the security of skill and experience, brings the despair of obsolescence and questions about the meaning and value of our lives.

So now the world has flip-flopped. Rather than providing us with constancy, it has removed all constancy. The only effective buttress against this lack of external constancy is the emergence of the constancy of the self.

Omni consciousness does not change. Omni consciousness knows that we produced the dazzling external changes. Those changes are superficial in that they are the playing out of human potential—the enduring, unchanging human potential. Like the clay ball being rolled into a sausage, the essence does not change. It is only a firm grounding in the essence that can confidently stand up to the external changes and be master of them. Without it, you will be prone to anxiety and despair like a powerless ship at the mercy of capricious winds.

### Looking for Yourself
One of the surest signs that constancy of self is absent is when a person is looking for himself or herself. If you are looking for yourself, you are focused outward, where the self cannot be. Just focus on who is doing the looking. You will find that the looker or seeker (omni consciousness) is the answer. You are home and just don't know it. Looking for yourself means that you have rejected yourself and are split off. As long as you maintain that posturing, the world will threaten or overwhelm you—you are ready if not eager to be whipped around; you have not achieved conservation of the self.

### Emotions
Emotions are states of activation that are associated with feeling tones and specific expressions. At one time, infants were not thought to be capable of much emotional expression aside from gross expressions of fear and pleasure. More recently, researchers have discovered a wide range of emotional responses, even in very young infants, that include joy, surprise, anger, fear, disgust, and sadness. Different cries have even been identified for revealing pain and anger.

Emotions provide the most important early experiences for locating and defining a separate self. These powerful emotions are experienced as unquestionably "my" emotions. It is in this manner that emotions become essential for the "me" experience. After all, what is more "me" than my emotions? Conversely, in order to maintain the sense of "me," the activation of emotions becomes necessary. Emotions and "me" are so intertwined that we are not about to question their validity and will certainly resist giving them up. They are deeply grooved into the very tissue of "me." Giving up emotions is experienced as giving up the self. This will prove to be a formidable barrier against returning to omni consciousness.

### Emotions and Reality
Aside from fear, which may alert us to a danger, emotions tell us little if anything about the real world. The relative world is neutral and unaffected by

emotions. We are always confusing our feelings with reality. When we feel something strongly, we are so impressed with the power of "my" feelings that we forget that feelings are the product of a nervous system that is structured to produce certain effects. Intense feelings reflect the nature of the nervous system and the needs and demands of the ego, not the nature of reality. Emotions lead you to objectify the self. In an emotional state, you become an entity that needs to do something to answer the emotion. Anger directs you one way, passionate love another way. But the true self is not in charge.

## Emotions and Self

Emotions become the motivational center of the self. The problem is that a self directed by emotions is very limited in the scope of its field of play. Yet we still yearn for that wide field of play. We fail to see that feelings are often self-created and that letting go of them clears the way for the larger self to emerge. We believe we are at the mercy of our emotions and therefore will not take any action to disarm them by simply not paying attention to them. We feel we have to confront them directly or yield to them. Both of these strategies abandon the higher self and suck us into the prison of experiences and appearances.

Simple observation reveals that you can withdraw energy from emotional reactions. We do it all the time when something else absorbs our attention and we drop a consuming emotion. Let's say you are angry with someone and really engulfed in that feeling. Then you get a call that a sought-after promotion came through or some other uplifting event occurred. Suddenly, you are in a whole different field of feelings. You will argue that you didn't do it. It just happened because of events. Can't you see that it is *your* mind that did it and that *you* have the power to register and react to events or not? The external event can only activate what the mind—your mind—is capable of doing. When you clearly see this process, you can begin to get control of your mind. But this is not an easy process until you are willing to break the addiction to emotions. As long as you allow emotions to rule, they will continue to be the springboard for empowering the ego self. Taking charge of emotions signals the demise of the ego self.

## Unreality of Emotions

"What do you mean my emotions are not real? I really feel them. And things happen to make me feel that way. What is it then that I am experiencing?" Of course you are really experiencing your emotions, and in that sense they are real. They are not real in two important ways. First, as I have taken great care to explain, you and your emotions are not the same thing. There is you, and there are the emotional experiences that are channeled through the nervous system. You have come to believe that you and your emotions are one, so you don't question the identity—you don't see that *experiencing* emotions and *being* emotions are entirely different. There is, however, space between you the experiencer and the emotions. You can, therefore, detach from them, assess them, ignore them, or get distracted from them—as often happens. If you don't accept delivery of the emotions, where are they? What is the nature of their reality?

Furthermore, emotions rarely tell us anything about reality. They almost always distort reality. There are no emotions in the world. They exist in your mind and your ability and willingness to receive them and act on them. That is not to say they don't feel real or generate interesting, engrossing, or frightening dramas. By taking action based on these emotions, you are further convinced of their reality. Let's look at the situation another way.

Imagine that you took a psychotropic drug that made you feel euphoric, frightened, threatened, angry, or happy. Now the world out there is the same no matter which of these feelings you may have. It is a happy or frightening world only in your mind via the drug working in the structure of the nervous system. Why then do you think that your emotions produced by other chemicals working on the nervous system have some different relationship to the outer reality? It is difficult to see this because everyone shares the same emotions, providing another example of consensual agreement being consensual distortion, not fact. It is all an egocentric view that we cling to in a desperate effort to believe that our inner experiences reflect and control the world. We are so reflexively married to this assumption that we are not aware of the huge amount of energy required, like all delusions, to maintain them in the face of constant evidence to the contrary.

### Emotions and Addictions

As long as human existence is based on the ego and its emotions, civilization will be in trouble. Powerful emotions require powerful sedatives. As we keep escalating the delusions—big successes, big money, big material acquisitions, big worries, big disappointments—we need bigger doses of alcohol, food, sex, drugs, or anything else that can soothe the pain of the ego's deprivations and longings, anything that can even offer temporary relief and the good feelings and euphoria that we feel is the ego's birthright. Eventually the system collapses in on itself so that we can begin over at lower levels of emotion and smaller doses of fixes. This pattern has been repeated throughout history. If the great materialism of the twentieth century has not made people feel good about themselves and at peace with existence, what will? Nothing, because pleasure is not the real game. It is the future concept of pleasure embedded in wanting. The wanting state generates the belief that the actual acquisition of its object will produce profound pleasure and peace.

## Emotional Games and the Split Self

The ego has many convincing and plausible tricks to get into emotional states. The dramas that produce emotions seem so real and irresistible that the ego is convincingly portrayed as helplessly swept into the flow.

Recently, someone said to me, "I want to spend more time with myself so I can get to know myself better. I'm cooling it with relationships right now so I can be in my own space." Lots of people say things like that. Perhaps you have. You might even wish that you could make such a bold and self-serving commitment to personal growth.

But let's take a closer look at the statement to understand its actual meaning. It may not be as clear as it appears at first blush. First, it's important to note that the statement was made with an obvious expression of sadness in the tone of the statement and the near-teary eyes of the person making it. This is a hurt, needy, and searching self. By isolating itself even more in the quest for finding itself, it can only intensify the very needs it presumes to be addressing. Now this more isolated self feels even worse, confirming and justifying its neediness and giving it a wider platform for intense emotions.

Looking at the statement itself poses some troublesome questions. First, if we are to take the statement at face value, how can we locate the "I" that is referred to? Actually, there are two. There is the "I" that wants to know itself better or find itself and the "I" that needs to be known and found. But there cannot be two. Consciousness and the self are unities that can only be artificially and conceptually divided. There is only one consciousness. Furthermore, this seeking "I" seems to be a wise and knowledgeable "I." It presumably knows what it wants or will recognize it when it sees it. Why does it need any other "I"? If you stay with the state of the seeking "I," you will realize that is where higher consciousness resides. In that state of higher awareness, there are no emotions. It is outside of or above experience. However, we yearn for the object self and we can only get there by splitting the self and generating emotions so we can be back in the prison of familiar delusions and dreams.

There are many life situations and actions in which the primary purpose of emotional states—once you look beyond the narratives and dramas—are the emotions themselves. Sometimes these states have other consequences once generated, but to be infused with emotions is the lifeblood of the ego self.

The ego latches on to personal experience and personal history to generate intense feelings: "I'm little; I need; I want; I was deprived; I wasn't loved enough; I'm angry." If you reach into mind for action you can only find the past grooves and projections into the future. That's all the mind knows. You must get beyond mind for truly new, unconditioned action; you must drop thought and go to pure awareness. The mind moves so quickly that we are always in the vortex of its thoughts. It takes a very powerful effort to break away from this pattern. This is especially true since fragmentation of the self has become part of our mindset. Counselors will even direct you to your "inner child," "inner adult," or other mythical fragments. You must stay with "I am," not "I am this" or "I am that." To be a thing is to be fixed, historic, and inflexible. "I am *no-thing*" is when genuine and creative action can emerge. A thing is programmed. No-thing is not.

## Struggle- and Conflict-Free Action

We really don't want achievement without struggle and suffering. Without struggle and suffering, there is no confirmation that there is a "me" who achieved things and owns those accomplishments. When you give up "me," it is difficult to accept that you can have many of the things you want without the feeling of "me" ownership. We actually want the "me" more than the things and accomplishments. The bind is that the "me" exists in oppositional relationship to the not-me. Therefore, the moment we invoke or seek "me," we are immersed in conflict; and when we have conflict, the "me" is right there to note its presence. At the same time, we desperately want a conflict-free "me." But that's a contradiction. Peace is beyond thought and mind.

## Ego and Time

The mind seeks continuity of the conceptual ego. The ego self is a product or projection of mind and, therefore, is mind. Nevertheless, we want to feel that the ego is a concrete, enduring entity of past, present, and future. Mind seizes on time for that continuance and sense of enduring reality. As stated before, the ego needs to keep moving to maintain its illusion. Time gives the ego a history (past) and a direction of movement (future). The ego, then, is a mental concept of past projected into future. As such, it does not relate to reality (the present). As J. Krishnamurti states, "a continuous process (one that flows from past to future) cannot be creative. Its responses are always old and conditioned by the past." The ego self is always reacting in terms of the past carried into future projections. Only when the self is born anew in each moment can it respond spontaneously and creatively. But for most, mental life consists of inert, dead concepts and memories of the past projected into the future. As a total mental projection, the self is, therefore, a dream state.

## Genuine Action and Time

Genuine action can only take place in the present. All other action is conditioned by concepts and past memories. In that sense, action is restricted and not focused on the reality of the moment. The emergence of the mind's ability to conceptualize time (past and future) at around age five, while introducing a developmental advance, enables delusion. The ego cannot escape from the present and its dissatisfaction with its limited nature and vulnerability. Now with the concept of time it can relive the past and its hypothetical possibilities: "Look what I was, what I had; look what I could have been." It can also then project into the future: "I will become, I will do, I will have." The present is forever lost as it pales against the appealing unreality of past and future. Yet neither the past nor the future exist. They are concepts of the mind that become our reality, while the only reality (the present moment) vanishes. Even when we think we are acting in the present, we are really being guided by the dreams of past and future. As the mental concepts of past and future generate other concepts that produce still more concepts in a never-ending process, we get mired in this dream world of our own creation. How can this dream lead you to reality when its nature is to race further and further from reality? How can you get outside of the lifelong imprisonment and plant yourself in reality? How can you wake up and return to omni consciousness?

Later, in chapter 6, we will learn about a wakeup call that rings loudly at about age forty when the aging process begins to deliver a fatal blow to the very foundation of the ego. With the contraction of time closing down the future, the crisis of aging will make the leap to omni consciousness a life-and-death issue for the ego.

## Love

There is voluminous and indisputable evidence that love is an essential ingredient for successful personal psychological development. The child must feel a bond and the support, affection, warmth, approval, and acceptance of a stable parenting figure for secure grounding to take place. Perhaps most revealing of the vital importance of love in personal development is the research on the devastating effects of the loss of parental love and bonding through separation in infancy.

The classic work of pioneers such as Renee Spitz and John Bowlby showed how separation of an infant, especially between six months and two years of age, typically results in severe pathology including emotional, physical, and intellectual retardation. In some cases, these children exhibit extreme withdrawal and become totally unresponsive to their environments. Many even seem to lose the will to live. One famous case, portrayed in a film made in an orphanage for children separated from their parents during World War II, depicted an infant girl whose withdrawal was so extreme that she was thought to be deaf and blind; neither was actually the case. It's striking that the effects of separation often occur even if the new environment is a good one with warm and supportive caretakers. Although the most extreme cases are relatively rare, they dramatically illustrate that the loss of the exclusive love bond between infant and parent cannot be easily replaced when the parent is absent during a critical period of development.

It is clear in observing children who suffer from separation in infancy that there is a deeply embedded rage that colors all their experiences and cripples their functioning. For example, it seems paradoxical that these children who suffer from the loss of love will shun efforts to hold or comfort them. It is as if they have made an organismic decision that good feelings are too dangerous. Good feelings may elicit the pain of the losses due to separation, and they threaten to disarm the rage that is the child's only basis for feeling alive and powerful. Rage then becomes the child's reality. The outer world is dissociated, and there is little connection between the child and the environment. Consequently, there can be no learning from experiences, accounting for the stunted development.

Love then not only soothes and feels good, it maintains the child in a balanced state. The child is then not dominated by anger or rage, which distort experiences and lead to strategies that support a state of intense emotionality that in turn sets off a string of defensive maneuvers. One persuasive example of how love reduces negative emotionality is in the comparison of children who are "securely attached" and those who are not. Securely attached children are less frightened by strangers. This shows how love generates a calm that allows the child to assess the surrounding world of experiences without the intrusion of distorting emotions. If you are in a state of fear or anger, your world is colored by those emotions.

Research in social psychology in the 1950s called "the new look in perception" showed how all emotions, as well as other arousal states, influence what we "see." One study, for example, found that hungry children tend to see food-related things when presented with ambiguous pictures. Similarly, researchers using projective tests that require interpretations of vague pictures or ink blots that can be variously interpreted have shown that angry people will see anger-related themes, illustrating how our perceptual experiences are regulated by emotions. Consequently, what one sees in the "real" world is determined not only by what is out there but also by the properties of the receiving apparatus (sense organs) as well as emotions. The more intense the emotions, the less correspondence between reality and perception.

Love, through its meditative effect, is likely to result in a greater correspondence between reality and perception. However, love is not immune to distortions as well. The secure, well-loved child may imbue the world with love and trust whether it deserves it or not. The trusting child who is not afraid of a stranger may be misreading the messages. But still the child is in a better position to reassess information in a calm state than the frightened child who is driven by the surging forces of panic.

Love, therefore, is essential for the development of the ego self. Without love, there is a flooding of the ego with intense emotions that inhibit development. While the ego self has its limitations and is addicted to emotions for the "me" feeling, a "me" that is overwhelmed by emotions is even more limited in its ability to function. It also becomes identified with those overwhelming emotions. This makes that ego more prone to suffering as it clings to its intense emotions while at the same time trying to rid itself of these painful agitators.

**To Ego or Not to Ego**
Ego development may be a necessary step in development and an important bridge to higher consciousness. As faulted as the ego is, it remains for most people, and certainly for the child, the main vehicle for negotiating the physical and social worlds. While the ego self has all of the limitations described in chapter 2, the child has little choice but to identify the self with the ego object. All its experience directs it toward ego, and there is usually no available teaching or guidance for perceiving omni consciousness. However, once established, the calm, more highly developed ego is in a better position to transcend ego because the path to higher consciousness is not blocked by intense debilitating emotions.

Psychologist Jack Engler believes that people with weak, fragile, or shattered egos cannot readily move to higher consciousness. In his therapy with these patients, he wisely first works on developing a coherent ego self before proceeding to direct patients toward higher, ego-less consciousness (you can't give up what you don't have). Intense emotions tend to heighten the focus on the experiential self and force the self to shore up and defend its boundaries for survival. Furthermore, intense emotions exaggerate the self-world distinction, thereby creating greater feelings of alienation, which generate escalating delusions.

Once the self is defined by experience, it must seek experiences to maintain the me-self feeling. Experience then becomes an addiction. Experiences are needed lest the self slip away. Since love soothes and generates good feelings, the need for love evolves. When we feel anxious, we get insecure and angry about not having received enough love. Wouldn't sufficient love prevent or ward off bad feelings? This thinking opens the gate for blaming others and external circumstances for feeling states. It is also a way of protecting the vulnerable ego by providing explanations that seem to make sense, giving reasons why the ego is not invulnerable. It also implies the conditions under which the ego would be invulnerable. If we had enough love or support, the ego would be master. Sometimes we substitute other circumstances for love when we feel we can't get love and are fearful of rejection if we pursue it. In such cases it is easier to *need* substitute things—money, power, exaggerated self-sufficiency, pleasure, and so forth. In all of these instances, the focus is outside—on experiences or getting something.

When the developing child has been immersed in genuine love, there is less grasping and defensiveness. The ego is calmed, and it knows how to effectively get the love that it needs for its definition and security. Although this ego is no less addicted to love, it pursues it in an orderly and predictable fashion. This ego may still feel unfulfilled and alienated, but it is not frenzied. It can find many satisfactions and good feelings to buoy it through life. If inclined, it is positioned to let go of its relative security for a higher state of consciousness where its security and field of play can be vastly expanded.

Paradoxically, the relatively secure and loved ego is less likely to look further because it can cope effectively with the limitations and frustrations of ego existence. On the other hand, the unloved ego that has developed elaborate delusions suffers more and, therefore, is more likely to seek relief and new answers, opening the door for omni consciousness. Prisoners who are well fed, well treated, and offered perks and periodic gratifications are often not as rebellious as the ones who are grossly mistreated. This is especially true if the well-treated prisoners don't even have the concept of a better place outside prison. But the mistreated and suffering ones will seek freedom even if they are not sure of another place. There are, of course, the rare ones who dream of liberation and tenaciously seek it no matter what their circumstances.

# CHAPTER FIVE

# Beyond Counseling, Psychotherapy, and Self-Help

Needy Mary, short-fuse Henry, Bob the manipulative one, perfectionist Kathy, Tom with the perpetual half-empty glass, and cheery Nora who always sees the bright side. These general descriptions of individual differences are just a fraction of the unique personality fingerprints that set each of us apart from all others. Psychology's task is to explain how unique individuality comes about. Counselors and therapists then draw strategies from those understandings for helping people grapple with problems and conflicts, promote growth, and initiate change.

Doesn't that sound neat and simple? It isn't! Just how Mary, Henry, Bob, Kathy, Tom, and Nora become so distinctly different is hotly debated.

Everyone has a pet theory to explain personality—it's almost unavoidable growing up in our psychologized world. And you might be surprised to learn that your "theory" is not much different from the popular professional ones in textbooks. That's what I discover each time I pair young college students and ask them to construct a list of questions they would pose to their partners to write a psychological profile. "What would you need to know to understand what makes your partner tick?"

I'm always amazed when time and again these teens and young adults come up with lists of questions that implicitly reinvent Freudian psychology, as well as notions from other prominent contemporary psychological thinkers. I've tried it with adults of all ages with the same results. Typically, they want to know about personal experiences, particularly in infancy and the early childhood years: "Where did you grow up? Were you rich or poor?

How many siblings did you have? Where were you in the birth order—old-est, youngest, only child? Did you get along with your siblings? Were you a planned or wanted child? What was your relationship with your parents? Did you feel loved or rejected? What kind of emotional supports did you have? Did you feel deprived? Any personality conflicts at home or in school? Did you experience any emotional traumas? What did you worry about? What were your experiences of success, achievement, inspiration, failure, and dis-appointment? Did you have a life plan? What were your dreams and ambi-tions? Were you happy? What made you angry or frustrated? Any mentors or role models?" And the list of possible shaping experiences goes on and on.

At this point you might be scratching your head and thinking, "All that is obvious—why even make a point of it? After all, biology may tip us in a particular direction, but it's well known that who we are is to a great extent a statement of our experiences—what happens to us as we grow up." That's what the man or woman in the street would confidently say. But it's obvious only if you were born in the last century, when modern psychology and psy-chiatry began to flourish. The further back in history, though, the less likely that many of my students' questions would have been asked at all—and some of the queries might even have seemed strange, if not bizarre.

That's what researcher Lloyd deMause discovered when he sought to in-vestigate childhood going back through the centuries to antiquity and even biblical times. Much to his surprise he found that virtually nothing was writ-ten about childhood through most of history simply because those "obvious" questions were never asked—and not because no one was on the case. Every period of history had writers, commentators, and historians who wrote about contemporary life and people—but almost never about the lives of children.

Historian Elizabeth Wirth Marvick notes that as late as the seventeenth century, when there was extensive writing of correspondence and diaries by learned men making comments and observations about their times, they "continued to overlook the lives of children around them." Even French imaginative literature, she says, "ignored the infant and small child."

What about Bible stories? The Bible chronicles the lives of many individ-uals. Yet what do we actually know about the childhoods of even towering figures like Moses and Jesus? The Torah (Old Testament) tells us about Moses' birth after Pharaoh's edict to kill all newborn Jewish male children. We learn that he is saved when his mother places him in a basket and floats him down the shore of the Nile past the spot where she knows Pharaoh's daughter is bathing. The princess rescues Moses and raises him as her own in the royal court as a prince of Egypt. This sketch about the childhood of Moses is told in a few hundred words in the book of Exodus. We next encounter Moses as an adult. The Bible then gives us a rapid-fire sequence of events: Moses kills a guard who is mistreating Jewish slaves. He goes into exile, fearing for his own life. Then he marries Zipporah, who bears a son, Gershom. Soon afterward, God speaks to Moses and he becomes Moses the prophet who God sends to Egypt to set the Israelites free.

We learn about the birth of Jesus in two of the Gospels (Matthew and Luke). After the manger scene and the escape to Egypt to avoid King Herrod's edict to kill all children age two and younger, we hear nothing about the childhood of Jesus. He appears again as a twelve-year-old at the Temple in Jerusalem, where he is found debating Torah with Jewish sages. Then he again disappears from the Gospels—for eighteen years—and reappears around age thirty to begin his ministry after he is baptized by John the Baptist in the Jordan river.

This sketchy information would be very unsatisfying to my students for constructing psychological biographies of Moses and Jesus. There's nothing about early experiences that might provide clues to understanding how their personalities were shaped. The Bible leaps from the skimpy chronology of events, in the case of Moses, to Moses morphing into Moses the adult prophet. Did any early life experiences prepare him for his monumental role? Did it matter if he was toilet-trained early or late or how long he was breastfed? What about the impact of adoption? Did he feel rejected by his parents? Children often do when given away, no matter what the circumstances. Did he experience other emotional traumas or interpersonal influences that might forecast future traits and behaviors? Would any of that information, if available, shed light on Moses the man and prophet? If so, why weren't we informed? We can ask the same questions about Jesus.

Is it possible that my students and others were smart enough to know what information is needed to explain the personalities of Moses and Jesus but that the author of the Bible—God, the Gospel authors, other sages, or whoever—didn't? How can we explain the "obvious" omissions?

## Different Time, Different Lens

Throughout most of history, the prevailing belief was that people are shaped not by experiences but by destiny—meaning that who you are is predetermined. In the Bhagavad-Gita—the Hindu scripture dating back thousands of years—personality is attributed to the mix of the three inborn personality types called the three gunas (tamasic, rajasic, and sattvic) plus the karmic traits carried over from previous lives. Today, we call that view the biological or nature explanation: you're wired to be who you are with inborn tendencies and characteristics that supersede personal experiences, or even shape and direct experiences.

According to the destiny view, if you survive to adulthood—no small matter with huge infant mortality rates through much of history—you will become the person of your inborn and predetermined destiny. If that's the case, why even bother to examine personal experiences, except out of curiosity? Experiences would have little explanatory value. Moses was simply destined to be a prophet, and Jesus the Messiah (according to Christian scripture).

That way of looking at personality changed with modern psychology. At the beginning of the last century, psychology started placing its bets heavily on experience to explain who we are. Every nook and cranny of personal experience was then put under the microscope. The experiential view offers hopeful strategies if you are unhappy with yourself and seek to make changes. Simply put, if experience got you into your mental suffering, conflicts, and neuroses, then manipulating and changing experiences should bring relief, according to this view. And who knows what subtle experiences from the past might be the culprit holding you back.

When psychologists first discovered the power of experience, some extremists, like the behaviorist psychologist John Watson, boldly proclaimed that we are shaped solely by experience: "it's nurture, not nature," Watson insisted in 1913. Carrying his principles of classical conditioning (based on laboratory experiments fashioned after those of the Russian scientist Ivan Pavlov, who trained dogs to salivate to the ring of a bell), he flamboyantly proposed: "Give me a dozen healthy infants, well-formed, and my own specified world to bring them up [his conditioning laboratory world] and I'll guarantee to take any one at random and train him to become any type of specialist I might select—doctor, lawyer, merchant-chief, and yes, even beggarman and thief, regardless of his talents, penchants, tendencies, abilities, vocations, and race of his ancestors." For Watson, infants were all the same: "when I look at infants in a crib all I see is a glob of protoplasm." Watson insisted there were no inborn tendencies, personalities, talents, or abilities—just the same globs waiting to be shaped by experiences. What a turnaround from the historical view that it's all destiny to it's all experience. Watson's radical behaviorism had an irresistible appeal. First, it looked scientific—none of that wishy-washy mind or consciousness stuff, just observable behavior and observable measurable experiences (stimuli). And who could resist Watson's ultimate proclamation of psychological equality? All humans were not just equal before God and the law; they were equal in ability and potential. Anyone, in his view, could be anything. All that was required would be the right experiences applied to the protoplasmic glob.

Other theories, as we will shortly see, had a less radical view of the role of experience but still gave prominence to various takes on the central role of experience.

## Played Out and Tapped Out

As these theories played themselves out, failing to deliver the promised results, personal transformation seemed as out of reach as ever. This was made strikingly evident to me a few years ago by the words of an eminent psychologist speaking at a meeting of the American Psychological Association. Number one on his list of the most important things he had learned about psychotherapy over his long and distinguished career was this: "We should eliminate the term *cure* from our psychotherapy vocabulary." Other panelists and the audience of mostly therapists applauded in agreement—and perhaps relief. A stunning reversal from "we can change anything" to throwing in the psychological towel. The shift from cure to help might come as a surprise to clients who are putting their money where neuroses are in the expectation of cure. It is only *now*, when these therapies seem to have reached a barrier, if not a dead end, that modesty and denial of any expansive applications have replaced earlier hopefulness and grandiosity.

Is it any wonder that people in droves are embracing alternative views of human existence that provide a vision of self beyond the ego and the confines of a limited range of experiences? Nevertheless, the experiential theories are still ingrained in our culture and pervade our worldview despite the quest for ego transcendence. That's why it's worth the effort to learn the details of these theories and how they have shaped your thinking about yourself. It might just get you worked up enough to confront and challenge them directly while seriously considering the alternative of omni consciousness.

## Part 1: Me and Self in Popular Western Psychologies

We have already looked at the ways in which forces in personal psychological development compel us to identify with a narrow range of experiences. Now we will see how popular psychological theories work to keep us on that track, leaving little room for omni consciousness to shine through and making us lifelong prisoners of the limited self—the only self that most of us have ever been schooled in. It's crucial to understand how our visions have been narrowed so we can harness the determination to break out of our shackles. In sketching these theories that have shaped our world- and self-views, some names, like Sigmund Freud, will have a familiar ring. Other less-known thinkers have receded from center stage, but nevertheless, notions they introduced are woven into the very fabric of the way we think about ourselves.

Some may take offense with what will appear to be my simplistic reduction of complex theories to the singular focus on the role of personal experience in shaping the self. "Isn't that an injustice to Freud and others who produced volumes of writings about the intricate workings of the mind?" you might say. Granted, some of these theories are comprehensive, with twists and turns that could be explored endlessly. But that's exactly what I want to avoid. As I stand back and look at the basic assumptions, I see a common foundation and thread that unites them on the side of ego consciousness. If these theories rest on a common flawed principle, the voluminous details lose interest and, worse, can take you far afield from the essence of your being.

Make no mistake about it, there's a monumental difference in looking at self strictly as ego and personal experiences versus a higher, more inclusive pure consciousness. These oppositional perspectives mark a deep rift in spiritual and psychological views of self that cannot be easily glossed over or casually reconciled. Sogyal Rimpoche's renunciation of the ego, discussed in chapter 2, dramatically makes that point.

While several psychological thinkers have departed from a strict reverence for experience and recognize the possibility of introducing changes in behavior by directly accessing another consciousness, they have not shaped our thinking about the self in the formative years. For example, Carl Jung, a contemporary of Freud, spoke of the influence on individuals of a *collective unconscious* stemming from ancestral and ancient sources outside of personal experiences. His colleagues, who favored the rationalistic, scientific model of psychology that was just taking root in the early twentieth century, gave short shrift to Jung's spiritual ideas about the human psyche. He was tagged as mystical or even kooky. Jung's ideas are currently attracting considerable attention as the shift to more spiritual conceptions of human existence gains respectability.

## Same Song—With Variations

The "self" so beloved in Western psychology is clearly born and molded out of personal experience. True, there are different definitional twists and emphases depending on whether one is talking about Freud's ego, Erickson's ego, Kohut's self, the self of ego psychology, or a host of other formulations that worship at the altar of the ego. There are also arguments as to whether the seed of self or ego is an inherent given or whether it evolves totally from experience. In any case, Western ideas of the self are all largely cut from the same cloth, even if details appear to set them apart.

The examination of these theories may get a little heady, but bear with me. It will be worth your effort in revealing the assumptions you have passively adopted that will throw wrenches along the spiritual path.

## Freud and His Discontents

For Sigmund Freud, development proceeds through various stages that he called "psychosexual." Accordingly, libido, the life-force energy, focuses sequentially on different erogenous zones: the mouth, the anus, and the genitals. The period of time that energy is focused on a particular area comprises a stage. The resolution of the crisis of each stage then determines lifelong character traits. For example, during the oral stage (focus on the mouth), the crisis deals with security. Will the infant's need for nourishment through the mouth be satisfied? The degree of satisfaction or dissatisfaction will depend on a complex interaction of biology (the degree of need and irritability) and experiences (will the breast be there and nourishing enough?). Whatever outcomes occur during this stage determine future reactions when issues of security arise. So the oral-aggressive person might respond with "biting" and oral abusive reactions to stress situations. Similarly, resolution of the anal period crisis (submission vs. autonomy) and the genital stage (sexual identity) will also yield fixed personality characteristics that determine later behavioral and response styles.

Within the Freudian scheme, "me" is defined as the experiences that are assimilated, identified with, and then assumed to be permanent aspects of personality: "me" and my experiences are one. It's easy to see why radical change cannot occur within such a framework. "Me," or at least my "character traits," as Freud called them, become fixed by age five or six. From then on, only modest modifications within the fixed system can take place. Consciousness, in this view, is not separate from experience. Yet for true change to take place, consciousness *must* detach itself from the imprisonment of its experiences and identifications. In the Freudian scheme, treatment methods say experience got you into your mess, so the analysis or manipulation of experience will get you out of it. Nowhere is there even a hint of a consciousness beyond experience. In fact, when Carl Jung championed his theory of a transcendent transpersonal consciousness (collective unconscious), that innovation marked the end of the previously close collaboration between Freud and Jung.

While other associates and critics of Freud challenged some of his ideas, they still remained within the fixed system of the unity of self and experience. They largely quibbled over which experiences were more crucial for defining "me" or self. Erik Erikson, for example, emphasized a broader *social context* for the crises of the different stages as opposed to Freud's biological emphasis on oral, anal, and genital erogenous zones. In expounding his "eight ages of man," Erikson spells out the social forces and experiences that fix personality. Erikson calls his first stage "trust vs. mistrust" rather than the oral stage. Although this stage bears many similarities to Freud's oral stage, Erikson goes beyond the feeding situation to emphasize the entire social context for meeting the child's nurturance needs.

Erikson calls his next stage "autonomy vs. shame and doubt." For Erikson, this stage, though corresponding to Freud's anal stage, is not shaped solely by toilet training, as Freud insists, but by the whole array of social situations that embody the potential for autonomy or shame and doubt. Children have many other demands made on them during this period pressuring them to conform to rules and conventional standards in addition to toilet training. The former freedom to "let go" in all areas is replaced by rules and regulations at every turn. All of these, according to Erikson, affect the psychological outcome of this stage. Similarly, his discussions of other developmental stages target the social contexts and experiences that in sum define personality. While Erikson's concepts are very appealing for their broad humanistic emphasis, there is still no way of accessing consciousness free from personal experience. Again, consciousness and experience are one for Erikson—consciousness is in lockdown with the ego.

Karen Horney, an early follower of Freud, broke with him over his biological emphasis (*instinct theory*) and female psychology. For Horney, *basic anxiety*, a term that has worked its way into popular language, is the driving force behind human behavior. The "me" is the outcome of how the early mother-child relationship relates to basic anxiety. Horney described ten neurotic needs that derive from high levels of basic anxiety: the needs for affection and approval, prestige, personal admiration, a partner to take over one's life, restricting one's life within narrow borders, exploiting others, power, personal achievement, self-sufficiency and independence, and perfection and unassailability.

Within this system, personality is shaped, then fixed, by particular experiences relating to basic anxiety. It's another instance of "me" and my experiences forming a unity.

From the perspective of omni consciousness, "basic anxiety" is not basic at all but rather an interpretation of the experience of consciousness in the personal world of the individual. Where did this basic anxiety come from? Can a nonexperiencing person have basic anxiety? The very starting point of Horney's psychology excludes the pure state of consciousness.

Alfred Adler, another early follower, broke ranks with Freud, insisting that *social interest* was more central to human behavior than the aggressive and sexual drives favored by Freud. Nevertheless, guiding this social interest is a *striving for superiority* because of an underlying *universal basic feeling of inferiority*. As in the case of the basic anxiety of Karen Horney, the ways in which one strives to overcome feelings of inferiority define "me." Again, it is personal experience that contracts consciousness into a fixed personality. Just like basic anxiety, inferiority feelings are interpretations of experience. How did one come to feel inferior? Can a nonexperiencing person feel inferior? Adler's self with its stamp of inferiority sets the stage for lifelong searching for experiences to fill the bottomless pit of incompleteness. Again we see a starting point of human psychology bypassing pure consciousness prior to experience.

Harry Stack Sullivan, a psychiatrist who founded the interpersonal theory of psychiatry, introduced ideas in the 1940s and 1950s that continue to flourish and influence many in the mental health field today. Personality or "me," said Sullivan, is born and rooted in the infant and child's relationships with *significant others* (doesn't that term have a ring of familiarity?) in his or her environment. Sullivan's self-system arises from anxiety prompted by the inherent insecurity of the parent-child relationship. To ward off this anxiety, the child develops "security operations" for self-protection. Once these security operations are in place, personality becomes fixed since efforts at change expose the person to the anxiety he or she is defending against. This is an especially clear example of how the very strategy for security that Sullivan describes becomes a self-contained prison that allows little opportunity for parole. Pure consciousness is lost in the misunderstanding of a self that attributes exclusive importance and validity to personal experience while not acknowledging the consciousness behind the identifications that could offer true liberation from suffering.

## The Beat Goes On

*Ego psychology* was another outgrowth of dissatisfaction with the classical Freudian notion that the infant is all id (aggressive and sexual energy). The id-driven infant is impulsive, nonsocial, and uninvolved with reality. The ego (the adaptive structure) presumably developed only because the id didn't work very effectively in achieving satisfaction. Yelling, screaming, or demanding instant gratification does not reliably get you what you want and need, even with the most doting parents. Frustration is inevitable. Consequently, Freud reached the unflattering conclusion that the ego emerged only because the id was ineffective. Thus our so-called civilized side—the adaptive, social, and reality orientation of the ego—emerges as a grudgingly reluctant addition to our personalities because the preferred primitive id mode of functioning simply wasn't successful in securing maximum or reliable pleasure (the *pleasure principle*)—not a pretty portrayal of human motivation.

Then the ego psychologists, led by Heinz Hartmann, came along to propose that a rudimentary ego is present right from the start. It then grows and expands its domain through its ability to survey and assimilate a widening world of personal experiences. This presents a somewhat more flattering picture, but even so, the ego is still clearly an experience addict thirsty for experiences to gain a sharper and more expansive self-definition. In this model, all the defense mechanisms that lock individuals into their styles of functioning and the ways in which they view and distort the world are determined by the interaction and interpretation of the ego's limited world of experiences.

A more recent twist in the realm of the experiential self is self psychology, developed by Heinz Kohut. Self psychology postulates two concepts of need, "mirroring" and "idealization," that center on the significant parenting and caretaking figures in a child's life and the ways they validate—or fail to validate—the child's developing self. Whether and how these two needs are met will determine the definition of self through adulthood. Although self psychology therapy can lessen the impact of negative early experiences and faulty mirroring and idealization, the basic identification of self and experience remains a fixed unity. Pure consciousness is out of the picture, still nowhere to be found.

Behaviorism, another dominant Western psychology, particularly popular in the United States, is totally removed from any notion of higher or pure consciousness. Behaviorists cringe at the very idea of consciousness and the ways in which people experience and talk about it. The only psychological reality, they say, is behavior that can be directly observed and measured. While there are some exceptions to this, behaviorists are uncomfortable with anything they can't see and touch. They ignore the message from quantum physicists at the cutting edge of science that "what you see is not what you get" and continue to insist, "what you see is all that you get."

From its inception by John Watson and further development by B. F. Skinner, behaviorism clashed with the psychologies that spoke of "invisible" processes such as mind, personality, id, ego, self, and the like. Any intangible structures or processes inferred from behavior they call intellectual "constructs" that behaviorists should not recognize or be concerned with. Human functioning, according to the behaviorists, is controlled and guided by rewards and punishments—mostly external—rather than internally driven needs or motives. This view led to the characterization of behaviorism as the "empty organism" theory by its opponents. Whereas you may experience thoughts, feelings, mind, and other internal processes that don't have material extension, the behaviorists will say you are deluded and confusing those experiences with concrete behaviors. The concept of pure consciousness lies entirely outside the scope of the behaviorist approach to human psychology. Behaviorism is a pure experience play. The behaviorist "me" is strictly a creation of its mostly immediate circumstances and experiences—there is no behaviorist self apart from experience.

### Change Beliefs, and Behavior Will Follow
Cognitive theorists like Aaron Beck and Albert Ellis offer another twist on the experiential menu. Neurotic behavior and psychological conflicts, they will acknowledge, spring from personal experiences. These behaviors, they explain, become entrenched because we develop belief systems around the conclusions derived from our experiences. For example, if you were subjected to severe rejection, criticism, and other negative communications, you might reach the pervasive conclusion "I'm inadequate, stupid, needy, dependent"— or all of these. In this way, Ellis explains, we "disturb ourselves" by invoking beliefs we have adopted from the messages of our experiences and the significant people around us. Cognitive therapy strives to expose and challenge these beliefs with the goal of mobilizing the person to alter his or her beliefs—to replace negative, self-destructive beliefs with positive, self-enhancing ones.

Nice idea, but there's a problem. We are back to the confusion of a number of selves tripping over each other. There's the screwed-up self with the faulty beliefs—the self that Ellis says has been disturbed by the presumably primary self (remember, it wasn't screwed up to begin with—it became screwed up). Then the primary, initially un-screwed-up self, is conscripted to correct those beliefs. But if that's the self that did the screwing up, wouldn't that be like hiring the thief to catch the thief? So there must be another wise, observing self, or an aspect of the primary self—perhaps a subself—that can detect, learn about, and then expose the fraud. This wise self knows what needs to be done (or can learn it) and then can generate still another self (or morph into a transformed self) with better beliefs that will neutralize or cancel the screwed-up self. This crowded, fragmented consciousness makes little sense. If there is a wise, observing self that can witness and detach from personal experience, why the need for rest of the gang? Furthermore, that wise self sounds very transpersonal and much like omni consciousness. That may explain why cognitive approaches appear to be more successful than other treatment modalities.

Ellis's wise self is rational—it's the rational part of his Rational Emotive Behavior Therapy (REBT) that counters the distorted beliefs generated at the personal ego level. In numerous discussions with Ellis over the years, I've enjoyed provoking him by declaring that he's America's leading spiritual psychologist. (Ellis disdains anything religious, spiritual, or transpersonal.) Once Ellis gave me a copy one of his books that had just been released and inscribed it with "For Bernie—who I hope is too bright to get really hooked on mystical claptrap!"—meaning anything spiritual. But backing up my view that Ellis taps into the transpersonal dimension, pastoral and other religious counselors and therapists have enthusiastically embraced REBT. Not surprising, since rationality, if it is true rationality, must be the expression of a consciousness that is not corrupted by personal experience, because personal experience colored by the I/me/ego cannot be purely rational. If rationality is outside personal experience, then it must be transpersonal. Religious counselors have flocked to REBT, sensing, I believe, that it validates a transpersonal consciousness in rationality that resonates with spirituality. Once, when I thought I had cornered Ellis on this point, he thought for a moment and retorted, "We are never totally outside personal experience"—an interesting, arguable theoretical point. But then, Ellis would have to acknowledge that if there is no pure rationality, his therapy would be compromised and limited—just another case of expecting the thief—that is, the irrational ego driven by its experiences and beliefs—to turn in the thief, or an even more outlandish expectation, that the thief dissolve itself—commit suicide.

This logical dilemma may explain why Ellis more recently dropped the term "rational" in favor of "functional." Either way, he can't dodge the implication of a rational or functional self that is at the core of being and outside of experience.

## Flirting with Spirituality

While Freudian and related psychologies and behaviorist theories were flourishing in the early and mid-twentieth century, shaping the Western view of self and reality, several theorists flirted with spirituality. Most notable among them is Erich Fromm, who fled Germany in the 1930s, settling in New York City and Cuernavaca, Mexico. Like many early devotees of psychoanalysis, Fromm broke ranks with Freud's biological determinism, favoring social influences in shaping personality. Fromm was also deeply interested in nontheistic religion. That perspective explains his attraction to Buddhism. Late in his career he met the great Zen master D. T. Suzuki, who was teaching at

Columbia University in the 1950s. They struck up a friendship and eventually jointly hosted a conference on Zen Buddhism and psychoanalysis. There's no doubt that Fromm was well versed in Buddhist philosophy. Quite remarkably, he wrote a number of books on religion and spirituality. Yet surprisingly, little of his spiritual knowledge infused his formal writing on personality development and psychotherapy practice. Jeremy Safran, author of *Psychoanalysis and Buddhism: An Unfolding Dialogue*, comments that spiritual leanings of Fromm and other therapists of his era (like Karen Horney) went underground only to resurface in a currently more receptive spiritual environment. Perhaps they understood from Jung's outcast status that psychotherapy was suspect enough and that spirituality would only discredit them even more in the eyes of those colleagues desperately seeking scientific status.

Abraham Maslow, an academic psychologist, introduced humanistic principles that identified transcendent human characteristics. Many of his themes resonate with spirituality—mission, detachment, inner autonomy, striving for growth, and others. For Maslow, self-actualization is the pinnacle of human motivation after basic human needs of survival, security, social acceptance, and self-esteem are fulfilled. Self-actualization is the central driving force for achieving human potential—to become what you are capable of becoming. His ideas are inspirational and have encouraged other investigators to explore and expand ideas about human motivation beyond reduction to biological and social forces. But Maslow did not develop a comprehensive theory that recognized different levels of consciousness. While his exercises and suggestions for developing and moving toward self-actualization are useful, it's unclear who is to do the self-actualizing. If it's the ego, we're back to square one. Nevertheless, Maslow provides a distinct bridge between traditional and spiritual psychology.

## Positive Psychology

Positive psychology is a recent development that exploded on the psychology scene with the publication in 2001 of *Authentic Happiness* by its founder Martin Seligman. Since then, positive psychology has generated a buzz and significant momentum in psychology.

What is positive psychology? Bing Crosby's recording of the Johnny Mercer and Harold Arlen tune of 1944, "Accentuate the Positive," could be the positive psychology anthem that captures its essence. The song goes on to play out the theme of positive psychology: "eliminate the negative, don't mess with mister in-between . . . you've got to spread joy up to the maximum, bring gloom down to the minimum." In citing the biblical story of Jonah and the whale, the song then restates the positive psychology mantra: "just when everything looked so dark, Man, they said we better accentuate the positive, eliminate the negative, latch on to the affirmative."

The launching pad for Seligman's romance with the positive is an outgrowth of his observation that contemporary psychologies have historically focused almost exclusively on the negative: depression, aggression, problem behaviors, pathological personalities, and a host of self-destructive and maladaptive behaviors. Changing or dissolving some of the negative so that a degree of happiness can emerge has been the goal. Positive psychology offers the appealing proposal, in the spirit of the song, to forget the negative and go directly for the gold—happiness. In the service of the universal high priority on happiness, positive psychology promotes development of the noble human traits such as wisdom, courage, love of humanity, justice, temperance, and, yes, even spirituality and transcendence (although light over). In therapy, it strives to identify, nurture, and develop strengths. Get positive and the negative will recede is the message.

Who wouldn't elect happiness over depression or pathology? Since that's obvious, positive psychology begs the questions: Can you do it? Does it work? It's the same question that I have raised throughout this book. Can the ego, the common modus operandi or operating system, merely on Seligman's command, eliminate or bypass itself to engage authentically in selfless acts? Or are these acts like rituals that do not penetrate to the core without any lasting effect? Remember, the ego is slippery and can play the positive game as well as the negative. Can you simply drop the negative, "accentuate the positive and be happy"? Many believe the answer is yes—Seligman has signed up more than 400,000 people for his authentic happiness Internet program.

Positive psychology has also attracted a corps of talented researchers who have already rolled out a bevy of impressive studies supporting many of its themes and hypotheses. Studies have shown that engaging in positive acts like altruism, kindness, helping others, and a growing list of prosocial behaviors elevate, at least temporarily, contentment and happiness.

Critics of positive psychology charge that Seligman overstates his "j'accuse" sweeping indictment of traditional psychologies for negativity. They point to psychological research on resiliency that illustrates the possibility of overcoming negative environments and experiences. Also, the popular self-actualization principle of Abraham Maslow speaks to the positive—and Maslow studied almost exclusively "normal" subjects, not patients or pathological individuals. Other outstanding thinkers like Victor Frankl and Paul Tillich have championed the importance of humanistic traits such as courage, determination, willpower, and positive thinking. Then, of course, almost all of the themes of positive psychology resonate with spirituality: love, meaningfulness, purpose, service, compassion, loving kindness, embrace thy neighbor, charity, helping others, selfless service, and the list goes on, echoing through the spiritual literature reaching back many millennia. Nor is happiness exclusive to positive psychology.

Indian sage Sathya Sai Baba tells his devotees: "Happy, happy, happy—be happy." He adds that to be enlightened, you have to be happy. This challenges the usual assumption of spiritual seekers that first you get enlightened—overcome your obstacles, issues, and conflicts—and happiness will follow. Sai Baba says yes, do sadhana (spiritual practices), but at the same time you must be happy (with faith in the protective spiritual dimension) and embrace and live *all* the given spiritual human qualities, and that is enlightenment—it's a return to your source and who you really are.

The Dalai Lama, as well, has a fondness for happiness and places it high on his list of priorities. Just look at the titles of his books—they could comprise the handbook of positive psychology: *Live in a Better Way: Reflections on Truth, Love, and Happiness*; *An Open Heart: Practicing Compassion in Everyday Life*; *The Path to Tranquility: Daily Wisdom*; *The Art of Happiness: A Handbook for Living*; *The Wisdom of Forgiveness*.

The success of positive psychology may rest on the same foundation and mechanism as spiritual traditions recommending the same behaviors. In selfless acts we forget or relax the ego and open a door allowing higher consciousness—omni consciousness—to peek through. Thus far, positive psychology is playing its cards close to behavior and not fully acknowledging a distinction between ego consciousness and higher consciousness. Nevertheless, positive psychology dressed up in research, technical analysis, and a largely secular posturing may be tiptoeing toward a rapprochement between psychology and spirituality—a healing of the distancing that dates back to the inception of scientific psychology.

### The Secret

Another version of "positive" grabbed attention in 2005 with the release of the video *The Secret* followed by the publication of Rhonda Byrne's book version. Its effective infomercial-type marketing campaign that looks like the power of positive thinking merged with MTV and the shopping network is sweeping the world. While *The Secret* is hardly in the same league as the theories that I have reviewed—and its shelf life uncertain—its popularity merits it some commentary.

*The Secret* is a one-size-fits-all simplistic version of "accentuate the positive" and "the universe" will deliver all that you wish for. The law of attraction is the lynchpin of *The Secret*: it proclaims that everything that happens to you is brought on by your thoughts—stick to positive thinking and all that your heart, or rather your ego, wants will be delivered by your friend "the universe." Health, wealth, and happiness are just a positive thought away. Its theme is an updated version of the popular 1936 Depression-era Bing Crosby tune, "Pennies from Heaven": "Every time it rains, it rains pennies from heaven—you'll find your fortune falling all over town." Corrected for inflation over the last six decades, *The Secret* offers much more from above—and all you have to do is think positively:

Struggling with weight loss? Forget about Atkins and the Mediterranean diets:

"To lose weight, don't focus on 'losing weight.' Instead, focus on your perfect weight. Feel the feelings of your perfect weight, and you will summon it to you."

Do you have one of those sub-prime mortgages and are worrying how you will make the next payment? Why not just pay off the entire mortgage? "It is as easy to manifest one dollar as it is to manifest one million dollars."

Need a new car but can't afford it? "You put yourself in the feeling place of really being in that car."

While *The Secret* freely tosses around terms like "God," "the universe," and "energy" to give it a spiritual spin, make no mistake about it: *The Secret* is all about ego—harnessing thought and desire to get stuff for me. When the Buddha said, "You are what you think," he was not suggesting that you think Lexus, a three-million-dollar home, or a Rolex watch. Spirituality resides in formless consciousness that is beyond the voices of the ego.

The fact that millions of people have bought the *Secret* video and book exposes the persistent wish for a quick fix and easy path to nirvana. It dramatically affirms that the ego is alive and kicking—kicking with furious desperation for *more*.

### Neuropsychology

Neuropsychology, a branch of neuroscience, is another school of psychology totally grounded in material reductionism. Neuropsychologists will tell you there is no independent consciousness, either higher or lower. Their mantra boldly proclaims that all behavior, mental or otherwise, is strictly a product of brain activity. You may believe you are actively conscious, exude awareness, have feelings, exercise free will, make moral and ethical decisions, and initiate other "invisible," mentally driven internal and external behaviors that are the essence and core of your being. Neuroscientists will smirk at your naïveté. They will even wonder why you don't grasp the obvious—that all your conscious experiences are illusions. "Why can't you see that conscious experiences, or 'the person' traced to the source, are just other names for brain?" They are confident that when the brain is fully mapped out and completely understood, psychology as we know it will be unnecessary clutter.

While neuroscientists cannot currently explain consciousness or how the brain produces this incredibly unique and mysterious phenomenon, they have a firm conclusion and have closed the book. This illustrates one of the principal dangers of doctrinaire theory. A theory can explain and account for a lot—and surely neuroscience has—but it can also narrow vision when it mandates an all-inclusive worldview in the absence of the last word.

That's not to say that brain science isn't important or that it hasn't delivered valuable knowledge, with the promise of much more that will enrich us behaviorally and medically. But is it the whole story? They keep beating the drum of their successes to smugly justify their *belief* that they have the whole picture in hand. Should it even be a dispute or contest over who is totally right or totally wrong? Remember from positive psychology there's that pesky "mister in-between," which fortunately we do have to mess with.

Neuropsychology brings our historical excursion full circle. We started with the belief that behavior and personality were governed by destiny—predetermined and wired in. With John Watson and the entry of scientific psychology, that view was abandoned in favor of experience—"it's nurture, not nature." Neuroscience has returned us to biological extremism—"it's all brain."

Only time will tell if neuroscience is on the right track (neuroscientists will acknowledge that we are at the very beginning of our understanding of the brain), or if it's stuck in pre-twentieth-century materialistic science with its neuroscience head buried in the quantum sand unable to see the quantum for the sand that is filing its eyes.

In our pursuit of omni consciousness, though, we should note that naysaying neuroscience, today's dominant academic psychology, has filtered down into our culture and will be another discouraging wrench in your path. Neuroscience is totally antithetical to spirituality—"everything spiritual is neurons firing." Neuroscience is outside the psychological debate on the role of experience for its rejection of the very notion of a meaningful or independent consciousness.

From this brief sweep of the most influential modern psychological views of the self, we can see that both the developing human being and the professional researchers and theoreticians are riveted to personal experience for the location and definition of the self, the only self that either can imagine.

As I've shown previously, when the self/ego is seen as independent from omni consciousness and totally dependent on experiences, life is perforce confined to a narrow range of pleasure and pain with only very limited possibilities for change. The increasing realization of the bankruptcy of traditional psychological approaches is what, in my view, has begun to turn people away from Western psychology to broader conceptions of self and consciousness.

## Therapy and the Transpersonal Self

*Transpersonal*, meaning beyond the person, or outside of personal experience, is one of those terms like *spiritual*. It causes no trouble for some people and no end of trouble for others. It's what got Carl Jung into trouble with his contemporaries and rendered him fringe status. Only recently has traditional psychology begun to take Jung seriously. Jung's notion of an inherited collective unconscious embodying themes and images, even motivations emanating from the history of the species and previous civilizations and cultures, seemed outside science, if not totally in the realm of the occult. To a degree, Jung's collective unconscious endorses the Lamarckian notion of the inheritance of acquired characteristics.

Although Jung's collective unconscious introduces influences outside of individual personal experience, it differs from omni consciousness. Omni consciousness is pure consciousness prior to experience. It is contentless and timeless. It is the ground of consciousness. Jung's collective unconscious drawn from the history of the species, and even evolutionary prehuman experiences, provides content from early species experiences. There's no assurance that these reflexive, instinctual, or ego experiences passed down from the past are any less mired down in all the distortions that our current individual egos are subject to. Nor is there any reason to believe that species experiences from the primordial past embody any greater wisdom than ego experiences today. Wisdom from the spiritual perspective is a priori, that is, outside the distortions of the I/me/ego. Nevertheless, to speak of a self shaped by experiences outside of "my" experiences, as Jung did, seems to imply, at least for many people, something unreal or mystical. Those who cringe at the notion of a transpersonal self assume that nothing beyond one's personal experience can be real or meaningful to an individual. Not so surprising now that we have seen the exclusive experiential diet we have been raised on— food for a narrow consciousness. We are so firmly committed to personal experience to define the self that there is simply no room for any other view. Omni consciousness is staring right at us but remains invisible. A *transpersonal* view of the self is rejected out of hand because it threatens what we believe is our security base—the bind we keep returning to: If something is out-side my personal experience, how can it be mine? But a self mired in its own limited range of personal experience is the problem, not the solution.

In fact, when we rise above or resolve conflict and suffering, we do so by going to the transpersonal realm. *Whenever therapy or counseling of any kind is successful in mediating genuine change, it has tapped into the transpersonal dimension. The personal dimension alone cannot bring lasting resolution of conflict.* As I pointed out in chapter 2, when you are identified with your experiences you can't let go of them because then you would in effect be obliterating your self—the only self you feel your existence rests on. Inasmuch as we define ourselves by our conflicts, we need our conflicts to be ourselves.

*Case Illustration*

"I'm angry at my husband and feel distanced from him. We avoid any sex-ual contact. I feel as if my anger is eating up my life." This is Joan talking about her unhappy marriage. She goes to a therapist (of whatever persuasion) and "works out" her anger. We will not go into the particulars of the coun-seling process but will accept that, for the moment, people like Joan some-times do "work out" problems in therapy. We might say, and Joan would likely agree, that therapy "changed" her by helping her get rid of her debili-tating anger. But if she dropped the anger ("changed"), then she was *not* the anger in the first place. She didn't *change* (this is an important distinction) but merely *disidentified* with the anger. In the process of disidentifying, she transcended her experience—she separated herself from her experience. She most certainly experienced anger, but the anger did not define who she was. Once she fully realized that, she was able to let go of the anger ("change"), just as she might discard an old set of gloves she would no longer use. The gloves do not define who she is, and neither does the experience of anger. If one can do that, then the self *is* transpersonal. Even if we choose to say she has attached to other experiences, we are still affirming the separation of self and experience. Indeed, the ability to choose among experiences, dropping some and keeping others, assumes a subjective entity that can make such a choice. Between letting go of one experience and attaching to another there is a space. That space is where the choosing entity, the transpersonal self—omni consciousness—can be found.

What an extraordinary revelation! We have the power to let go of our ex-periences! We can pick and choose among them. One practical implication of this revelation is the realization that instead of dealing with conflicts by "working them out" one at a time (which for many is a lifelong process), we need only turn to the transpersonal self and latch on to it. When we firmly

identify with the transpersonal self, we are in omni consciousness where conflicts can fall away (not resolved). *Conflict can only exist in personal experience,
and personal experience is not the genuine self.* Beating the drum of experiences
plants an obstacle in the path of change that blocks escape from the prison
of the self. Here's why.

## Part 2: The Validation of Delusions

In traditional counseling and therapy, therapists typically unwittingly participate in the delusions of their patients. Instead of taking clients to a higher
level of consciousness where the problems dissolve, counselors and therapists
validate the delusions when they address them on their own level. And, as I
have pointed out, psychological problems cannot be resolved on their own
level because that level of understanding is the problem. In effect, patients
and therapists share the same delusional systems or views of "reality"—delusional because they are based on false notions of reality.

These notions are inventions of mind in response to the needs of the ego
and the mind's conclusions about how to give this conceptual, nonsubstantial
ego objective existence, security, happiness, and mastery. The delusions are designed to serve a "me" that, in fact, has no objective existence—yet we insist
that it must. It is this focus on "me" that keeps us rooted to a narrow self defined by limited personal experiences. Various inventions of mind are required
to sustain the delusion of an objective "me." The content of the delusions may
vary, but their origin and intent are almost universal. It is this universality, or
what scientists call *consensual validation* (when most observers agree on a phenomenon), that shields us from seeing through them. We have all been raised
on them. They seem so real. That almost everyone—patient and therapist
alike—shares them is what makes them so resistant to serious critique or rejection. It's a major stumbling block to transformation. Let's be clear, though,
on one point. It's not that that therapy or counseling at the ego level is useless
or that it can't relieve anxiety and help patients function better.

On the contrary, as psychologist Jack Engler has emphasized, for seriously
disturbed patients with overwhelming conflicts and intense emotions, therapy is an initial must before they can readily transcend ego and embrace
higher consciousness. The good feelings generated by supportive therapy
could eventually open a door to omni consciousness.

Then many people seeking help want relief and support, not
transformation—sometimes just a bridge to get them through stressful times.
Sensitive talented therapists are artful and often successful in mediating
those goals. True, these benefits may be temporary, and even the more last-

ing ones will not deliver transformation or liberation from the most painful psychological sufferings. Reality keeps intruding to contradict the delusions, necessitating bigger and better delusions and more powerful allies to confirm them.

**Case Illustration: "Napoleon's March on Russia"**
Let's look at a concrete example illustrating how the counselor or therapist can become part of the problem, thereby assuring the continuation of the problem. To make my point, I'll first describe an extreme example depicting a situation where the therapist *doesn't* participate in the delusion because the patient's story is so clearly delusional.

A man enters the therapist's office and announces he is Napoleon and that his troops are getting ready to march on Russia. He adds that he's very nervous about this campaign: the cold Russian winter, the length of the supply lines, and so on.

It's obvious this person is delusional, and the therapist wouldn't try to reassure him by discussing alternatives to long supply lines and options for coping with the Russian winter. Doing so would be participating in the delusional system, making it impossible to address the patient's distortion of reality. Whatever method of therapy is employed, the ultimate goal would be to get the patient to see through the delusion and recognize that he is not Napoleon.

Now let's look at a more typical therapeutic issue. Ralph complains that he is depressed and angry over his relationship with his wife. He feels she puts him down and doesn't respond sexually the way he would like. That's why, he explains, he doesn't respond to her needs. "She just goes through the motions and doesn't turn on." Furthermore, he feels that he wants more and is entitled to it. "There are plenty of women out there, and I can get whatever I want." Now where is the delusion in this scenario?

Actually, there are a number of delusions:

1. That someone is responsible for your feelings.
2. That you have to get what you want or you will be depressed or angry.
3. That you are entitled to things, and you will inevitably have bad feelings if you don't get your entitlement.
4. That you must retaliate to achieve good feelings.
5. That getting what you purport to want will make you happy.

The problem in recognizing these delusions as delusions is that most people endorse and accept them and base their lives on them. Of course, underlying all of these is a needy and dependent "me" that relies on experiences for its validation and happiness. We can start with this "me," which I have shown to be an invention of mind with no substantial existence—just a projection of consciousness. We want this object to be the subject. The subject (omni consciousness) lies behind "me" and mind, but we don't see it because we are so dazzled by the sensations and experiences that divert our attention.

Once the "me" is defined as needy and dependent, the very problems that it perceives (like the man's complaints above) are necessary for its existence. If I am not needing or angry, how do I know who I am? This dynamic tension is what makes me feel my presence. So I need reasons to justify these feelings, and the reasons are drawn from personal experience. I have trouble relating to my wife, and this causes me to be angry and unhappy. What can you do for me?

Because we all believe that our personal experiences give us these problems, we analyze and scrutinize them searching for solutions or better beliefs. The therapist may offer more insightful analyses or better reasons for our experiences than we can create, but all the talk, analysis, or altered beliefs miss the point. Even strategies that may reduce conflict—talk it over, share complaints, and so forth—do not challenge the underlying assumption that moving the chairs around will bring peace and contentment with the self. *It is not the content of the experiences that counts but the whole structure of the belief in the experiential causal system.* It hardly matters what reasons are injected; the false structure and system will not be touched. This is totally unlike the case of the would-be Napoleon, where the delusion would not be implicitly endorsed by addressing it on its own terms as presented. In the case of more everyday problems, however, we can't readily see the delusional structure because of the universal acceptance of commonly shared, more mundane delusions. It also reveals how thoroughly we have been conditioned to distorted thinking about ourselves and reality. Like Ralph, we think experiences mandate our problems—another version of "the devil made me do it."

### Case Illustration: "The Flat-Earth Anxiety"

Here is another example that exposes how traditional efforts to defuse conflict work at the level of the problem and, therefore, can only yield small gains. It also shows the difference between insight at the level of the problem and higher-order insight, which is akin to revelation.

Imagine a sailor on one of Christopher Columbus's ships who is terrified about falling off the edge of the earth. He is in constant dread, frequently breaking out in cold sweats, and is unable to sleep, and when he does manage to fall asleep, he is plagued by terrifying nightmares. He also poses the danger of infecting the other men with his terror. As the journey takes longer and longer and the ship enters uncharted waters, the apprehension all around is building.

What would a skilled therapist do in this situation to reduce the sailor's anxiety and calm the others as well? The success of this historic voyage may very well depend on the outcome of the treatment. First, the therapist can reassure the sailor and offer him opportunities for catharsis—releasing some of his pent-up emotions. By getting his feelings out and having them received sympathetically, he may feel some relief. Often patients in therapy do feel comforted by this process, even when they are facing real dangers and anxieties. "I'm terrified I will fail the exam and never graduate." Well, that's a possibility. But we still can reassure and calm the student although we can't guarantee that the fear will not come true.

In the case of the sailor, using another therapeutic tool, we can impress him with the skill and charisma of Columbus. After all, Columbus is no fool, and he's one of the greatest sailors. If Columbus thought there was any real danger, would he continue? We might even have the charismatic Columbus speak to the sailor. Sometimes the personal power or persuasiveness of a leader or a respected therapist can allay fear. Finally, we might get all the men together for a group therapy session in which the mutual sharing and support can help keep anxiety manageable. But whatever gains we make will always be threatened by the underlying belief that the earth is flat with the imminent possibility of the ship suddenly arriving at the end of the flat earth and falling into the abyss. Within this belief system, the terror is real and well founded.

But what if we could place this sailor in a rocket ship and fly him fifty miles into space where he could see the true shape of the earth. In one flash, the fear of falling off the edge would evaporate. Now back on the ship he would have total confidence that no matter what other dangers the voyage may face, the ship will not fall off the earth. His conviction on this score will be unshakable. No further therapy, or support on this issue, will be necessary. The fears of the other men will seem ludicrous, if not primitive and childish. Revelation has superseded analysis. This is true insight that occurs in a flash and is irreversible. There is no step-by-step progress and no backsliding. It's instant and firm—much like the man described earlier clinging to a ledge and then discovering he was just a few feet off the ground. And don't confuse this "knowing" with switching beliefs or adding a new manufactured concept as in cognitive therapy. It's directly perceiving and knowing reality.

## Therapies, Psychological Birth, and the Flat-Earth Anxiety

The anxiety associated with psychological birth (chapter 4) has similarities with the flat-earth anxiety. In both instances a fixed false notion about the nature of reality locks the individual into an inevitable and unrelenting anxiety state that cannot be resolved on its own terms within its false system of assumptions. All the therapy in the world can only distract and soothe—but not eliminate—the flat-earth anxiety. Only direct, accurate vision of reality can do that. Similarly, psychological birth generates anxiety because of the perception of a fragmented, isolated, and vulnerable self that is a mere speck against a vast and overwhelming world. On close examination, most of our anxieties will be revealed as flat-earth anxieties tied to the basic false assumption of psychological birth. All efforts at release will be ineffective or temporary as long as conclusions drawn from psychological birth are locked in place. Only a glimpse of the whole with the locus of consciousness in omni consciousness offers the possibility of escape from this prison of false assumptions.

## Therapies Glorify Feelings and Emotions

Interpretations in counseling and therapy have meaning only within the orbit of the treatment itself. For example, I was watching a demonstration film recently of group therapy. It was clear in these sessions that there was a reverence for feelings. When emotions, especially wrenching ones, came out, there was the sense that something important was happening that validated the process of reinforcing personal history and narratives.

The therapist keeps things within the phenomenal orbit by persistently reinforcing the process. Little strokes along the way ("Oh, that was very helpful" or "you're so courageous") feel good and make the process seem convincingly real and on the right track. We learn in therapy how to manage our problems and how others react to them. We can, therefore, modify our behavior to make our scripts less abrasive and more subtle without abandoning them. We in effect become better neurotics.

It was apt that actors playing a script portrayed the patients in this film. These scripts are the very ones that people live, and are lived by—scripts they have no control over. The scripts immobilize omni consciousness in favor of the phenomenal self. For progress, it is important to get outside the phenomenal self and shift focus to the chooser or witness consciousness—omni consciousness. Otherwise, there is only the illusion of change by overvaluing the very products of the problems and conflicts—intense emotions.

## Drowning in Emotions

John has been feeling depressed and lethargic for the last six weeks since he broke up with his girlfriend. She said she "needed space," but he just can't get his mind off her and keeps brooding. He yearns for the relationship the way it was. Currently John is preparing for a civil service exam, but he is unable to concentrate on it, even though the job is extremely important to him.

John is obviously not in charge of his emotions. We don't like to look at the situation this way because it seems so "human" to be sympathetic and understanding of his imprisonment in his hurt feelings. Heaven knows, the feelings are real and the pain is real. How can we just ignore or escape from those facts? Yet staying with these intense emotions does John no good, and probably does him a lot of harm both psychologically and physically. More important, it may actually prevent him from doing well on the exam and achieving a long-sought-after goal that would serve him (if successful) for many years.

John believes he *is* the hurt feelings and therefore only passively observes and experiences them as the feelings live him. There is no way to resolve the feelings by wallowing in them. That only intensifies the pain, reinforcing the need to get deeper into the bad feelings to "resolve" them. That is the course taken by traditional psychological approaches.

As we've seen, it is possible for the transpersonal self to take charge and not accept delivery of these harmful, experiential feelings. It can do so by seeing the split—the "me" that is suffering and the "me" that is the witness (whose mind is it, anyway?). Trouble is, we don't believe or know that we can unify the self in omni consciousness, and therefore we remain split and paralyzed.

## Therapies, Emotions, and Personal Histories

Attempting to deal with hurt by immersing yourself in personal narratives that only serve to trigger the emotions will most likely sink you deeper into bad feelings. But if you are not defined by your emotions, then you can let go of your past emotional experiences without losing your true self—omni consciousness.

### Case Example

Mary had a very traumatic childhood. She was abandoned five times and shuffled around to different relatives. She felt deeply hurt and rejected throughout her childhood, and these feelings persist in her as a twenty-five-year-old adult. Now whenever she experiences stress, she immediately returns to those feelings and gives up. She believes that those bad feelings are her destiny. "I get very teary when I talk about myself. So many bad things happened to me that I feel I can never succeed."

When a person is exposed to the terrible childhood that Mary experienced, there is a flood of intense feelings, especially anger, very early in life. Because of the intensity of these feelings, the person identifies even more with the emotions evoked by recollection of the past and the messages they convey. The task of transcending these emotions and finding omni consciousness is, consequently, more difficult, but omni consciousness is present as a given—it is the ground of consciousness. In cases like Mary's, however, attention is fragmented, and the refusal to take delivery of the unhappy past with its negative emotions is just that much more difficult.

What Mary can't see or acknowledge is that she has had many successes in her life *despite* her history. Who accomplished those things and how? She accomplished those successes by herself through omni consciousness. In the end, all successes are driven by an inner source. Personal history—positive or pernicious—will make it easier or more difficult for inner power to shine through.

Once you identify with the bad feelings and the belief that you are stuck in your past and your emotions, you surrender omni consciousness and become lived by the past. Personal insight can only be effective if it is lodged in omni consciousness. If it is lodged in the ego and directed by emotions (at the level of the problem), change will be negligible and illusory. The compelling personal narratives that make up so much of therapy will pull you back into the imprisonment of your mental concepts of the past. When you are in charge of your mind, you control the past. But intense emotions will be a barrier to taking charge. For Mary, like others who are caught in the grips of intense emotional traumas, it will be a formidable challenge to come to grips with disabling emotions in therapy before she will be ready to uncover omni consciousness.

We live in two worlds: the spiritual (higher consciousness) and the relative (ego consciousness). The two must be integrated for total effective functioning. That is difficult at best for most of us to accomplish without help and guidance. There are increasing numbers of therapists who span both dimensions. For example, the National Institute for the Psychotherapies (NIP) has a division of spirituality and psychotherapy with highly trained therapists dedicated to the integration of traditional and spiritual treatments.

## It's Mommy and Daddy's Fault

Blaming mommy and daddy for our woes has fallen out of style. We are supposed to take responsibility for ourselves in the here and now. But in practice, when conflict persists, there's a strong pull based on the experiential ground of our being to blame and point fingers out there—and mommy and daddy are often closest to the finger. Listen to people talk and you will see that mommy and daddy are still convenient dumping grounds for constructing delusions out of personal experiences and narratives. There is a plausibility embedded in all the experience-based therapies that allows one to shift the blame for distorted, exaggerated, and unjustified needs and wants to others. If you trace problems and conflicts through the maze of early personal experiences, mommy and daddy will surely pop up. Remember how my students were reflexively, if not magnetically, pulled to the past to create a template for constructing and explaining their partners' present psychological profile. But such ascriptions of responsibility must be explored from another vantage point to clearly see how common delusions are formed and how they operate.

When we understand the origin of such delusions as blaming our parents or others for perceived flaws and discontents, we do not try to work them out, correct, or solve them. We must rise above them to see how we use them to lend plausibility to a flawed self system, just as we wanted to take that sailor on a space trip so he could see the way the earth really looked. Our past is not us; our parents are not us. If we remain at the level of the perceived problem, blaming our parents—or others—for what we see ourselves to be, we cannot make significant progress or evolve to higher consciousness; we can only hope for temporary relief—we may pass Go, but we don't collect $200, and we swiftly return directly to jail: the prison of the self!

## Primal Therapy

*Primal therapy* rests on the theory that childhood and even prenatal experiences traumatize us, leaving scars that remain throughout our lifetimes. Trauma, according to this view, is unavoidable because of the inevitability of frustrations, rejections, unfulfilled longings, and feelings of vulnerability. The goal of primal therapy is to have patients vividly—both physically and emotionally—relive these traumas in order to recognize the associated feelings of a buried "me." Throughout the repeated reliving of these experiences, the feelings eventually become neutralized. Both catharsis and the "soothing" of the hurt child within are believed to contribute to the healing process.

I first became interested in primal therapy in the 1970s because it broke the logjam of the therapeutic practice with its fixed 50-minute session, strict rules of distant formal interaction between therapist and patient, and highly restrained verbal communications. Therapies, after all, were aimed at uncovering hidden unconscious conflicts, and primal therapy seemed to me to offer a much more direct approach. Indeed, it proved to be so. It cut through the verbiage and got to the hurts in a few sessions, where traditional methods would have taken months if not years to accomplish as much.

Traditionalists warned that cutting so quickly through defenses could be disastrous, but those working with primal methods didn't find that to be the case. It was in fact amusing, in light of this reluctance to attack defenses openly, to observe patients go right through their defenses to the underlying feelings, writhing in the reliving of their early traumas, regressing to infantile levels, and then at the end of the session snapping right back to the present. Many even returned directly to their responsible executive positions without missing a step. This showed me the following:

1. Defenses are not as fragile as thought (except for those of the extremely disturbed); they come right back, and reliving them does not destroy or remove them.
2. There is an underlying control mechanism.
3. We have an incredible ability to split the self.
4. There are severe limitations in addressing problems at their own level.

If traditional therapy endorsed personal experience, then primal therapy did so with messianic zeal. It was appealing for its no-nonsense, direct approach to raw experience. Early primal experiences stretching from possible intrauterine assaults, the birth experience itself, and other traumas in infancy establish templates that translate into self/world views (e.g., conclusions on an organismic gut level that the world is a dangerous, threatening, and painful place) and behavior patterns in response to them. Primal therapy presumed that dramatically reliving painful experiences would provide release from the grips of the primitive experiences and interpretations that shape personal identity. Like other less dramatic techniques, the approach totally endorsed personal experience as the sole definer of the self. We've seen over and over again the dead end of this road, with nowhere to go. If self and experience are one, how can you extricate the self from experience? If, on the other hand, you *can* extricate the self from experience, then why take those experiences so seriously? You can choose not to take delivery of them.

## Traditional Therapies: Wrong Place, Wrong Time, Wrong Person

It may be true that reliving painful experiences, as in primal therapy and other affective evocative modalities, can reveal the powerful raw hurts, identifications, and interpretations that hijacked your identity. Nevertheless, at some point, there must be recognition of the true self—a shift to omni consciousness—in order to remove the self from the imprisonment or the identification with those experiences and interpretations. In looking at these experiences through the lens of omni consciousness, you can witness them, know them, accept them as events that happened, but realize that they are not you—they happened to you but don't define you. Otherwise, the knowledge gained by reliving primal or other experiences will be of limited value.

Likewise, the perception of a self divided into many selves—infant "me," child "me," adult "me," and so on—that interact and do battle with each other will prevent any real progress. A *self divided and turned against itself cannot be victorious in its struggles*. The illusion of victory can only be at the expense of another part of the self. *Self defeating self cannot be a victory for the self*. Only when the self is unified can conflict end. Psychological conflicts are largely manifestations of a split self acting in lower consciousness.

## Destruction vs. Construction

Psychological therapies assume that understanding the destructive process of conflict and problems will tell you about reconstruction. But theories of destruction and construction are not necessarily related. For example, if I showed you the rubble of a collapsed building, you might ask how it was destroyed. Well, it might have been blown up, torn down, hit by a tornado, or razed by an earthquake. Whatever the cause, none of that knowledge could instruct you about rebuilding. The media has played and replayed the painful details of the tragic destruction of the World Trade Center. But no amount of understanding and analysis of how the buildings came down will help reconstruct the site. For that we need the largely unrelated knowledge of architecture and construction—with a strong injection of imagination.

In traditional psychological thinking, we cling to the belief of a bond between destructive and constructive processes. If factors in the parent-child relationship led to conflicts and problems, we believe that somehow understanding, talking about, analyzing, fighting, or evoking the hurt feelings and destructive forces will reconstruct a new and stronger personality. Not likely. Even constructing new beliefs to counter the faulty ones from your negative experiences will keep you in the orbit of the destructive forces. As in the case of the collapsed building, the details of how it happened may be interesting, even fascinating, but they will not get us closer to a new structure no matter how long we persist in exploring every nuance of the destructive process. Psychological therapies are masterful at examining the ruins of personality but have much less to offer in building new personalities or effecting real transformations. Construction is not their strong suit.

Basically, it's the marriage between you and your experiences that causes your problems and conflicts. You believe you can't let go of the marriage because it is "normal" and breaking the bond is "abnormal," yet you still strive to solve your problems. Don't you see the absurdity of this? Repudiate the bond! *Refuse to take delivery of experiences and you will discover another locus of consciousness beyond conflict—omni consciousness.*

## Watch Your Language

To begin moving away from identification with our experiences, we have to think differently and use words differently. For instance, in everyday talk about emotional life, the words "detached" and "impersonal" are pejorative; we recoil from them. We want to be personal and attached so we can be close and committed to others. A woman said to me: "It's inhuman to be detached and impersonal. I wouldn't want any part of it." Like most, she misunderstands the terms *detachment* and *impersonal* as they are used here and in Eastern psychology. The misunderstanding poses a formidable obstacle to getting beyond conflict.

In glorifying attachment to personal experience, we forget the addiction it entails. There is nothing fresh, spontaneous, or truly responsive when we are conditioned by personal experience. Only through detachment at the impersonal level can we generate creative responses and genuine feeling. It is unfortunate that we don't have better words, minus the negative connotations of *detachment* and *impersonal*.

## Going Out of Mind or Into Mind?

Psychoanalysis and other traditional therapies are based on mind looking at mind through concepts of mind. You simply cannot transcend mind in this fashion. Remaining at the level of mind insures imprisonment within mind. Change requires transcending mind—going to a level beyond conflict. "Going out of mind" in this case means giving up the limited experiential self. When you lose psychological balance, you are running *deeper* into mind in a desperate attempt to preserve the illusion of the omnipotent, fragmented, limited objective ego self. More and more fragmented concepts have to be added to defend the fragmented self that feels under assault and losing its grip on the imaginary concepts it believes it needs to preserve wholeness. You are not losing your mind when psychologically disturbed; you are *imploding in mind and drowning in mind.*

To gain true psychological balance, it's necessary to "go out of mind" to omni consciousness. In doing so, you let go of personality binds and the fragmented ego self. When out of mind, you are in pure consciousness where you are "no-thing," just pure-awareness. There is no-thing to defend. What a re-

lief! So much energy and work is required to keep the myth of the conceptual personality going. In omni consciousness, on the other hand, you have
control of mind because mind is a projection of omni consciousness. In omni
consciousness, mind cannot control or disturb you—there is only "I am." Remember, it's *your mind,* or is it?

$\backsim$

# The Spiritual Emergency of Aging: Surviving "Thirtysomething" and Beyond

## Part 1: The Crisis

"Birth is spiritual emergency," Stephanie fired back when I first told her the title of this chapter.

What a great insight! Stephanie, like many of us on a spiritual quest, regrets not discovering that very early in life. You are probably nodding in agreement. Her astute comment also calls attention to what this book is all about: unveiling the experiences from the moment of psychological birth onward that point us away from our spiritual core—omni consciousness.

We have seen how the human condition immerses us in me/body experiences that fuel the celebration of ego identity. So indeed, birth—the starting point for the prison of the self—should signal a spiritual emergency. Unfortunately, it rarely does. In some respects it can't, for the reasons spelled out in chapter 4. The demands of "normal" psychological development drown us in personal experiences that we need for acquiring the cognitive and social skills to function effectively in the everyday world. Then, the powerful early drive for attachment to a nurturing caregiving figure for feelings of security and psychological balance spills over into attachment to an ever-widening web of personal experiences. Paradoxically, these same feel-good and developmentally productive experiences become the breeding ground of an oppressively exclusive ego consciousness that constructs a barrier to spiritual consciousness—omni consciousness.

Along the way, some do awake to spirituality—typically on the heels of a personal crisis, trauma, disappointment, or the experience of emptiness and loss of meaning in life. My friend Hal Honig got his wakeup call at age thirty when he achieved most of the material goals that he set for himself, with even more in clear view. Still, he could not shake off a gnawing sense of something missing. For Maggie, it was a life-threatening illness that got her thinking about a bigger picture. Kate's auto accident left her with permanent physical disabilities that devastated her self-image of youth and vigor, launching her on a spiritual quest. The breakup of a long-term relationship was the catalyst that put Rita on the spiritual path. Getting "downsized" from his high-powered job on Wall Street prompted Matt to reassess his values and join a spiritual group. Helen was loosely on a spiritual track from her teenaged years, but the death of a friend from breast cancer deepened her commitment to spirituality.

In the throes of these shocks, there's the feeling of running out of gas—the usual modus operandi doesn't work. The ego just won't crank up and your sense of being comes to a grinding halt. That's when the age-old questions are likely to erupt: Who am I, where did I come from, what is my purpose and mission in life, and where am I going? The spiritual search can then begin in earnest.

Some like Hal, now many decades on the spiritual path, will stay the course and genuinely shift their locus of consciousness beyond the ego. For Hal, spirituality became a central focus of his life, even as he managed a family business. He became a devotee of Sathya Sai Baba and made frequent trips to India to deepen his understanding and practices. Later, after he retired, Hal devoted his life entirely to spirituality. Eventually he accumulated twenty-four trips to India, often taking others along. His home in New York City became a gathering place for discussion, spiritual practice, and a sense of community that helped many others initiate and stick to a spiritual focus, particularly young people whom he mentored. Now most of those young people are married with children, and their families continue to be part of Hal's spiritual family. But unlike Hal, others will drift back into the old grooves as their immediate life crisis wanes—the brief awakening to spiritual insight fades. Then aging sneaks up.

## Why a Crisis?

Aging poses a special crisis that brings the term *emergency* into high relief. For one thing, as much as you may try and try, aging won't go away. You might get over other losses and disappointments, but aging is your copilot for life—for a long time a silent copilot while the ego's dog and pony show of power and invincibility enables you to dance through life with great expectations of a bigger and better ego *in the future* (I emphasize this phrase because it will figure prominently in the crisis of aging). Then aging, the spoiler, hits you with reality checks at every turn that stop denial in its tracks.

## Friend or Foe?

Have you ever met anyone who loved to age or, better yet, was looking forward to growing old? I haven't. Yes, there are the joys and compensations: maturity, wisdom, and all the other questionable and perhaps gratuitous positive stereotypes. But let's be honest. If given the choice, wouldn't you pass on old age and freeze life at youth, or some point in early or middle adulthood? Deep down, most of us don't actually expect to grow old. What a shock when it actually happens. A *New Yorker* magazine cartoon poignantly captures the feeling. A woman of "a certain age" complains to her friend: "Somehow, in all the confusion I aged." Aging wouldn't be so bad, if you just didn't have to grow old or die—two events that don't sit well with an ego that seeks never-ending expansion with a secret agenda of immortality.

Yet, early in life we don't mind aging—we may even yearn for it. As long as aging and the ego are in sync—teamed up for bigger and better things—aging will be friend, not foe.

## Hurry Up, Future!

As a child, didn't you long to "age"—weren't you in a rush get to the future? When I was in grade school, I longed to leap into the future when I could work with my father in the drugstore. Four-year-old Nora can't wait to be six when she can begin real school like her ten-year-old brother Jacob. And Jacob is already talking with great excitement and anticipation of aging to sixteen when he can drive a car. Looking ahead to college age, with all its attractive perks, can rev up the next enthusiastic wish to add years. Then full-fledged adulthood may have the most enticing pull of all with its promise of independence, exciting career choices, romantic relationships, marriage, family, and more.

But about thirtysomething the prospect of aging starts getting dicey and not so cute. "Where's the brake pedal?" many start frantically asking. That tension accelerates as forty approaches (it's more than coincidental that almost all theorists, commentators, and observers of human developmental stages cite age forty as a crisis point). Later, retirement might have its appeal of freedom, leisure, and independence. Chances are, though, you would prefer retirement if you could put the aging part on hold. Unfortunately, life isn't like your favorite sandwich: "I'll take the chicken and vegetables—hold the mayo and bacon."

Comedian George Carlin brilliantly captures the shifting attitude toward aging throughout the life cycle. Children, he said, are so eager to age that they think in fractions: "How old are you? 'I'm four and a half'—you're never thirty-six and a half. Then he pointed out that teenagers are so focused ahead that they jump to the next number: "How old are you?" "I'm gonna be sixteen." A few years later, Carlin says, "you *become* twenty-one." After that, aging begins to labor: "You *turn* thirty." That sounds like bad milk, Carlin comments. But aging turns even more sour: "You push forty, reach fifty, make it to sixty, hit seventy as aging speeds up," and possibly "get into your eighties" if you don't run out of gas.

## Shifting Gears

So the first crisis of aging is simply that it looms as an enemy that no one wants anything to do with. Most, in fact, hate it. When you first start noticing aging and tune in to messages of our youth-worshiping society, the ego will not like what it sees and hears, adding to the dread of what you begin to suspect lies ahead. Prejudice and stereotypes will pop up at every turn, puncturing the ego with blow after blow. You'll get an uncomfortable feeling of heading toward oblivion on the radar screen of life—insignificance is not exactly the ego's cup of tea. And the assaults will be everywhere.

It might start with the morning glance in the mirror revealing a new wrinkle or one gray hair. "How could this happen to *me?*" Next you're on a bus, on a train, or at a toll booth and someone calls you "sir" or "madam." You wonder, what happened to "young fellow" or "young lady"? Even "girly" would be welcome—to heck with sexism. Then you turn on the television and learn that your favorite program has been cancelled—not for lack of a sizable audience but that too many viewers are like you—over age fifty, or approaching it. That's a big no-no in advertising and the media—despite the known fact that the over-fifty population controls 75 percent of all liquid money assets. "Yes," the advertisers will tell you, "but you're getting old and probably keep your money in the mattress, don't spend, and don't change brands" (all proven untrue). More to the point, behind these stereotypes lurks a deep dislike of aging and the elderly that you will begin to sense. It's a club you don't want join or be identified with.

When I was on the talk-show circuit with my book (coauthored with Dr. Marcella Bakur Weiner) *The Starr-Weiner Report on Sex and Sexuality in the Mature Years* (about sex after sixty), a young news anchor, about my age at the time, preparing to do an interview with me asked what the book was about. When I said "sex and aging" he reflexively blurted out "uck" and looked a little nauseous. He tried to make amends by quickly apologizing. Too late, his reaction spoke tons about his prejudice—and perhaps fear. More significant, he was speaking for countless others. On reflection, his reaction shouldn't have surprised me. After all, the book noted that older people are sexual neuters in the popular mind. Even the experts, I discovered, often fueled those stereotypes.

For example, Alfred Kinsey, who gave us much of our basic information about human sexuality, wrote two volumes (one about men, the other about women) comprising 1200 pages of data and information drawn from 20,000 subjects. Yet, he included only a handful of adults over age sixty—and they were not even given his full interview. His omission screamed out, "Why bother with people on the sidelines of life, devoid of sexuality or any vital involvements?" Not surprising, therefore, that Kinsey devoted only four pages to older women and three to older men. The image of the sexless older person stubbornly persists today.

Another revelation came a few years later when I was seeking a sponsor for my radio feature, "Update on Aging." To me, aging wasn't ugly or strictly about old people—rather a natural process that begins at birth and remains with us throughout the life cycle. My features were mostly human-interest items about adults age forty and over. Yet radio programmers, potential sponsors, and ad agency executives routinely cringed at the word *aging*. After listening to a demo tape and liking it, the media director of a large Madison Avenue ad agency looked right at me and said, "It's good material and I like your voice and presentation, but the only thing you can sell in America is youth, longevity, and greed." I thought I was in a scene from the film *Wall Street* talking to the Michael Douglas character. The word *longevity*, though, stuck with me, and eventually I reluctantly changed the name of the feature to "The Longevity Report." Same material, but a much warmer reception. Who doesn't welcome the illusion of living forever?

Still, colleagues, and even friends, would say from time to time, "Are you still doing that geriatric stuff on radio?" Geriatrics is the medical side of aging. To them, as to most in our society, aging means geriatric, and geriatric means old and deteriorating—or, worse, the flesh-eating virus. It's an image, I learned, that you can't erase once you utter the word *aging*. Explanations don't help—maybe they don't even register. When I explained to these same people that over the seven years that I was on the radio with "Update on Aging" and then "The Longevity Report," I only broadcast one item on Alzheimer's and one or two on nursing homes, they were astonished, as if to say, "What else is there about aging?"

Hugh Downs, former announcer on the *Tonight Show*, host of the NBC *Today Show* (1962–1971), host of *20/20* (1978–1999), and author of *Fifty to Forever*, told me an amusing—and revealing—story about his groundbreaking, ahead-of-its-time television show about aging called *Over Easy*. Public television reluctantly agreed to do the show in 1977 a few years after Downs left the *Tonight Show* because, after all, it was Hugh Downs. They assumed that after a few shows, *Over Easy* would fail and then Downs would be ready to do something really important. The private buzz among the producers was that after three or four programs he would have said everything there was to be said about aging and would run out of material. The show ran for four years and would undoubtedly be a smash hit today. Hugh Downs, where are you?

## You and Them

Didn't you once think thirty was over the hill and old people were members of a different species? Chances are, you've held many of the negative stereotypes about older adults—hard not to, growing up in an ageist society. If so, those deeply ingrained prejudices will come home to roost, adding to the obstacles in facing your own aging when *you* become *them*—a process you will begin to feel creeping up when you hit the thirties.

So you see, dealing with aging will be an uphill battle. The enemies will be within and without. Don't expect much support "out there." You will have to find inner strength. But how will you muster that strength when your own ego, the very structure that guides your existence, is on a collision course with aging? *Aging is the ego's Armageddon.*

## Advance or Retreat—Your Choice!

Crisis, yes. But that doesn't mandate a frightening downturn in your life, or a call to arms for a life-and-death struggle. Crisis can also offer a choice point for growth. Zalman Schachter-Shalomi in his book *From Aging to Saging* illustrates the many ways that *conscious aging* can enrich the later years. And Deepak Chopra notes, "draining away of vitality, curiosity, and the will to live is controllable and in fact has nothing to do with normal aging."

The crisis of aging actually opens a window of opportunity for discovering the spiritual self—omni consciousness. And the spiritual choice can make all the difference between successful, productive aging and painful despair over an ever-increasing period of later life as we keep adding years to the average life span. Others have discovered spiritual consciousness—some without knowing it by that name or concept. You can too. In identifying and accessing spiritual consciousness, you can accelerate and enhance the process of getting beyond the ego. Best of all, you don't have to look very far. Omni consciousness has been with you all along—another very silent copilot that needs to take the controls to avoid a crash landing. And *now* is the moment to do it. You have everything to gain. With the longevity revolution persistently driving up the limits of life expectancy, you have lots of years ahead in the *third age* of life. If you are thirty, you may have as much as seventy more years ahead of you. Your ego will not get you through those years optimally. What can deserves serious attention. First you need to recognize what you are up against. That will help you muster the courage to battle the obstacles rather than defend a dead-end strategy.

## Longevity Revolution

It's remarkable that just a hundred years ago, average life expectancy in America from birth was just about forty-seven for men and fifty-one for women. That didn't leave much time for an aging crisis. Then thanks to improved public health measures (better water and sewerage), the advent of antibiotics and vaccines, as well as improved nutrition, life expectancy has grown in leaps and bounds throughout the world. Today, in the United States you can expect to live on average to 77.9 years—males to 75.2 and females to 80.4. That's a whopping 50+ percent increase since 1900. In some parts of Europe and Asia, life expectancy is even greater. And the over-eighty crowd is the fastest-growing age group. With expected breakthroughs in medicine and the genetics of aging over the next decades as our "golden age" of biology kicks in, hundred-year-plus life spans will soon be commonplace. Today there are about 72,000 centenarians (age one hundred and older) in the United States, and that is expected to swell to 834,000 by 2050.

What will your third age of life be like? If age thirty or forty terrorizes you, how will you handle fifty, seventy, or ninety? Are you equipped to thrive and survive? A big slice of life is at stake.

## Serious Business

The later years, call them the retirement years, leisure years, the new-me years, the over-the-hill years, or whatever label you've assigned to them, should not be taken lightly. In fact, the third age could be a quarter of a century or more—the biggest chunk of your life—longer than infancy, childhood, adolescence, young adulthood, or middle age. Surely, too many years to treat casually, throw away, or label unimportant. Yet, our youth-worshiping society pushes the later years off the stage of life in almost every arena:

work, love, romance, the media, you name it. Often it's older adults themselves who abdicate equality and willingly fade into the shadows of life. Leading the retreat is the defeated ego.

## The Ego's Showstopper

The crisis of aging is basically a crisis of the ego. The ego is a time bomb. Ego consciousness or personal "me" consciousness breaks down with aging. Aging, marked by time, is the archenemy of the ego. The ego doesn't comfortably accept limitations, let alone decline and death. Remember, the ego is driven by the assumption of an independent, separate "me" rooted to "me" experiences and dedicated to growth, development, and expansion to achieve security and mastery of the environment. The ego's mantra is all about personal power and invulnerability. It lives in a linear world moving from past to future, barely touching the present moment. The package of past, present, and future is essential for sustaining the ego's illusory sense of a concrete entity. What could be more real than a "me" that has a history, a presence, and extension into the future? The future is particularly vital to the ego's survival—that's where its grandiose goal of wholeness and immortality will be achieved. Then clock time runs down, threatening to puncture the ego balloon. Where can an expansive ego turn as its forward movement slows with the prospect of stalling or, worse, coming to a halt?

An inert ego stuck in the present with no substantial future is a dead ego. In the "now" moment, the ego must squarely face the deficits it has always assumed to be its nature—and doesn't like it. Worse is the scary feeling of not enough time to fix it. That's why the ego will run helter-skelter from the "now," into the future. Incompleteness in the "now" is tolerable only if there is movement toward a fantasy of future rescue. Where can the ego turn to fulfill its lifelong mission in a world without the crutch of time? "If I am not lodged in the here and now and the future is fading, the only other familiar haunt I know is the past. So I'll jiggle the past in an effort to jump-start the old engine." Dwelling on past successes can offer some solace. But that past has nowhere to go—it is no longer a springboard to the future. From the ego's perspective, aging tarnishes the prospects for golden days ahead. The very foundation of its existence is challenged as it loses its grip on time.

## The End of Time

Philosophers and scientists have long pondered and debated the nature and meaning of time. Some say time is nonexistent, a construction or illusion of mind—in a sense, a figment of our imagination. Albert Einstein declared that space/time—his fourth dimension—is a continuum with the implication that all time, past, present, and future, coexists. If so, then past and future are here and theoretically accessible. In Einstein's universe, everything is in motion, so time and motion are relative—there are no fixed reference points. As speed increases, time slows down, according to Einstein. In our earth dimension, most of these differences are imperceptible. But if you were traveling in a space ship and could approach the speed of light (186,000 miles per second), time would slow down considerably. If you were a twin and returned to earth after a few years of high-speed space travel, you would find your twin on earth was elderly while you remained young.

Physicist Julian Barbour disagrees with the motion view of time and space. In his contrarian book on the underlying reality of the universe, Barbour not only refutes the existence of time, he insists that the entire universe is static and motionless—all motion, he says, is an illusion. If there is no motion, how can time move at all?

While these intriguing concepts will continue to absorb scientists—and baffle the rest of us, even more than "way out" spiritual notions—the fact is that clock time, illusion or not, is a concrete reality in our everyday lives. Moreover, our perception of time is a powerful driving force in how we frame and conduct our lives—perhaps the most powerful. Yet on close examination the concept of time does little for us. It tends to work against us. We would be better off without it. While we may not be able to figure out if time actually exists, we can choose to ignore it. Later we will find out how. First, let's look at the confusing, if not bizarre, ways time plays out in our lives.

## Conflicting Meanings and Perceptions of Time

We perceive time moving in a straight line from now, which is a continuation of the past, to the future in regular units. Time can be broken down into seconds, milliseconds, minutes, hours, days, months, years, or innumerable possible categories and subdivisions. Whatever units we choose, they are conceptually equal. In our everyday notion of time, a minute now should be the same duration as a minute at any other time. A month is a month of time and is the same quantity of time this year, last year, or a hundred years from now. But in living and experiencing time, that's not at all the case. Even though we are not accelerating to speeds approaching the speed of light, our experience of time is individual and widely variable. You may perceive time to be fast, slow, or even standing still. Although the units of time are always the same, we sometimes feel we have lots of time or little time. Like a rubber band, time can seem to stretch out or shrink. An hour might fly by for you while that same hour feels endless to someone else. On a laid-back vacation, haven't you felt time slowing down or dragging? Then back at work it seems to pick up speed, even race.

The experience of time is also colored by age and the season of your life. Young people often feel they have so much time they can waste time, postpone decisions, and try out different roles. But once on a fast-moving work, professional, or corporate track, the frequent complaint is "I don't have enough time." Time becomes precious, so you make careful, measured decisions. "I don't have time for that, it's a waste of time. How can I afford to relax and reflect? Time is running out and I won't have time to get where I'm going." Then the forties strike, and you may still be flowing with time, eager to get to the next rung on the ladder that someone will be retiring from, or to some other goal while you feel time is still on your side. Suddenly you're in your fifties and time seems compressed, with many feeling they're reaching the end of time and are desperate to slow time down. Then retirement sneaks up, and despite the fear that time is rapidly vanishing, you find that you have time on your hands, even too much time—time to kill. But tell these same people to do something new, like learning to play a musical instrument that they never had time for, and they'll say, "That doesn't make any sense; how much time do I have left?"

Does this picture sound familiar to you? If so, you are not alone. Most of us are senselessly whiplashed by time. How would your life change if you dropped out of time—eliminated it from your mental vocabulary? In a timeless world where only "now" is real, there's time for everything. Do you yearn to embrace the "now"? If so, you must first shake off the grip of time. Later we will visit some everyday activities and decisions in a timeless world where only "now" is real to learn about the value of dropping out of time when it doesn't serve us.

## Numbers Count—or Do They?

At some point in everyone's life, the ego's familiar options for "fixes" narrow. Exactly when that will happen isn't the same for everyone. The process can begin as early as *thirtysomething*. Individual timing will depend on many factors such as goals, achievements, disappointments, illness, rejection, the biological clock ticking or expiring, children leaving home, or death of a spouse or friend, among an endless list of possible turns in life circumstances. Complicating matters for the ego, the longevity revolution has blurred the very notion of aging. What with John Glenn blasting off into space at age seventy-seven, granny skydivers, senior surfers stalking giant ocean waves, and ninety-year-old marathon runners, who, in fact, is old?

Of course, there's also another side to aging, especially in advanced old age when life can become monastic. Some old people live in a world of silence not based on a vow of silence but due to disabilities and immobility that narrow their social world. Others live in poverty not through a Franciscan vow of poverty but due to unfortunate life circumstances. Then there are those who are celibate, their state not initiated by a vow of celibacy or the quest for a priestly monastic life but due to the loss of a lifelong mate, absence of suitable partners, or social isolation.

Our concept of "old" also shifts with age. A young child may think all adults are old, with some just older than others. Actress Brigitte Bardot said as a teenager that she could not imagine growing old—meaning thirty. For many adults, "old" is someone else but surely not me—usually someone at least ten years older than me no matter what my age. I once overheard an eighty-five-year-old say, "I don't eat in that restaurant—that's where the old people eat."

Perceptions of "old" and "young" are also dictated by professions and life roles. Thirty-five is old and over the hill for dancers and athletes. But it's young, even suspiciously underage, for politicians or corporate executives. A few years ago a veteran pitcher for the Atlanta Braves baseball team became a free agent and was sought by many teams despite his advanced age of thirty-seven and his thirty-five-million-dollar price tag for three years—his skills held up despite his "advanced" age. He chose the New York Mets over the Philadelphia team because he felt that he would be more comfortable with the elderly pitching staff on the Mets (ages thirty-seven to forty-two) than the youngsters on the Phillies (ages twenty-six to twenty-seven). When tennis champion Andre Agassi announced that 2006 would be his last U.S. Open, the press was rife with speculation about what the aging "old man" of tennis (age thirty-six) would do with the rest of his life.

Perhaps "old" means time remaining in life. But how do you calculate that in an uncertain world that can throw nasty curves? Life time is not a guaranteed account balance. At age ninety, Jeanne Calment sold her apartment in the south of France to a young lawyer, Andre-Francois Raffray, with the provision that he pay until her death, at which time he would take possession of the apartment. The lawyer thought he made a shrewd bet with time on his side. He died thirty-one years later at age 77, the same year that Jeanne cut her first rap CD, *Time's Mistress*, at age 121—she died at 122.

When Senator Strom Thurmond ran for reelection in 1984, some critics thought the octogenarian was too old for public office. His opponent Melvin

Purvis thought so and made age an issue in the campaign. Thurmond won, and two years later Purvis died of a heart attack at forty-six. At age one hundred, Strom Thurmond was still strumming along in the Senate.

When I met John F. Kennedy Jr. at a fundraiser in Manhattan, you could not look at this impressive, bigger-than-life young man without thinking of his glowing future—and all the time he had to play it out. Time certainly seemed to be in his court. You could see the admiration, and even envy, of the onlookers as the paparazzi snapped away. He died a few months later in a plane crash. Measured by time left, JFK Jr. was an old man the night we met. So it was with many extraordinary people throughout history who died young, reminding us that we only own the present moment (Alexander the Great, thirty-three; Mozart, thirty-five; Chopin, thirty-nine; James Dean, twenty-four; Marilyn Monroe, thirty-six, to mention a few).

Even if you imagine yourself to be John Glenn, Jeanne Calment, or other long-lived super agers, there still will be those gnawing reminders that life time is finite. Under the best of circumstances there will be losses—friends, relatives and spouses, roles in life, and more. Although you may be healthy and active, you will see many examples of your peers who are not, reminding you of your vulnerability and throwing a wrench in the ego's usual upward and onward trajectory. Nevertheless, the blurred picture of who is old leaves lots of room for denial to thrive.

## The Boomers Are Coming

Birds do it, bees do it, and even kings, queens, presidents, popes, and billionaires do it! They all age and die. But don't tell that to the baby boomers. The huge, 77-million-strong post–World War II generation (born between 1946 and 1964) seems to believe that the fate of all creatures on the planet will not happen to them. Bigger and better ego-driven strategies, they think, will be bring them to the proverbial fountain of youth that eluded fifteenth-century Spanish explorer Juan Ponce de León (although he did discover Florida). This upbeat generation of aging adults that are beginning to cross the senior line are fighting back. They have declared war on aging.

Their strategy is to whip the ego into action, believing the aging horse can continue to jump through the same old hoops. And American industry and corporate America have been quick to feed the youth frenzy. Just read the headlines and captions in popular magazines: "Stop Aging Now," "Beat the Clock," "Reverse Aging," "Stay Young Forever," "Erase Wrinkles," "Create the Age You Want to Be," and the best one: "Cure Aging," as if it were a disease.

To fulfill the promise of "young forever," there are the spas where you can fight the clock with miracle herbs, hormones, secret formulas, crash diets, intestinal cleansing and detoxification, intensive exercise, yoga postures, breathing exercises, hair transplants, breast implants, breast reductions, tummy tucks, other cosmetic surgeries, and endless practices and procedures to win the age war—desperate egos in a life-and-death struggle to survive intact and unchanged.

Economist and writer Sylvia Hewlett, in her book *Creating a Life: Professional Women and the Quest for Children*, reports the shock of women who postponed family for career discovering that fertility drops dramatically at age thirty-five and that by forty-two the average woman only has a 5 percent chance of getting pregnant. Many women believe that fertility can routinely continue into the forties and fifties, and if there are problems, biotechnology will come to the rescue. Sadly, many find out, as reported by Hewlett, that their eggs are gone or vastly diminished and that pills and procedures don't reliably work magic. Still a group of young career-track women listening to these facts and the desperate quest for fertility by aging women on a TV magazine show retained the conviction that they will be able to start a family in their forties and fifties. Their unshakable faith is reminiscent of the twenty-eight-year-old young man I met who had the diet of choice for those whose arteries lack cholesterol. When I pointed out to Stanley the risks of his junk-food diet, he said, "By the time I'm fifty they'll have a pill to ream out my arteries. So why should I worry?" Lots of luck!

Now that's not to say that we haven't made inroads in making longer lives healthier lives, and we have postponed or vastly reduced many chronic conditions associated with aging. Aging is not a disease. The early onset of chronic conditions such as arthritis, diabetes, and arteriosclerosis is often tied to diet and lifestyle. The surgeon general reports that a third of all cancers, most cases of cardiovascular disease, and a large percentage of adult-onset diabetes cases can be prevented or slowed by diet and lifestyle.

And surely, the new generation of older adults has knocked down some age-old stereotypes, helping them forge more active and productive lives. For example, at one time menopause was considered the end of sexuality for women, if not the end of femininity. If you bought into that, the self-fulfilling prophecy made it a reality. But boomer women on the heels of the feminist movement have turned that around. Now many women call menopause "the pause that refreshes"—in no way diminishing femininity and in fact allowing for greater freedom in sexuality without the fear of pregnancy or the need to take pills with their uncertain long-term collateral damage. They have not defeated aging but have taken charge of aging by aging optimally.

Still, there are eventually changes with age. The gift of birth forecasts death. And between birth and death there's aging. Ultimately, reality in-trudes with the realization that aging is for real and you can't get out of this life alive! We're back to the crisis of aging.

## Ego Plus

We live in two worlds—the relative and the spiritual. We are the ego—but we are more (see the discussion of conservation of the self in chapter 4). Without the spiritual higher consciousness—omni consciousness—the ego is stranded and lost. The ego, if it works at all, is designed for the young. Its youth-based operating system can't effectively cope with aging. That's why it's no coincidence that Freud, with his ego-centered psychoanalysis, con-cluded that people could not be effectively analyzed after age forty. In Freud's day—the late nineteenth century and early twentieth century—forty-year-old egos would begin to sputter given shorter life expectancies than today. Now the ego may have legs until fifty, sixty, or later before the prison of the ego's self-conception moves into a lockdown mode with diminishing options for its usual gratifications projected into the future.

Contrast Freud's view with Eastern spiritual traditions that say age fifty is the ideal time to embark on the spiritual path to discover the higher self. Why not? At fifty you are more likely to be in a position to get off the tread-mill and make conscious choices that can open the way to discover your omni consciousness. The forty/fifty divide reveals the radical difference be-tween Eastern and Western conceptions of human existence. Western psy-chology is ego based, Eastern psychology omni consciousness based.

## Save the Ego

Western psychology says you're stuck with your ego, a view that you have been nurtured on, have absorbed, and live by—like it or not, or believe it or not. And now, as you age, you're up against a wall. The ego simply does not have the tools for penetrating that wall. Face it, the ego is not designed for aging or old age. While the ego will get you into trouble at any age, it's a dis-aster in the later years. Ego strategies may work more or less effectively through early adulthood, especially if you were fortunate enough to have good health, were lucky in love and relationships, achieved success in work and professional life, had kids that did all right, and were able to navigate through a host of other life events that minimally challenged the ego's game plan. Most of us aren't so lucky and will suffer, even when young, as the ego is challenged or thwarted at many turns. For almost everyone, the ego will begin to sputter as the ugly face of clock time running down looms ahead. Strategy will then shift to defensive damage control, ultimately leading to desperate hand-to-hand combat.

## Part 2: Mobilizing the Troops

Denial is one of the ego's most ferocious defenses to maintain its illusions. Ultimately, even denial cannot fend off aging, particularly advanced old age. Aging chips away at denial until it collapses. A big piece of the ego's world is vanishing: time. No wonder the desperate war cry of the oldest baby boomers as they lead the charge across the age line: "Save the ego!"

Why not? If psychological existence begins and ends with the ego, what choice is there? But how do you preserve a self under assault with a vital part—the future—fading? If we look into the ego box, there are just so many psychological self pieces to play with. Essentially, the box contains the "me" experiences held together by memory over time. The future part of that time line is particularly vital to the survival of the ego. Remember, the ego needs to be on the move toward the future. With the future fading, what's left in the box? There's the present that the ego never warmed up to. At best, the "now" was always just a fleeting moment on the way to the future. So the present will not be a comfortable resting place. On the contrary, without the future, the present will be a constant irritant calling attention to the lack of completeness, but without hope of filling the hole. Ah, but there's the past— past achievements, and successes, and just plain past experiences to beef up the feeling of a concrete, enduring entity called "me." And, surprise surprise, the past is exactly what experts looking at aging through the lens of the ego have seized upon for preservation of the self. No small task given all the assaults on the self as we age.

### Ask the Experts

Until fairly recently, there was little written about the psychology of the later years and old age. There just weren't enough old people around in earlier generations to excite anyone's interest. Prior to the explosion in life expectancy, the world was largely young. Relatively few ever lived to old age. People typically started work early, married young, promptly had large families, then died at about age forty, which was the life expectancy through the middle ages in Europe. Those who managed to hang on beyond age fifty were commonly afflicted with chronic diseases, disabilities, and poverty—certainly not candidates for surfing, bungee jumping, or space travel. Social security, pensions, and retirement were unheard of until the late nineteenth century—"till death do us part" applied to both marriage and work. The first-ever social security was introduced by Otto von Bismarck, the chancellor of Germany in 1889.

One of the most startling statistics reported by Ken Dychtwald, author of *The Age Wave* and *Age Power*, says it all: through 99 percent of human existence on this planet, life expectancy was less than twenty years of age.

That picture dramatically changed with the longevity revolution ushering in the explosive growth of elderly populations. Social scientists started noticing a gray revolution rapidly unfolding and began spinning theories about aging over the past few decades. Some of the first notions were quite dreary but nevertheless resonated with popular stereotypes. For example, Cumming and Henry in 1961 introduced the disengagement theory of aging. Old people (meaning age sixty and over), they said, "naturally disengage from life," pulling back from people, roles, and activities. They even warned that continuing to engage in life as a full-fledged adult is an aberration. Disengagement in their view flows from the anticipation of death.

Disengagement theory is a forthright, uncompromising expression of the ego model—without knowing it. With the future out of the ego box (anticipation of death), what's the point of life? So pull back, pull in, and disconnect. It's also a dressed-up version of "if you're over sixty, be glad that you're still lucky enough to sit up and take nourishment."

Aside from disengagement being theoretically flawed—there's more to existence than the ego—it defies the fact that countless older people live engaged lives outside the ego box. How they do it reveals a revolutionary approach to successful aging beyond the ego that older adults are forging in defiance of the experts. It's part of the unfolding story of omni consciousness.

**Looking in the Wrong Place**
Just who were Cumming and Henry looking at to reach their conclusion? I raise this question because it's clear to me that most professionals in the field of aging that we turn to for insights, knowledge, and guidance—psychologists, psychiatrists, physicians, social workers, nurses, and others—make their living working largely with infirm, disabled, mentally distressed, dependent, hospitalized, and institutionalized older adults—most often the oldest old—who may exhibit more of the popular negative stereotypes of the elderly. Their observations give us a distorted view of later adulthood. In reality, only 5 percent of the over-sixty population—and that includes the very old and the very sick and disabled—live in nursing homes and other institutions where they require extensive care. The other 95 percent of the older population are relatively

healthy and live independently. As we look into the lives of this group, we will see an entirely different picture of aging that will shake the foundation of our assumptions about the aging process and call attention to a consciousness beyond ego that is the foundation of the *third age survival kit*.

## What You See Is Not What You Get

Disturbed by disengagement theory, sociologist Robert Atchley noted that when we look at the evolving lives of older adults, appearances can be deceptive, especially if you focus exclusively on the half-empty glass and ignore the half-full ones, which qualitatively may be overflowing. Yes, he acknowledged, older adults might pull back and consolidate or narrow their activities but not to withdraw or disengage from life. His continuity theory noted that older people continue engagement in life, even intensely, but may focus on fewer preferred activities rather than dispersing energy over a wider range of involvements as when they were younger. Or they may shift into new activities that use the skills, interests, and abilities that have always guided their lives.

Phil Sine is a good example of Atchley's continuity theory. On the surface, Phil is a retiree. He no longer has the role or responsibilities of executive vice president of a large international publishing company where he spent much of his professional life. You could say he's disengaged because he no longer manages thousands of employees or controls a budget of tens of millions of dollars. Nor does he travel around the world launching new publications. But if you look closer, while taking some postretirement courses at Marymount Manhattan College, he became part of a group of retirees, including a former CEO of a large corporation, that founded a new program for retirees—the Center for Learning and Living. Phil soon became the volunteer executive director of the program, which offered fifty-five courses a year with volunteer faculty members—all with extraordinary credentials. Phil also taught several courses in politics, history, and social issues, his lifelong interests, that required him to study and deepen his knowledge. Phil was using the same (continuity) take-charge skills that served him so well during his business career but in a new arena with different activities. Atchley got it right!

## New Wave

Then other voices entered the fray to rescue the third age from irrelevancy and give it legitimacy on a par with other stages of life. Psychologist Erik Erikson was first to offer a comprehensive psychological theory that took adulthood and aging seriously. Included in his eight stages of human development are three that speak to adulthood and later life. Prior to Erikson, all the popular theories of development, as noted in chapter 5, were exclusively about the childhood years, as if nothing of great significance happens developmentally after adolescence.

### Erikson's Adulthood

The crisis, or task, in early adulthood, Erikson said, is to come to grips with relationships. The possibilities range from isolation to intimacy. In middle age, the choice is generativity vs. stagnation: you give back to the young and invest in nurturing the next generation or you get stuck and psychologically disintegrate. Of particular interest for this chapter is Erikson's last stage—integrity vs. despair—that speaks to later adulthood. The task of this final stage is a life review to gain a sense of completeness, wholeness, and meaning that imparts a sense of integrity and coherence to one's life. It's a time to come to grips with disappointments, failures, missed opportunities, and other limitations of a lived life. Erikson warns that failure to achieve integrity will result in an old age of despair and bitterness.

We are indebted to Erikson for affirming transformational possibilities beyond the childhood years—that real qualitative changes and growth can occur in adulthood and even old age. Yet on close examination, integrity vs. despair puts us squarely back in the ego box still playing with the remaining pieces of self as time flies out of the box. Integrity is mostly about reviewing the past, evaluating the past, making peace with and reworking the past, and then reaching a conclusion about the worth of the self now. It's the ego struggling to assert its wholeness in the face of a lost future, the place where it always sought completeness. Erikson actually acknowledges this: "Despair expresses the feeling that time is short, too short for the attempt to start another life and to try out alternate roads to integrity" (*Identity and the Life Cycle*, p. 105). Anticipation and fear of death become the showstoppers that turn the ego to the past for shoring up its integrity, according to Erikson. But why the need for a psychological will and autopsy when vital living "now" is still possible (taking the term *vital* from the title of Erikson's book *Vital Involvement in Old Age*)? It's strictly the persistent obsession with the ego that directs us to the past as we desperately try to hold the conceptual self together when the future fades. All this work to maintain the dead past consumes enormous energy that takes away from the potential for continued fulfillment *here and now*. Integrity and wholeness are always "now"; they do not rest on the past—or the future. The most vital older adults that I know and whom others have written about, including Erikson, as we will shortly see, are vibrantly involved in life now. Why then the pull to the past? It's the ego, stupid!

Erikson undoubtedly sensed that there was more to life in later adulthood than the ego. In *Vital Involvement in Old Age*, after laying out his more traditional views, he surprisingly shifts gears: "But it must be equally clear that the sense of 'I' in old age, still has a once-for-all chance of transcending time-bound identities and sensing, if only in the simplest terms, an all-human and existential identity like that which the world religions and ideologies have attempted to create" (p. 53). This startling excursion beyond the ego grabbed my attention. Erikson was clearly flirting with omni consciousness—a timeless state where life goes on as long as there is consciousness. No need to establish the integrity of omni consciousness through happenstance personal experiences from the past. In omni consciousness there is unconditional acceptance. Wholeness and integrity are its nature.

Unfortunately, Erikson didn't follow through with the far-reaching implications of a transcendent "I." He promptly reverted to his ego mode, reaffirming and patching-up the integrity of the historic ego. Perhaps it was too threatening for him to run with the concept of transcendence. If there is a transcendent "I," wouldn't that force Erikson to rethink all his stages of development—and even the nature of development itself? If there is a transcendent consciousness beyond ego, why wait until old age to access it?

## Reminiscence and Life Review

Building on Erikson's stage of integrity vs. despair, Dr. Robert Butler has championed reminiscence and life review as an important and constructive task of later adulthood. He criticized those who called reminiscence in older adults a sign of senescence rather than a natural and useful activity. Surely, there is much to be learned individually and collectively from life histories. Butler went on to demonstrate the uplifting, healing functions of life review. It proved particularly useful in treating older people suffering depression, despair, or physical illnesses. Reviewing strengths, achievements, struggles, and the coherence and wholeness of a life can reaffirm the power of the self here and now by identifying and embracing enduring strengths and possibilities. From my perspective, it can trigger awareness of an overarching consciousness—omni consciousness.

But reminiscence and life review have become an institution—activities almost mandated for the elderly. Aside from the fact that they are not new— history and many psychotherapy schools incorporate them—overdoing reminiscence and life review beat the remains of the ego (the past) in the hope of keeping it going and compensating for the vanishing future. It also subtly devalues the self by making its worth and meaning conditional—"my life is meaningful only if I can extract some meaning from the past." Zealous advocates of life review will say they use it to motivate older people to act in and value the present.

Butler warns that reminiscence should not get caught up in nostalgia, which can be heavily colored with longing and regret that glamorize the past and devalues the present. But in practice I find that others working with reminiscence get mired down in the past. And I believe it has been obsessively embraced and promoted as a device to save the ego—"finally we have a tool to resurrect and deify the past. The ego can live!" Confirming this, I was astonished to hear one "expert" suggest that older people should change their stories—seeing and interpreting them in a more favorable or flattering light to beef up the ego—generously calling this "reinterpreting" the stories. Why not? If the ego is a mental construct to begin with and one of its support pillars for self-fulfillment—the future—must be abandoned, then inject any fantasy and distortion into the remaining pillar of the ego that will make you feel good in a marriage of desperation and delusion. But there is another choice called reality—the here-and-now reality, and unconditional acceptance of self: omni consciousness. What would life review and reminiscence mean in the eternal now?

## Good at Any Age

Keep in mind that life review, reminiscence, and autobiography are valuable at any age. Haven't you ever reminisced about "the good old days" in elementary school, high school, and college or about your early work experiences on the way up? People often like to talk about their struggles earlier in life and the obstacles they overcame. Even young children enjoy and benefit from life review. When four-year-old Nora found an album of photos of her and other family members that had been taken two years earlier, she enthusiastically scrutinized the photos with an ongoing narrative about her impressions. She asked if there were more pictures of "when I was a baby." Nora was engaging in reminiscence and life review. Her review was not just nostalgia for the past. Her review informed the present—"I'm not a baby anymore, I'm a big girl." But Nora doesn't want to hold on to the past—she is here and now and pointed to the future.

There's a danger of reminiscence falling victim to the aging ego's fear of the future or, rather, the lack of it. So use reminiscence and life review, but don't get lost in it.

## A Look Ahead

Back in the trenches of aging, the desperation of the boomers to hang on to youth tells tons about their present dread of aging. But what exactly is their vision of the future?

Sociologist Daniel Levinson provides an interesting glimpse into the fear of the future at middle age. Levinson's groundbreaking study of men and women between ages thirty-four and forty-five filled a gap in our understanding of adult development. In *The Seasons of a Man's Life* and *The Seasons of a Woman's Life*, he identified three stages of adulthood called eras, each with a transitional period: Early Adulthood (beginning at the end of adolescence and extending to age forty), Middle Adulthood (ages forty to sixty), and Late Adulthood (sixty and beyond). Eras are defined by life tasks and events of everyday living like separation from family in early adulthood and then entering the world of work, marriage, and family. Later tasks are making choices to strengthen commitments to work, community, and personal interests. Since Levinson's subjects were middle-aged, he could only speculate about life after sixty based on their projections—and fears.

Levinson's interviews revealed the life-and-death threat of aging as early as forty (again the number forty comes up as the turning point), when it is first recognized by many: "A man at mid-life is suffering some loss of his youthful vitality and, often, some insult to his youthful narcissistic pride. Although he is not literally close to death or undergoing severe bodily decline, he typically experiences these changes as a fundamental threat. It is as though he were on the threshold of senility and even death." Notice the intensity of the language that screams out the catastrophic terror of the ego faced with aging and anticipation of death—not physical death as much as ego death.

Levinson says that there is no one event that triggers this universal fear. But inevitably life will unfold many experiences that will call attention to mortality and the finite nature of the lifecycle: death of a parent, a child leaving home, divorce, or some other traumatic event. Obviously these can occur at various ages and don't apply to everyone. However, the powerful emotional distress of middle age that Levinson noted has a unifying feature that can be set off by a wide range of behaviors that occur in middle age, leading to the realization of ego death—that time is diminishing and the ego will eventually be thwarted in its quest for immortality.

**Train Wreck Ahead**

Levinson has tapped into the backdrop of what we have observed in the youth frenzy of the boomers. At the same time, we can see the older baby boomers marching toward disaster: you don't have to be psychic to clearly foresee that the war on aging will not be won. It's just a matter of when the time bomb will explode. The boomers have not heeded the warning of British writer and philosopher George Bernard Shaw, "You should not try to live forever, you will not succeed." How will the collective egos take this defeat? What actually happens when aging meets its Armageddon? Is it possible to have meaningful, joyous life on the other side of the lost battle? Or do the elderly keel over and wither away? Are the later years a wasteland of retreat from life as the boomers' fears would suggest? Not trivial questions for young and middle-aged adults that Levinson so graphically depicts looking at the enemy (aging) over the trenches at the battle line and wondering, Who will I be one, two, three, or more decades from now? A frightening query that often breeds desperation, if not despair. If a crystal ball could offer you a glimpse, would you even dare to look?

## Part 3: Beyond the Veil

Based on all that we know about the nature of the ego and the ferocious battle to conquer aging, we should not be surprised if the later years were rife with sadness, depression, despair, hopelessness, withdrawal, and anger. Young people would think so. As gerontologist Sheldon Tobin writes in his book *Personhood in Advanced Old Age*: "Indeed, young researchers and practitioners can not easily comprehend how it is to live with the kinds of physical impairments and interpersonal losses found among the very old; and certainly, most young people cannot comprehend how it is to live without an active sex life. If such adversities were to occur to them, life would be truly unbearable."

What, then, is life like on the other side of the battle line? Is it the disaster anticipated by the middle-aged ego looking ahead? Let's fast-forward for a peek into the world of older adults to find out the real story.

### Downbeat or Upbeat?
The good news, contrary to popular mythology tainted by fear, older adults aren't any more depressed than other adults. In fact, the incidence of serious depression is surprisingly less in older adults than younger ones. The gerontologist Dr. Michael Smyer notes that mental illness in general occurs less in the elderly than younger people: "Older adults of both genders have lower rates of affective, anxiety, and substance use disorders." These findings are even more remarkable since the many medications that the elderly typically take for physical ailments often have side effects on mental functioning. Also, many physicians believe that physiological changes in the aging brain can contribute to depression. Taking all these factors into consideration, we would expect far greater incidence of depression and other personality disorders with advancing age even if all else were equal. The statistics reveal the resiliency of older people and highlight that something dramatic happens be-

tween the war on aging exhibited by middle-aged adults and reconciliation with aging that is evidenced in the later years.

### The Plot Thickens

The mystery deepens as we look into the actual lives of older adults on the other side of the divide. It's strikingly different from the anticipated fears projected at midlife. A picture of satisfaction, peace, and active involvement is more the norm than the exception. How can we explain this? Egos don't dance to the music of self-satisfaction in the "now," especially with real losses and diminished prospects for the future. What, then, is directing these behaviors if not the ego?

### Ernst and Ethel

Let's look at a snapshot of two successful agers for some clues. My cousin Ernst (his father and my grandmother were siblings) is in his nineties, although he won't give his exact age—numbers don't count, he insists. Dr. Ernst Katz is founder and conductor of the Junior Symphony Orchestra of Los Angeles.

As a young man, he gave up his career as a concert pianist (he is also an accomplished violinist) who performed around the world to found his orchestra in 1940. Remarkably, he's still conducting, although he recently stepped down as concertmaster, passing that along to his nephew Gary, an attorney and first violinist with the orchestra. Recently, Ernst complained to me that his eyesight is so bad that he had to conduct a Beethoven symphony and a Schubert symphony from memory.

When I joined him in his office in Westwood, he went on and on with an endless number of fascinating reminisces (life review?) about intriguing friends like John Paul Getty, William Randolph Hearst, and movie stars dating back to his lifelong friendship with Mary Pickford, the silent-movie star, and the fact that he and Albert Einstein played the violin together in the years that Einstein was at Cal Tech. Einstein came over to his house once a week when he was in California—"He may have been a great scientist, but he was a lousy violinist," Ernst quipped. With all these stories, you might make the mistake of thinking he's lost in the past. I soon learned otherwise.

He talked about his next night's concert, the sixty-fifth anniversary of the "battle of the batons"—an annual Hollywood event in which he trains a number of celebrities from the entertainment industry in conducting. They each conduct the orchestra, and afterward the audience of invited guests votes on a winner. Ernst said that at the annual performance he usually tells the story about Marjorie Maine, the movie star who was an early winner of the battle of the batons. But, he said, he thinks people are tiring of that story so he'll tell a new one—"maybe about Henry Fonda." He then went into great detail about how nervous Fonda was about this performance—he came over to Ernst's house every night for a few weeks, listening and practicing diligently. The story continued with other amusing details like Fonda freezing at the performance when he raised his arms to conduct. Ernst had to go over and push his arm down for the music to begin. Just when I thought he would keep rolling with more reminiscences, he said he had to stop because there was business to do now. Ed Asner, one of the emcees for the concert, was on the phone, and they had to go over the script. It wasn't until the next evening before a filled house at the Dorothy Chandler Pavilion that I realized Ernst was not just telling a story, or reminiscing, about Henry Fonda the previous afternoon, he was rehearsing. As he addressed the audience, he told the story almost word for word the way he had reviewed it with me earlier—and no doubt with others.

At the reception after the concert, he was already talking about the next concert scheduled for a few months later. Despite his infirmities—poor vision and physical problems—he moves ahead with vital involvement with young people in the here and now. He says he feels twenty when he wakes up in the morning—that is, until he creaks his way to the mirror. Then when he conducts, he says, that youthful sensibility returns.

While you may say that Ernst is unusual with his musical talent and his associations with celebrities over the years that set him apart from more ordinary lives, that's not entirely true. Everyone who has lived a long life has a history, stories, involvements, and the potential for creative living now. We will keep returning to this conclusion as we explore the crisis of aging.

Ethel had a more modest history—no movie stars or celebrity parties in Hollywood (although her grandson directed a major Hollywood film)—but her life at ninety-six is vibrant, connected, and a valuable asset for everyone around her. When I called her a few days before writing this sketch, she had just returned to New York after a week in Oregon visiting her grandson and great-grandchildren—and she traveled alone.

I first met Ethel, a secretary in the Continuing Education Office at Marymount Manhattan College, when she was eighty. Ten years later, when she turned ninety, the school honored her with a party that was also celebrating her twenty years of service. Yes, she started the job at age seventy after a forced mandatory retirement from the New York City Board of Education, where she had worked as a school secretary. More remarkable, this was not a retirement party—and no one was even hinting that she retire. Nor was Ethel slowing down. There's always a spring to her step, a cheerful, alert demeanor, and efficiency in her work. It's well known that if you want to get something done right—and fast—you should give it to Ethel. And if you think all older adults have memory problems, think again. Ethel is the one we relied on to remind us of upcoming meetings and other events that often had slipped our minds. Ethel finally did retire two years ago at ninety-four, but not willingly. Continuing Education was closing down. She was offered a job in one of the academic offices, but the hours would have put her on the bus she took home to Queens during the rush hour. So Ethel reluctantly retired—or, more accurately, shifted her activities. She comes in to New York City three times a week to swim at a health club. She initially did some volunteer work in her neighborhood but now has backed off to concentrate on fixing up her house, which she said she neglected for many years while working—she has been living in the house since 1941, much of that time alone since her husband died in 1975. Ethel would like to do some volunteer work, but she says she doesn't have time right now—she's treasurer of her neighborhood homeowners association and is pressed to complete the annual report.

Although she is close with her family, regularly visiting her three children, four grandchildren, and three great-grandchildren, she likes living in her own space independently. Some family members live within short travel distance, and a bus or train ride is no deterrent for Ethel (her family persuaded her to give up driving at eighty-eight). Ask her what she thinks about aging and she'll tell you she is too busy to think about it.

Ethel and Ernst are not anomalies. Researchers probing the day-to-day lives and inner worlds of older adults find a surprisingly positive picture. That's not to say that all older people are thrilled to age and are dancing with joy. Others don't have Ethel's energy and good health, or Ernst's musical talent and determination to continue teaching and performing. But clearly peace with aging and active participation in life is more the rule than the exception. And there is growing momentum for older adults to embrace productive, positive, and creative aging—the self-fulfilling prophecy ("I can") is shifting to the plus side. Let's listen to some of the comments recorded by Erik Erikson in his interviews with older adults age seventy-five to ninety-five.

**The Person Within**

"I don't think I'll be here in ten or fifteen years. That's why I love . . . to do things now." "If you're going to keep on living, you better keep on growing." "I can't wait to get into bed at night with a good book. I can't wait to get up in the morning and have a cup of coffee. That's my life." "When you get to my age [age ninety], why, I am willing to die any time"—he is interested in literature and politics but regrets that infirmities keep him from other life passions. Others show pride in their accomplishments, come to grips with regrets and disappointments, see grandchildren as an extension of themselves, worry about the state of the world for future generations, and pursue old and new interests. What overrides the comments despite disabilities and limitations is a pervasive sense of peacefulness, self-acceptance, and focus on the present without the need for achievement to validate the self. Erikson's elders typically view the future as a time for activity, not achievement. He also noted that they are "more tolerant, more patient, more open minded, more understanding, more compassionate less critical and slower to anger."

Others have made similar observations. In their book *Life Beyond 85 Years* Colleen Johnson and Barbara Barer found that the oldest old (eighty-five plus), compared to the younger old (seventy to eighty-four), showed greater detachment from social irritants, had fewer emotional problems, accepted that they could not exercise mastery over much of their lives (mastery is one of the prime ego drives), showed increased acceptance of their inability to solve many personal problems or change important things in their lives, and were less emotional in talking about physical and mental limitations. The younger old complained more about advancing age. The oldest old were more likely to see age as positive—"Everything is smooth, but why shouldn't it be? At my age, it is natural to have lost so many family and friends." Another said, "I have outlived my worries." How can we explain the upbeat comments of Mrs. Albert, a ninety-two-year-old woman with numerous medical problems and disabilities: "I really enjoy life. I have my projects, so I feel I can accomplish something—I wouldn't change my life." Or the upbeat attitude of eighty-six-year-old Mrs. Carter, who is legally blind from macular degeneration and has arthritis and a heart condition—"I'm happy most of the time. I take one day at a time, and I'm thankful I've lived so long. I don't dread death." Another said, "Death, no big deal."

## Centenarians

A few years ago a CNN magazine story on aging and longevity featured young and middle-aged women in the throes of the antiaging, antiwrinkle war. One desperate thirtysomething woman seeking Botox and Resolyn treatments in the Caribbean said, "It's getting scary. It's all going downhill." Later in the program, the centenarian great-grandmother of the interviewer, appearing totally relaxed and comfortable in her original wrinkled (untouched) skin, attributed her longevity to "living in peace with that which you cannot change."

Adding similar eyebrow-raising examples, Dr. Thomas Perls and Dr. Margery Silver, studying the very oldest old—those living to one hundred and beyond, found that centenarians typically display positive attitudes toward life despite considerable physical impairments, limitations, and dependency. The ego mantras of mastery and invulnerability have little applicability to these centenarians. How can we compute that many continue active engagement in life, some even taking on new interests? There's Lola Blonder, who started watercolor painting at age 90 and was still painting at 104. And Lucy Boring was playing bridge and winning at 109. Listen to Marie Knowles, age 104, capture the positive outlook of successful aging with her wise advice: "Pick out the fine things in life, and if you can't find them there, pick them out of your own head."

The secret of successful aging revealed by these centenarians is to age well rather than to deny or fight aging, say Perls and Silver. But that requires letting go of the ego's tight grip. How do they do it?

Other researches have come up with additional baffling, counterintuitive observations of contented well-adjusted older adults. Given the ferocious age war fought by boomers in their thirties, forties, and fifties to obliterate all signs of aging and halt the obnoxious party pooper, how can we explain the finding that most of the older adults in a number of studies did not base their sense of contentment on physical appearance or disability? As we listen to the voices of these older adults, one conclusion is inescapable: we are not hearing egos talking. Nor are they singing songs of the ego. These *positive agers* are not obsessed with death, don't fear or measure the future, or seek escape into the past. What explains the new tunes? The ego doesn't change colors or throw in the towel without paying a heavy emotional price. What happens between the all-out war on aging and peace with aging to account for this remarkable turnaround?

**From War to Peace**
Terms like adjustment, adaptation, reassessment, acceptance, maturity, coming to grips with, wise decisions, and other descriptive terms that are glibly offered ring hollow when we grasp the enormity of the shift we have been observing. They describe but don't explain the behaviors—and almost trivialize the accomplishment. What we are witnessing is an astonishing phenomenon of *ego transcendence*. The profound shift from war to peace begins to make sense only when we recognize the guiding presence of another consciousness—omni consciousness. The I/me/ego consciousness has yielded to transcendent consciousness.

Ego transcendence is not an entirely new concept. You will recall that Erik Erikson acknowledged it and actually gave many examples of transcendence despite his emphasis on ego preservation. Unfortunately Erikson didn't fully embrace transcendence or give it center stage in his portrait of aging.

Psychologist Robert Peck is frequently quoted for his observations of ego transcendence in later adulthood. Although Peck does not offer a comprehensive theory of transcendence, he does note that the prospect of death is perceived as an assault on the ego. He calls anticipation of death "the night of the ego." He goes on to describe a number of life strategies for self-perpetuation after death by investing in children and grandchildren, making the world better for future generations, and a number of other activities to achieve significance "beyond the limits of their own skins and their own lives." While Peck's vision of transcendence is admirably humanistic, it is still fixated on the ego. It subtly wrestles with death—the overhanging Damocles sword that is its reference point. Peck then offers strategies for sustaining some viability to the ego—it's compensatory and still mournfully massaging of the ego. Passing a better baton to future generations should be an activity and ethic throughout adulthood, not only when the brakes are applied to the ego. Otherwise it casts transcendence as reactive. True transcendence is not about death. It does not stand in opposition to death. It's about life—here and now. Transcendence resides in omni consciousness, which is timeless—the only reality of the eternal now.

First to fully champion ego transcendence in later life is Swedish psychologist Lars Tornstam. He too notes that Erikson's theory is past oriented with emphasis on preserving the historic ego. Tornstam's detailed observations of ego transcendence in older adults (he calls it gerotranscendence) document transcendence as a genuine and frequent occurrence: "Simply put, gerotranscendence is a shift in metaperspective from a materialistic and pragmatic view of the world to a more cosmic and transcendent one." His probing interviews with fifty adults between ages fifty-three and ninety-seven about changes in attitudes toward life, oneself, and relationships produced impressive examples of his subjects' transcending conventional notions of body, self, and time.

But Tornstam does not offer a solid theoretical framework for understanding the origin and emergence of gerotranscendence. His "theory" is mostly descriptive. He establishes the fact of ego transcendence with numerous persuasive examples and then concludes that "the very process of living into old age is characterized by a general potential towards gerotranscendence . . . the final stage in a natural progression towards maturation and wisdom."

But there is nothing automatic or natural about ego transcendence. And then calling it "maturation and wisdom" perpetuates one of the positive stereotypes of aging. The fact is, if you go to sleep a jerk at age thirty, forty, or fifty-nine, you are most likely to wake up a jerk the next morning. Wisdom—and surely transcendence—do not come automatically by virtue of achieving a certain age. Yes, the crisis of aging opens a window of opportunity offering another chance to leap to higher ground. Some seize it. But gerotranscendence is not universal. It doesn't happen to everyone, and when it does occur, it manifests in varying degrees. Tornstam reports that among his fifty respondents, "some had come a long way toward gerotranscendence whereas others had not." Later he says, "the proportion who reach high degrees of gerotranscendence is small." Nevertheless, his powerful examples of gerotranscendence beg the question of how the I/me/ego existence switches gears to allow omni consciousness to kick in when it's been shrouded since psychological birth. How do older adults accomplish this leap to transcendent consciousness when young, determined spiritual seekers often fail?

The process of ego transcendence begins to make sense only when seen in the context of a struggle and crisis of aging in which the ego level of consciousness and functioning is mortally challenged, framing a genuine and important stage of development unique to later adulthood.

**Real Stage**
Ego transcendence represents a real stage of adult development. All genuine stages begin with a crisis. As in all genuine developmental crises, a new reality disables old modes of functioning. In the case of the crisis of aging, the viability of the ego is challenged with eventual realization that it can't survive. Successful resolution of the crisis results in *qualitative* changes that introduce a *new structure* for assimilating and responding to the new reality. Omni consciousness awakens from its dormant state. Failure to resolve the crisis leaves you in a state of stagnation, unable to respond appropriately—you're stuck with square pegs (the ego) for round holes (the new reality).

**What Is a Real Stage?**
The childhood stages described by Freud and Piaget more clearly reveal the nature of true stages. In Freud's oral stage, for example, the crisis centers on nurturance. The infant will passively receive nurturance and requires minimal tools and skills for obtaining gratification. Toward the end of this stage, the child's world becomes more demanding. To obtain nurturance the child must develop new social and cognitive skills to maximize his or her ability to

generate nurturing responses from adults. Passive expectation and impulsive demands cease to work effectively. In developing the new structures for interacting with the environment, the child's world is expanded and enriched. Similarly, in Piaget's framework, the concrete operational child (age seven to eleven) cannot think abstractly. Toward the end of this stage, the child's world (school and social world) bombards the child with demands and challenges that can only be met effectively by developing abstract thinking.

The sequence of genuine stages is a state of equilibrium with the environment that is upset when the demands of the world exceed the present capability. The tension of this disequilibrium sets off a crisis that is only resolved when a new structure emerges, establishing equilibrium at a higher level. From this analysis, you can see why many of the proposed adult "stages" offered by Erikson, Levinson, and others are not true stages. The behavioral and attitudinal shifts they describe use old tools and old structures. An outlandish example will make the point clearer.

### The Massive Brick Wall

Let's say you were confronted with a giant wall of huge proportions. To continue with your life you must get to the other side of the wall. So you start planning and trying out various strategies. First you attempt to blast a hole in the wall (familiar tool and strategy) but discover that it's too thick, perhaps even stretching miles. Next you decide to build a giant ladder (also an old tool). But as you climb far up, the top of the wall doesn't seem any closer—maybe it's miles high as well. You then try a variety of other strategies using modifications of tools and methods that have worked in analogous situations in the past. When none succeed, you experience a number of stressful states including frustration, anger, despair, determination, and desperation—it's a crisis. In the course of struggling with the crisis, you discover that you possess the rudiments of wings. At first your rudimentary wings take you only a few feet off the ground. But as you work on developing them, their size and strength grow, taking you higher and higher. Success makes you work harder at developing your wings. Then at one point your wings develop to maturity and you find yourself soaring higher and higher, eventually finding the top of the wall and easily flying over it.

In developing wings you not only overcome the immediate obstacle of the wall but you have added a new dimension to your being that opens up a wider reality—and a *qualitatively* new way of relating to it with the added dimension. That's what a genuine new stage accomplishes, not just adapting to or overcoming difficulties and obstacles using old tools and structures.

Ego transcendence has all of the qualifications of a genuine stage. The crisis of aging threatens and immobilizes the ego operating system. Old tools and strategies are applied but can't resolve the crisis. Only when omni consciousness is recognized, embraced, and developed, offering a structure that can assimilate the new world of later life, is the crisis resolved, opening the gate to a new reality. With the wings of transcendence, you can now soar in ways you couldn't before. Soaring is expansion, not contraction or reaction.

## Finding the Way

There is growing suspicion that elders who are called successful agers, especially many of those who are long lived to the nineties and beyond, achieve this spiritual consciousness—often without ever recognizing or calling it spiritual. It appears to be something that is easier for some—perhaps they have greater *spiritual intelligence*—while others discover it through prolonged searching and struggle. Then there are those who deepen their awareness of omni consciousness as they age, having identified it earlier in life, perhaps while on a spiritual quest.

Now don't get me wrong. All successful agers are not enlightened or wise. How much ego is dropped will be a better measure of progress. But something clearly happens in the course of aging that sets off a crisis challenging the very foundation of lifelong ego existence. That crisis is the focal point of a genuine stage of development that offers the choice of ego stagnation vs. ego transcendence. In ego stagnation, you are stuck in the ego box with its limited resources for coping with aging—time consisting of past, present, and future and personal "me" consciousness. Outside the box is omni consciousness that offers renewal.

Omni consciousness is not defined by time or form, explaining why successful agers do not dwell on shrinking clock time. Nor are they obsessed with physical changes and decline. Like all stages of development, resolution is not all or none. Where you wind up on the continuum from stuck to liberation will mark your degree of successful aging. Many achieve degrees of success and the term *spiritual* never enters their vocabulary. The crisis of aging simply leads them to their omni consciousness—and they go for it! Not surprising, since omni consciousness is a given—it's the ground of existence that needs only to be uncovered, not created or invented. A better understanding of the nature of omni consciousness and the limitations of ego consciousness could help individuals accelerate and deepen the shift. As researchers continue to examine the lives of successful agers, we may find clues that could provide new insights into the process of ego transcendence that could benefit people of all ages at all stages of development. Why wait for the crisis of aging to return to our nature?

## Mourning Ego Death

Dr. Elizabeth Kubler Ross describes five stages that people go through when faced with life-threatening illness and death: denial, anger, bargaining, depression, and acceptance. The ego's antics, so evident in the boomers' desperate war on aging, parallel these stages in coping with the anticipated death of the ego.

Implicit denial of aging and death peaks in the teenage years and early twenties. That's when the ego is riding high on invulnerability and the fantasy of eternal youth. From that perspective, the elderly are another species whose lives and aging process have little bearing on the younger generation's path of ascension. By thirtysomething, aging begins to look like a serious reality, but still the belief persists that it can be fought, stopped, and possibly reversed. Denial is still pretty firm, but some anger is beginning to break through. For women, denial suffers a serious setback with the realization that the fertility clock may be ticking down. But there's still time to beat the clock—and then there is hope that medical breakthroughs will provide a magic bullet or will be in place just in time. So denial maintains its platform, even if it's a bit shaky. At this time men may experience an occasional incident of erectile failure and other physical signs of decline, but there are temporary external reasons that can be cited—fatigue, tensions, alcohol, and so forth. Even so, no cause to worry—there are Viagra, Cialis, Levitra, and even better elixirs on the way.

With the thirties advancing, the troops start setting up the battle lines and begin marching. The forties bring a rising crescendo of fear and anger as the walls of the fortress expose evidence of infiltration. Signs of aging pop up on a number of fronts—wrinkles, graying, muscle tone loss, a little arthritis, and potbellies as well as the various social markers—kids leaving home, retirement looming, and so forth. But denial isn't about to quit—restoring youth is just a matter of greater diligence in paying attention to getting back in shape (a shape that most were never in) and sticking to other regimens.

Then at fifty anger peaks for many: "How can this be happening to me?" Now it's time to do battle in earnest, pulling out all the stops, as the older baby boomers are doing. Bargaining enters the picture with promises to devote oneself more earnestly to the aging battle—to stick to a plan, start a diet, get a trainer, investigate vitamins and herbs, do brain calisthenics, and pursue spiritual or other programs and pilgrimages to put an end to aging once and for all. At sixtysomething, it looks like the enemy will storm the barricades and face few defenses—the realization sinks in that aging is here to stay. The ego despairs. That's when denial and bargaining can give way to depression. The healthy resolution of depression and sadness will lead to acceptance—the realization that aging is part of a continuous process beginning with birth, that the gift of human existence forecasts aging and death. But acceptance is not the end of the line for the aging crisis.

In coping with ego death, unlike physical death, acceptance is not a final resolution. The next step is ego transcendence. That can only happen when omni consciousness is embraced. Just acceptance of aging can leave you frozen with no effective operating system. To resolve the aging crisis successfully, you must proceed to ego transcendence—finding your omni consciousness. Acceptance without transcendence is not a solution, only the failure to progress—it's the pathway to despair. With ego transcendence, the ego is no longer the central driving force. There is a shift in the locus of consciousness to omni consciousness.

**Friend of Aging**
Spiritual consciousness—omni consciousness—is more suited to navigate aging, since it is not defined by achievement, expansion, or particular attributes. The spiritual self is whole and timeless. It rests on the I-am-ness of being, living neither in the past or the future. The spiritual self isn't on the move. So there's no need to dwell on regrets or yearn for an elusive future. Omni consciousness requires no defense since it is no-thing. It needs nothing to add or develop to become whole. If the ego self missed this or that, it's not significant. Ego stuff is incidental and transient. No validation of self is required. The worth of the formless, timeless spiritual self is unconditional. It is *always* the spiritual self's time. That time is now as it always has been. Embracing the spiritual self can dissolve many of the issues and dilemmas of aging. "Now" is a great equalizer—it offers equal-opportunity fulfillment. The "now" moment belongs to no one of any age more than you!

CHAPTER SEVEN

# Going Home

## Part 1: A Journey Without Steps

Every magician knows that to pull a rabbit out of a hat, there must be a rabbit in the hat. The magic is knowing that the rabbit is hidden while the audience sees nothing but an empty hat. That's not much different than accessing omni consciousness, which may seem mystical or magical if you can't see anything beyond the wall of the ego. But when you know who you are, you reach with confidence. Better yet, finding omni consciousness is easier than the magic act. You needn't even reach, just become it—the seeker and the sought are one.

At first, there are three ways of looking at the spiritual journey. If you don't know where you are going, any road will take you there. If you think you know where you are going, many roads can take you there. If you fully understand where you should be going, no road can take you there—the journey is within. You are bound for your home, which is waiting for you in the very place where you are. Roads will only take you away from home; this journey is without steps.

That's why the greatest leaps of progress in the spiritual domain often happen through ignoring what we see and feel in favor of what we "know." This principle runs counter to our popular faith in sensory knowledge. True, what you *see* may be what you get, but what you get from seeing may not be what you need for spiritual nourishment. To reunite with omni consciousness, you must resist the siren song of searching "out there"—of getting on the road, of seeking new experiences in the quest for "home." It's this addiction to sensation

157

and experience, starting with psychological birth, that contracts our consciousness and creates the limited "me" that imprisons and all but lives us.

Does that mean we should stand still in an immobilized, robotic state? Not at all. Just make sure you know who you are. Travel many roads. Have as many experiences as you can, and don't fear to use your experiences. Live fully in the world—you don't have much of a choice not to, as action is part of our nature. Always keep in mind, though, that the essence of your being is elsewhere, not really strictly in what you *do*.

Omni consciousness is not a sensation. Nor can sensory knowledge lead you to omni consciousness. On the contrary, withdrawal from the senses (including emotions) enables omni consciousness to enter awareness—to be awareness. Then you will know that the journey home begins and ends in the same place—exactly where you are, here and now. That's why so many sages say you don't have to travel to find your true nature. A Buddhist teacher put it this way: "If you see the Buddha on the road, kill him." This seemingly violent advice is just a dramatic way of saying there is no Buddha "out there"—the Buddha is within. If you think you see your goal along the way, it's a mirage invented by the ego mind to lead you astray—to keep you in the prison of the self.

The "journey" is a metaphor for a shift in the locus of consciousness from "out there" to "in here." In fact, you must abandon the very concept of a journey (or searching) for omni consciousness to emerge. Once you have a firm understanding—an inner knowing—that you are home, you can begin to peel away the layers of personal experience that shroud omni consciousness.

## Knowing

The purely objective worldview of reality fostered by science has been tempered of late, and even scientists are opening up to other ways of knowing. What we call the hunch, gut feeling, or just deep sense of knowing is increasingly credited for astute decision making, inventive insights, and successful business decisions. "Knowingness" often contradicts popular wisdom as well as factual and observational information. Thomas Stewart, writing about decision making in the business world, cites numerous examples of successful ventures coming out of deep "knowing" that defied conventional wisdom, even logic. A grade of C for his college paper proposing an overnight delivery service didn't deter Fred Smith. He "knew" it would work and later proved it with his determination that launched Federal Express. Similarly, Howard Schultz shook with excitement when sitting in a café in Italy when he conceived the idea for European-style coffee shops in America. "Crazy," critics would say. "Americans won't pay $3 for coffee—most don't even know what real coffee is like." But Starbucks proved otherwise. In science, Einstein did not shy away from untestable insights that seemed at first glance preposterous. Some were supported by experiments decades later. Dark energy, proposed by Einstein to explain why the universe was expanding rather than contracting due to gravitational pull, was all but discarded, if not ridiculed by scientists. Surprise, surprise, in November 2006 new images from the Hubble telescope validated Einstein's insight. And isn't inner knowing rather than facts and experiments what we embrace for the most important decisions of our life—choosing a mate, selecting an occupation or profession, embracing a philosophy, and much more. We "know" and make the leap—proof comes later, if at all.

A few years ago, I took a course in quantum physics for laymen given by an outstanding physicist, Richard Plano, who had a gift for explaining complex theories in plain language. Plano repeatedly said that a number of the "darling" theories embraced by contemporary cosmologists are admittedly unprovable—and possibly never provable. A current popular "darling" theory, string theory, proposed to explain some of the mysteries of creation from a scientific perspective, is one of the theories that has divided physicists, with one camp maintaining that it defies testing. Isn't that the very reason why spiritual ideas are summarily dismissed as "unscientific"?

Dr. Plano's lectures on several discoveries of quantum physics were liberally peppered with comments like "that's weird, mysterious, doesn't make sense," or "we don't know." I thought that language was exclusive to spirituality and mysticism. Then I recalled a quip from a noted scientist: "I do experiments to convince other people, not myself."

Spiritual knowing taps into the deepest inner knowing, perhaps the same pool that germinates other intuitive "knowing." In the case of knowing the self, as long as you seek it "out there" you will be driven by the faulty assumption of an incomplete self that must constantly expand by accumulating more and more experiences. That's the ego's trip. And the more you go along for the ride, the further you will be swept away from the shore of home. Omni consciousness will eventually fade, replaced by the ego's thirst for "out-there" experiences that will flood your radar screen. So enjoy the ride through the dazzling fields of experience, but don't expect to find yourself there.

Experiences change; they come and go. When they inevitably fade, you are left with a sense of a fractured identity that will persist until your next attachment. The desperation generated by this loss of identity will addictively push you into new attachments that you can only hope will offer a lasting security blanket this time. Vain hope. A firm foundation can only be found in omni consciousness, where your identity is an unshakable rock of wholeness bigger than temporary experiential identities. Then when things come and go there is no profound loss; omni consciousness remains the unchanging ground of being. To restore the primacy of omni consciousness, your initial task is to allow it back into the picture. For that to happen, you have to start emptying the screen of experiences to give omni consciousness room to enter.

Although it's the ego that is filling up the screen and distracting you, it's not necessary to fight or destroy the ego. There's no merit or gain in beating up on the ego. The ego is you; that is, one manifestation of your consciousness. The ego becomes troublesome only when you give it total jurisdiction—allowing it to be the tail that wags the dog. The remedy? Seize every opportunity to recognize and expose the ego fraud and reclaim omni consciousness. To do this, you must defuse your ego identity and open a channel for the release of omni consciousness from its dormant resting place in the ground of being. Then you will be on the path home—without taking any steps. You will clearly see that omni consciousness is the force behind all ego manifestations. In that awareness, your locus of consciousness will shift. You will begin to know deeply and unshakably that all ego manifestations are superficial transformations of omni consciousness—the principle of *conservation of the self*. Conservation of the self will become your default setting and the base for your operating system.

Remember the four-year-old who ignored the superficial transformation of the clay when it was rolled from a ball into a sausage shape? The sausage looked bigger with more clay, but the child who achieves conservation knows the amount of clay is the same despite its appearance. Knowing about conservation of mass, the child favors what he knows over what he sees. Once in omni consciousness, you will know that the I-am-ness of pure consciousness has always been with you and has not changed over the years despite all the external changes that have taken place in your life. You will realize that the pull to go "out there" has linked you to the superficial "out there" changes rather than to the unchanging ground within.

Aging is often shocking because of the dissonance between the unchanging inner self ("I still feel young in spirit") and the outward appearances. In omni consciousness, you enjoy conservation of the self, enabling you to transcend all the superficial plays and transformations of omni consciousness into particular ego manifestations. You will not take your ego self and its external manifestations and appearances so seriously. "Out there" will have less pulling power and only limited reign when the balance shifts to "at-homeness" with omni consciousness. You will then discover that you can comfortably be the actor in your play of consciousness but know that omni consciousness controls the script—that omni consciousness is the source of all the scripts. Because omni consciousness is our nature, it's omnipresent. If you haven't noted this before, you were not looking in the right direction. Now the "journey" home begins by recognizing omni consciousness in the background of all activities. You can start the moment you awake in the morning.

## Wake Up to Reality

As soon as you wake up in the morning—even before you smell the coffee—omni consciousness will often be staring right at you. If you allow it, there's usually a brief moment of pure awareness when omni consciousness is in the foreground. You are present but not yet lodged in your ego self. It can be an exhilarating moment. Unfortunately, we don't usually stay with it for long. You might even dismiss the encounter, thinking it's meaningless empty space. More likely, the egoless state of pure awareness frightens you. "Who am I? Where am I? This feels like nothingness." So you anxiously rush into the familiar grooves that restore the "me" feeling—you quickly dress yourself in your identifications. You remember who you are (or think you are supposed to be) and are off and running: there are the appointments, the overdue reports, unpaid bills, phone calls to make, meetings to attend, chores to do, other things you forgot, war plans for your next move up the ladder of life, and much more. "Now I remember who I am—I'm Bob, that busy person in the vortex of pushes and pulls that make me feel real and concrete." In short, you invoke all the themes and narratives that give life to the conceptual entity "me" and reconfirm the character in your play of consciousness.

That's when the tension begins. You feel weighted down and burdened, but reassured that you exist. Jumping into the ego-self persona is very much like the actor recalling the play that he's performing in and then falling into character and reciting the lines. But unlike the actor who goes home to another identity, leaving the character behind (or in the background ready for the next performance), we remain stuck in our characters, forgetting our real home. The actor knows he is not the character even though he may live it intensely for a period of time. Because we think we are the ego character, we have no urge to get outside it; we strive only to improve it and make it a better character. Not surprising then that you, on awakening, are eager to get into character and away from the weightless open space of omni consciousness. It's a topsy-turvy world that reverses illusion and reality. But you can change that by noticing what is real and what is invention—your invention!

## Greet a Friend

Hold on to the expansive consciousness upon awakening. Greet it as your friend. Get to know it better. Understand and observe the process that pulls you away from omni consciousness. That will help you resist rushing to suit up in your ego. Recognize that you can pause in that pure awareness. Note that you are making a choice to switch from the omni consciousness moment to ego identity. Watch as your ego persona starts taking over. Observe the gap or space between pure consciousness and the ego self that you cross to become the "me" self. You will then realize that there is a choice—that you as omni consciousness are beyond your ego object on a higher plane. You will know that you run to your identifications because you have unquestionably believed that your self-created character is all you are, even though you frequently struggle to get outside it. When you know that omni consciousness is real—and your real home—you will gain the confidence and the courage to loosen the grip of the ego. At that point you will be empowered to have real choices of identity. You will have the firm conviction of another, more potent home to lodge yourself—a higher consciousness that is the ground of existence. It will then be *your* consciousness, *your* mind.

As smooth and simple as the shift to omni consciousness may seem from this appealing sketch, don't expect total success in one move. For most of us—at least at the beginning of the quest—there will be glimpses and tastes of omni consciousness only to see it slip away as we resume the familiar, safe "me." Be aware of what you are up against and note the defenses you have constructed to protect the ego self. Recall the long history of building the edifice of the ego from psychological birth through all the stages of development. As you reexamine and challenge everyday experiences, you will most likely face the formidable obstacle of "the void."

## Facing the Void

Letting go of your familiar identifications—those things that define you and were built up through a lifetime of ego construction—can temporarily leave you with a feeling of emptiness, of being lost and floating in space. Your psychological world may feel like a frightening void. To regain your moorings, you rush back into your self-imposed prison, like your first impulse on awakening in the morning. There is a pattern or pathways (grooves) that you always return to when you begin to stray too far away from familiar "me" grooves. Omni consciousness lies on the other side of the void. But how to get there?

Your biggest ally on the road home is the conviction that omni consciousness exists and is you. Knowing this consciousness in a variety of experiences, even briefly, will help you own that conviction. Eventually the void will also become your friend rather than a frightening barrier. It will increasingly signal that you are close to home. You will begin to welcome it, and when you do so, the void will lose its power to scare you into retreat. Once unmasked, you will begin to sense that actually there is no void—it is all in your mind, a trick to keep you imprisoned. Your focus will be beyond—to the home you know is yours.

## Taking Charge of Your Object Self

As long as you are identified exclusively with a particular object self, however you strive to change, you will feel stuck or in conflict. "But how can I let go of myself?" is the question that will persistently nag you. As valid and compelling as it may seem, it's the wrong question because it presupposes that the experiential self is the only you. The question removes omni consciousness from the picture. The question is a reaffirmation of your self-imposed imprisonment. It's reminiscent of the person described earlier who was hanging from a ledge holding on for dear life. All his energy is focused on that tenuous grasp, wearing down the flesh on his fingers. But he doesn't feel the pain. "How can I let go when my life is hinged to the ledge?" Then, he happens to look down and discovers that he is only two feet off the ground. In a flash his consciousness is transformed, and he lets go of the life-and-death grasp. A fraction of a second later, he finds himself firmly planted on solid ground. Similarly, omni consciousness is right there. Change your fixed lens focus and it will appear, and you will find yourself standing on the firm ground of being—the ledge, and clinging will become unreality and omni consciousness reality. Awakening to omni consciousness reverses figure and ground, thrusting reality to the foreground.

Once personal identification is loosened and you are in omni consciousness, you are free to move and become many objects without conflict or fear of losing yourself. Securely planted in "conservation of the self," you can be a particular personality without feeling stuck in it. You will be more adventurous in experimenting with new roles and will be less resistant to letting go of old roles—your identity and grounding will not rest on clinging to roles. You are free to just be. Being this or that doesn't change or threaten your essence. You are grounded in omni consciousness, which enables you to change and shift but remain firmly the same. You are you (omni consciousness) whether you take this form or that form. *Conservation of the self* reminds us that clay is the same piece of clay whether it takes the round or sausage shape. Its essence is unchanged. It is the same with water in the short, wide vessel and the long, narrow vessel. The subject can transform into many objects, but the short, wide vessel cannot be the tall, narrow one. They are fixed objects. As long as you believe you are a fixed object, you will feel limited and constrained with no option for liberation. The struggle to make the object into a subject is futile. The object is not the essence.

Now for the good news. As the fluid subject, you can flow into any vessel and not feel confined or feel you have lost your identity. The locus of consciousness makes all the difference. Do you choose to be the subject—omni consciousness—or a particular fixed object? It's obvious now that you can't overcome the limitations of the ego by seeking to create a more powerful ego—a bigger or better-delimited object. Taking charge of your object self means cutting your exclusive identification with a rigidly fixed object self and going home.

## Looking at Mind

Mind is the voice of the ego. The thoughts of mind speak the desires and cravings that fuel action and immerse you in experience. The spiritual teacher and writer Elkhart Tolle reminds us that "there is a me in every thought." The "me" mind directs you "out there," away from omni consciousness, to seek "me" enhancements. Much of this activity is on automatic as you passively accept the mind living you. In meditation you can get a glimpse of your out-of-control, ego-serving mind—what spiritual teachers call "the monkey mind." The flood of thoughts when you tried the meditation experiment in chapter 2 should have clued you in about your out-of-control monkey mind. When I first became aware of my monkey mind, it blew me away and made me determined to gain control. That's what encouraged and drove me on my path of self-discovery and the pursuit of omni consciousness. Even as I slip back after taking steps forward, I remain firmly committed to omni consciousness. The monkey mind is a constant reminder of where I should focus in consciousness.

What are your thoughts really like? Where do they come from? If you could get a printout of your thoughts for a day, you would be surprised, if not shocked, at the contents. It would certainly raise the question of whether or not you are really in control of your mind. Would you choose to be lived by the thoughts of your printout? What a waste of time and energy they represent. So start paying attention to mind. After all, if it's your mind, shouldn't you be able to control it? In the silent state of awareness—beyond mind—is omni consciousness where you will discover the source of mind.

## Resistance

Does the notion of taking control of mind put you off? If so, you are not alone. It's common to associate controlling, or being in charge of mind, with the dirty words "mind control" or, worse, "brainwashing." Then there's the fear that controlling the mind takes away spontaneity. Nothing could be further from the truth if we are speaking of controlling mind from the locus of omni consciousness. At the level of ego, consciousness control means obsessively or compulsively including or excluding certain thoughts. You judge some to be desirable and others to be undesirable. In the conditioning process that most people associate with mind control, desirable thoughts are reinforced and others eliminated (extinguished). The mind in this instance is divided against itself. By endorsing one part and rejecting another part, we validate and join the internal struggle. For example, if you try to eliminate undesirable angry thoughts, you might get annoyed at the thoughts and fight them, or even deny that they are your thoughts and verbally attack them: "Get out of my mind, angry thoughts. You are not my thoughts. I don't want to be angry." Compulsive acts like repeating a mantra or focusing on a pleasant image with the intention of keeping the bad thoughts out is another defensive strategy.

In controlling through omni consciousness, however, there is no judgment. Nor is there a fight or struggle. In fact, the control of mind occurs through the *absence of control*. This is true meditation. Omni consciousness stands back, letting go of mind—it merely observes the often chaotic flow of thoughts but does not get involved. Rather than fighting, it lets thoughts happen while taking a witnessing posture. In this manner you can clearly see that thoughts come and go while you remain firmly grounded in awareness. You disidentify with the thoughts although you accept them as happening in your mind but know they are merely occurrences in consciousness. It is only when you are not in control, meaning you identify with the thoughts, that they control you by getting you to run with or against them. In either case you are not in charge. When you can see these thoughts for what they are and deprive them of the ability to drive you, an amazing feeling of power emerges—the power of freedom. You will be astonished to realize that your life has been ruled by an out-of-control flow of thoughts that you never challenged—a lifetime of thoughts with no say in the matter of *your* mind. You experienced the feeling or illusion of being in control because the thoughts were *your* thoughts. The "me" is not a source of power. It is a source of addiction that passively masquerades as power. In omni consciousness, you are truly in charge. You can choose to act or not act, but the thoughts cannot make you dance to their frenzied tune. You are awake. The dream is over. You are home.

To accomplish this goal you have to watch your thoughts as the witness. The knowledge and conviction that there is a place in consciousness from which you can do this is essential. The affirmations in chapter 9 will also be an aid. Meditation is perhaps the most effective gateway to omni consciousness. Soon we will look at various meditation techniques.

## Omni Consciousness Throughout the Day

All religions and spiritual traditions have techniques for pulling attention away from everyday material concerns to focus on the spiritual. Muslims are called to prayer five times a day; observant Jews also pray a number of times a day and wear tassels that when touched are a reminder of the divine. Then there are beads, mantras, and other reminders of a higher or nonmaterial dimension. Unfortunately, these devices are prone to becoming mechanical rituals that can lose their deeper meaning.

In omni psychology, we seek constant recall of who we really are. Throughout daily activities, we get so absorbed in our limited identities in the service of the ego that we forget omni consciousness. To get out of the mess of ego entanglement, you have to shift awareness to omni consciousness throughout the day. Even in a busy schedule, you can stop for a brief meditation a number of times a day at specific times—surprisingly, you will find that three to five minutes can work in shifting awareness. At first, shifting awareness may feel forced or artificial. The ego will persistently draw you back to the prison of the self. Resist that pull and strive to be aware of omni consciousness. It will help you take your ego identifications and problems less seriously.

No need to concern yourself over why your consciousness projected a particular identity. We know that it was molded by a complex chain of personal experiences before we were aware of pure consciousness. When you go out into the world with your ego identity, note that you do so as a character in a play. You are playing a role that is you and is not you. Certainly it is not the *only* you. Be sure to remember that your home is omni consciousness. When you consciously focus your attention on omni consciousness, the balance will shift. The ego self will lose its power to pull and monopolize your attention. It will not sap your energy by getting you to mobilize to defend it. You will find there is nothing to defend. You are home.

## Witnessing the Chaos

In omni consciousness, you can clearly witness the constant flow of needing, wanting, running, getting, and perpetual seeking—for more of almost anything. Once you are aware of omni consciousness, none of this drivenness—the tail wagging the dog—will seem to make any sense. You will see that little peace or security is achieved when actions are ego driven. You will observe concepts building more concepts—like a shadow trying to catch itself. Both ego and shadow are inert projections of something else. To be identified with and driven by your inert shadow is absurd. Equally senseless is allowing yourself to be lived by inert projections, or dreams, of the self. But face it. That's what you do and that's how your life lives you if you are married to the ego.

## A Useful Anger

If you wanted to get angry at something, get angry at being lived by an inert object of your creation. At least such anger would show some awareness that you know the distinction between your genuine subjective consciousness and limited ego projections. I do not mean to say that all dreams are equally bad. Clearly, some dreams and projections are better than others. For example, it is better to project a dream of success, even if it is driven by anxiety and doesn't deliver enduring peace, than to project a dream of total dependence and helplessness. What is bad is to be encapsulated and controlled by the dreams. When you connect with the source of the dreams—omni consciousness—you can create whatever dreams you are capable of. You are not limited to the accidental character you have fallen into. Remember, a person's particular dream is the result of a confluence of circumstances. We go on then to accept that dream as the sole definition of who we are. Feeling limited by the dream, we then strive to change or improve it from within the dream. But the shadow cannot change itself and therein is the source of our suffering and dilemma. The power of omni consciousness is that it can observe dreams, ignore them, or create new dreams. It is not confined to happenstance dreams of our limited personal experience.

But we are blinded by our experience and senses and, therefore, fail to look beyond them to reunite with the omni consciousness that created them. The true self is outside your personal experience. This is difficult to grasp because it shatters our cherished notions of who we are. Our beliefs do not even allow us to seriously consider the possibility of a self outside of what we perceive and experience "out there" early in life. The good news is that once you get a glimpse of omni consciousness—the subjective source of living dreams—the locus of the self begins to shift and you will not let it slip away. You have come home. The bars can no longer hold you.

Let's take a fresh look at some common everyday experiences and ask: "Am I motivated by ego goals and assumptions that lead nowhere?" If so, then project an omni consciousness view of the same situations.

## Waiting for Life to Begin

How often do you find yourself on the launching pad of life looking to begin your "real life"? Each launch holds out the prospect of finally filling the hole that distinguishes the ego's sense of incompleteness. The excitement generated by this prospect can be intensely energizing. It's the engine that drives the ego. Stand back and witness the lifelong pattern of your quest. Observe that your behavior is driven by the ever-present hole that needs to be filled. Note that as long as that assumption is your motivating force, you will find new holes to fill in a never-ending cycle of excitation and frustration. Look at the hole through the eyes of omni consciousness. See that it's a black-mailer from the past. Reject it! Without the hole, where is consciousness? Know the completeness of omni consciousness.

By this time it should be clear to you that for the ego there can be no ultimate gratification. The ego is never ready to live *now*. As the spiritual sage and teacher J. Krishnamurti stated, "You will find that your desires are never really fulfilled. In fulfillment there is always the shadow of frustration, and in your heart there is not a song but a cry."

Therefore, much of our life is spent waiting for the real life to begin. This is especially true in childhood, adolescence, and early adulthood. Think back to all the struggles and suffering you endured while waiting to begin living. You will see that none of the struggles got you closer to your goal, except briefly. Many people talk about the disappointments of their landmark experiences: graduations, the prom, the first sexual experience, the first job, and so forth. While there may be an immediate lift, rarely do they deliver the readiness to start living that was expected. The disappointment sets in as the experience fades into the past and we point ourselves anxiously toward the future for the real thing. When you are totally identified with the limited ego, every occurrence can take on life-and-death proportions. It's like floating helplessly in the ocean on a small raft. Every change, every moment can seal your fate. Your entire being will, therefore, focus intensely on the experiences of that ego.

In childhood we feel so incomplete and unformed that it is easy to believe that there are many landmark accomplishments that will lead us to the real life. In adolescence, as well, we are often overwhelmed by the obstacles that stand in the way of full adulthood, and many people carry that same feeling into their adulthood. They maintain the theme of incompletion and searching so that the "real life" can begin. You may have even talked jokingly about what you are going to be when you grow up, that is, when the "real life" will begin. Some even continue to ask this into the retirement years—still waiting.

For me, a wakeup call came a number of years ago when I finished a book project that I had worked on with great intensity. When it was published, I experienced a big letdown even though it got good notices—even a major *New York Times* review—and I was in demand for many media appearances. I eventually realized that I was caught up in the ego that sought the "final solution" to the seeking. I now see that same trap in colleagues who suffer profound disappointment when the shine from a paper, article, or book wears off. From the vantage point of omni consciousness, every experience has a shelf life, sometimes very short—as expressed in the Buddhist mantra "Things come and go."

That realization and the pursuit of omni consciousness later enabled me to write commentary and op-ed articles for a news service. In the arena of newspapers, shelf life is a flash—sometimes just one day. Then it's "where's the next one?" Some call it a meat rack. But if you can't let go and move on, you will be tortured. The same is true for many life endeavors.

Others who have passed through all their sought-after rites of passage fall into despair because they cannot identify any remaining meaningful passages that will, even in fantasy, give them the feeling that the "real life" is at hand. So they continue to feel plagued by emptiness and yearning, but now may have lost or have given up the quest. Some continue to seek completion in artificial ways. They disrupt their lives to create what appears to be a legitimate basis for renewing the quest. Some discount their successes and start anew. Others find destructive courses that restore a sense of purpose. Look how often young athletes and performers who get to the top quickly turn to drugs and alcohol and then center their lives on getting back on course. Their purpose, lost at the top of their game, is recaptured in their new crusade at the bottom. The ever-tempting presence of drugs and alcohol assures that they can revive a purpose when all else fails.

Resist the pull and temptation of becoming. Don't confuse this with inertia. Planning, achieving, setting goals, and exercising talents and abilities for building and creating your life are all fine and can be useful expressions of the genuine self. It's when these activities are mobilized by the ego's deficiency model for the futile act of *becoming* whole that they will be frustrating and disappointing. But once they are separated from the ego and are expressions of pure consciousness, they become fresh and positive contributions. In your actions, be aware of who you are. You are the complete self that generates experiences. Experiences don't create or enhance the integrity or wholeness of the self—wholeness is given and unconditional.

## Life Changes

It's common to experience great stress when confronted with significant life changes. Moving to a new house or apartment, changing jobs, entering new relationships, switching careers, and a host of other moves can generate huge anxiety, even though the changes are desirable and were sought after. An apparently simple shift like relocating an office down the hall can be stressful and throw a person off balance. We all accept that changes are difficult. But why, especially when they are clearly positive?

We have to return to psychological birth to better understand this conundrum. Remember Margaret Mahler's comment that vestiges of symbiotic attachment persist throughout life. In changes, we can see in vivo the fierce life-and-death attachments symbolic of the quest to reestablish the sense of oneness prior to psychological birth. Letting go of attachments becomes symbolic of losing footing and control—a replay of separation induced by psychological birth. Attachments to things out there are the ego's effort to restore the earlier state of cosmic unity (see chapter 4).

So change speaks to the deepest yearning of the ego. It holds out hope. But it must let go to get reattached to something bigger to fill the hole of incompleteness. Inertia is resignation to a flawed ego. So the ego must be in motion seeking change—that "up to something" posturing that I spoke of earlier. Failure could be devastating, giving the frightening feeling that the hole may be permanent. Change confronts the ego with unfamiliar turf that threatens the very security that it is seeking for its survival. New turf is like the void, or where the "not-me" feeling flourishes. Change can temporarily remind the ego of its relative status in a vast universe of possibilities and other egos. So, for the moment, equilibrium and the very core of existence are under attack. When you get used to your new shell, you incorporate it and restore equilibrium. Then you return to your feeling of centrality as you develop new strategies for expanding the ego as the hole reappears, putting you back in your familiar prison.

When change is perceived through omni consciousness rather than the ego, equilibrium or balance cannot be easily upset. Conservation of the self says the self is whole and unchanging. External changes are witnessed not as real changes but rather as an expression of the infinite possible manifestations of the unchanging, unmanifested omni consciousness. Attachment is not a required condition for the wholeness of omni consciousness. The manifestations are temporary. You know you are not the manifestation but more. Since there is no particular identity or need for it, change does not threaten to topple a solitary fragile structure. Awareness merely shifts its focus of attention. People who move relatively effortlessly through changes do so because their identities are not lodged in particular experiences but in a higher, firmer ground of consciousness.

When confronted with change, note your reactions. See how you relate the change to your identity. What if your identity was not part of the equation? How would you feel then? How is this ego serving you?

## Navigating the Good and the Bad

Good feelings and outcomes are preferable to bad ones. Who would argue with that? Good feels right and just what we deserve and expect, even though we may want more. Aren't you less likely to question the meaning or mystery of life when things go your way? With bad feelings and negative outcomes, we are prone to reassess or question our philosophies, or we decry fate and curse our bad luck. Some rail against divinity or nature when things don't go right.

Spiritual traditions tell us to treat positive and negative events equally—the principle of equanimity. Equanimity is related to conservation of the self. The self remains the same despite all the surface ripples. In practice, though, few of us are able to match Job, the biblical figure who best exemplifies steadfastness and faith through terrible adversity. Maintaining equanimity or inner balance is difficult, so we should welcome small adversities as an opportunity to explore this issue. Become aware of the one-sided ego need for the positive and self-enhancing experiences and the rejection, if not terror, of the self-denying ones. Shift to the omni consciousness perspective of wholeness to experience equanimity in the situations. Practice will heighten awareness and reinforce this perspective.

## Feeding the Ego

We have to keep pumping up the ego because it doesn't exist as a real entity. We must remind ourselves who we are as an ego. This requires a tremendous amount of energy and attention. That's why it's so difficult for many people to go on vacations or get into settings where their ego identities are blurred. When the ego slips into an incubation mode of rest, it can feel like evaporation. Workaholism is often the obsessive need to reassert, "I am a doctor, lawyer, corporate chief. Look how intensely involved I am—this must be real and meaningful." You will run into people selling or advertising their ego identities in all kinds of inappropriate settings. They have to let others—and themselves—know who they are. This flimsy ego is so elusive and insubstantial that in a flash of inattention it is threatened and needs to go on the offensive. So we have to hang on for dear life and keep waving it—mainly for our own benefit. To let go of the ego "thing," you must taste the power of nothing (no-thing).

For the same reason, pleasure, success, good feelings, and the absence of pain or pressing needs pose big problems for most people. Satisfaction generates silence. Self-satisfaction is silent and interior. But in silence the ego vanishes. The ego needs noise—the noise of action. That's why it persistently renews efforts for greater and greater pleasure and success. Obtaining all the good things we strive and yearn for means we can now forget the self—it has what it wants; it should be complete and satisfied. Isn't that what we tell ourselves when we are driving toward our goals? "When I get to such-and-such place, or when I get da da da da da, then I will relax and bask in the sun of peace and contentment." But when we relax and forget ourselves, many feel lost and anxious. It's like a stretched-out version of the empty feeling of nothingness on awakening in the morning. "Who am I, what am I, what is the meaning of my existence if I am not doing?" So we invoke the pushes and pulls that return us to our ego home or prison. "I'm struggling for something. Now I feel alive." When you finally recognize that emptiness is omni consciousness, you will know that no-thing—emptiness—is everything.

The world at the level of the ego is a world of conflict and opposition. It can be no other way. How can a world of billions of egos striving, needing, wanting, and trying to get somewhere work smoothly? It doesn't on an individual basis and certainly not collectively. Do you want to be part of that frenzied world? Will you side with what you see and feel, fueled by the forces of psychological birth, or will you turn within and go with what you know? Will you fall through the trapdoor of experience or will you resist and embrace omni consciousness? Your senses and emotions may be irresistible, but they will not allow you the freedom to know yourself.

Part of your mindfulness and persistent effort to stay in touch with omni consciousness is to watch your ego and how it controls you. Stop feeding the ego, and you will see it fade. You can easily put this practice to the test.

## Part 2: Exercise in Nothingness

This exercise was prompted by an incident that my colleague Dr. Marcella Bakur Weiner told me about. A few years ago Marcella attended a retreat for psychotherapists. At the first session, the leader asked the therapists to interact and relate to each other in a getting-to-know-you fashion—like working the room at a cocktail party. But there was one restriction. You could not talk about your degrees, professional status, or professional accomplishments. "Me the therapist" was to vanish from the scene for this exercise.

The exercise was traumatic for many. In fact, few could do it. Some were frozen in noncommunication. Others violated the rule and felt compelled to establish a professional pecking order in which they were high up. Some were apologetic: "Let me just say this before I follow the format." The exercise, as you can imagine, led to lively discussion and, for some, soul searching. It surely was a powerful exposé of "me" the ego and "the world according to me."

The same exercise can be applied to many situations, giving you an opportunity to see the naked truth about your ego. When on vacation or at a party, social gathering, or professional meeting, make a conscious effort to *not advertise your ego*. Don't tell who you are, your "important" accomplishments, or ambitious and impressive doings. Make no self-references. Inquire strictly about others and praise them for their accomplishments. Ask for nothing and don't call attention to yourself. Try it. Note your reactions. Can you make peace with that or is your ego bursting at the seams? Your reaction will reveal how dependent you are on externals for your identity. Then look at this from a higher plane. If you can't feel it, pretend you are omni consciousness. Can you see how you are being lived by your silly ego?

## Content of Problems

Examine the content of your problems and begin to question their validity. The convincing content of our problems and conflicts magnetizes us to them, leaving no way out. When you live solely at the ego level of consciousness, everything about the personal ego and the "me" experiences take on immense importance. "Me" experiences are the lifeblood of the ego self. Even our problems are part of this "me" feeling, so we hold on to them for dear life—the "me" life. When we refuse to support this structure and see the ego and personal experiences as a limited projection of omni consciousness, our problems and conflicts are taken less seriously. You can note them, observe them, feel them, analyze them, or do whatever you want with them—then you can drop them.

"But how can I do that? The problems are me—they are mine. If I ignore them they will still be there torturing me." If that were the case, then indeed you never would be able to get rid of a problem and shouldn't even bother to seek change. But then, if you could shift the locus of awareness from the ego to omni consciousness, you would see that you are you and the problem is merely an appearance in your consciousness—one projection and interpretation of personal experience. When you can see the space between you and your experiences, you will begin a path to free yourself from the (not your) problems. Note that if you don't have to experience or deal with them, they cannot rule or imprison you. They are under your control rather than the other way around.

Have you ever left a job or relationship because of overwhelming problems that put you in a high state of anxiety, worry, or anger, then later, when comfortably ensconced in a new pleasant job or relationship, found that the previous problems had vanished? They may still be there, but you are not feeling them or reacting to them. Those problems, which were "your problems" at one time, did not disappear. Or did they? Where are they? Where were they? In any case, they are not your problems now. The fact is, they never *were* your problems. They were just problems that you allowed yourself to receive at one time. In your new job, you have disidentified with those problems, so in effect they don't exist. Then problems like those are not you. They only feel like you when you *accept delivery*. All problems are of that nature: *they are only yours if you accept delivery*. Psychological problems cannot flourish in omni consciousness—there is no entity to accept delivery. If you know who you are, and who you are not, conflicts will not take root. Omni consciousness does not accept deliveries. With that knowledge, you can return to your identity object with a different connection and freedom.

Perhaps detachment from the ego is the skill or natural state of those people who effectively deal with stress and problems. We try to emulate them: "I wish I could just take things in stride like Mary." Or "Why can't I get my mind off things and focus on the positive the way Bill does?" Another one: "Margaret can handle so many stressful situations without taking them so seriously." Yet, when you are told to do just that, you resist and insist that you must dwell on "your" content, which keeps you in the eye of the storm. Freud said, "Where there is id (primitive impulses) let there be ego," viewing this as the highest accomplishment of psychological development. We now have to extend the process upwards: *where there is ego, let there be omni consciousness—go home*.

## Powerful Emotions

Marriage to emotions will also keep you from going home to omni consciousness. Powerful emotions serve to validate the importance of the ego and personal experience. They are sure signs that the ego is in command. Powerful emotions also become guardians of the ego, widening the scope of fear, anxiety, and anger as the ego expands. The bigger the ego, the greater the need to protect it and the greater the need for emotionally charged triggers to justify the protective stance. It is this circular self-reinforcing system that digs us more deeply into ego consciousness and the lockdown imprisoned by experience. That's what happens when you have a "traumatic" experience: divorce, death, painful childhood, devastating war experience, and so forth. Some people get stuck. They keep going back and reliving the experiences with the aim of digging out. The conventional wisdom of psychology has encouraged people to work out their traumas—to get into them to get out of them.

Psychiatrist Sally Satel has questioned the knee-jerk reaction to immediately send teams of grief counselors to disaster situations to help victims promptly "work out" trauma and bring "closure." The route to healing in this model is to stay with the awareness of mental anguish, express the intense feelings and emotions, and, most important, to "talk, talk, talk." The problem is, according to Dr. Satel, that approach often doesn't work and can even make matters worse. She quotes another study by psychologist Dr. George Bonanno showing that expressing and talking about traumatic experiences can generate further emotional problems. The point here is not that counselors shouldn't be available for those who want them but that "one size doesn't fit all." Reliving trauma is not a universal path to healing.

Another fresh look at survivors of trauma reveals that repression, not diving back to the wrenching emotions, works better in many cases. University of Missouri psychologist Richard Gist studied intervention with victims of major disasters over the last few decades and found that the "let it all hang out" approach of reliving the details of trauma makes people worse. In a related finding, "repressors" recovered better from heart attacks than patients prone to opening the closets of their psyches. In a *New York Times* interview that revealed the benefits of repression, Gist said that victims of 9/11 who were promptly encouraged to relive their experiences with the intention of healing by catharsis were actually retraumatized: "Basically, all these therapists run down to the scene, and there's a lot of grunting and groaning and encouraging people to review what they saw, and then the survivors get worse. I've been saying for years, 'Is it any surprise that if you keep leading people to the edge of a cliff they eventually fall over?'"

Could the success of the "repressors" be not from repression—keeping the lid on—but the secret strength in the ability to detach from ego consciousness? Not surprising that the investigators did not consider this third possibility, since most of our psychological thinking excludes consciousness beyond the ego. Those who rebound from trauma may be less identified with their emotions. They are able to see the space between the self and emotional experiences. The more powerful the emotional experience, the easier it is to obliterate that space. Emotional resilience has also been noted in long-lived people—centenarians. They experience emotional pain but are quicker that most of us in letting go and snapping back.

Be mindful of your emotional reactions, remembering that they are only experiences and are not you. This will help you maintain omni consciousness awareness. As you gain the conviction that emotions are mostly destructive and don't work for you, they will lose their appeal. With that achievement, the ego's hold loosens—there is less need for debilitating emotions. Contrary to the belief that emotions are empowering, intense emotions give the *feeling of power*, but that's not the same as being powerful. We noted that contrast with infants prior to psychological birth who exude omnipotent cosmic unity but are in fact totally helpless and dependent on others for survival. The adults' sense of power often comes from the powerful presence that emotions generate—they expand the ego's feeling of me-ness, which is always intoxicating. No matter that emotions are not actually doing anything for you. Try something else: omni consciousness and its all-inclusive emptiness that allows choices and is not driven.

## Excitement

There are so many exciting things "out there" that it seems that the world was created for our excitement. Outlets and opportunities are everywhere. Some people say, "I need excitement—an affair really turns me on—especially when it's secret." Another person insists, "Making a hit on Wall Street is the ultimate." Still another, "When I feel down, what picks me up is to shop for some expensive clothes in a fancy shop. It makes me look smashing—it is so exciting—it energizes me." Or what about this statement: "Man, just getting in the car and going is exciting—it doesn't even matter where—I can't just sit around." Another variation: "You need some action or you feel dead—I need excitement in my life. Otherwise, what is there to look forward to?"

You might ask, what is wrong with this craving for excitement? After all, what else is there in life? Am I to just sit around and do boring things? I want to feel good and turned on. Is it better to feel turned off? The downside is not that excitement is bad—we must be clear on this point—but that it is fueling the deficit conception of self (the need for more and more to feel whole and secure) that will put you on the infinite treadmill. Your world becomes the universe according to "me" and "my" bottomless pit of needs.

Behind this outlook is the belief that boredom is the alternative to excitement. Without the craving for experiences and getting into states of excitement, we can't conceive of any prolonged state of feeling good. But let's look at what else comes with the turf of excitement and craving for experiences. The craving is never ending. It feeds on itself. Excitement is quickly over, and the craving reappears, begetting the need for more excitement, perhaps of greater intensity and frequency. "I just had it and I want it again, and more" (more may be necessary to get the same kick). Life without the excitement seems even duller after being there. We want it to last, but it can't last.

Bear in mind that excitement is not perceived as neutral or impersonal. It is "my" excitement. As such, it is filtered through the ego that uses these experiences to expand its delusions of grandeur. The greater the pleasures I can have the bigger and more powerful is "my" ego. This is an addictive process because loss of excitement feels like the loss or diminution of self. You are now dependent on external circumstances and events for your feelings of self. No good feelings can occur without experiences "out there." You work yourself into a frenzy or depression in focusing out there for something that will make you feel complete. The belief that you are seeking completeness is used to justify the addiction and to deny that it is an addiction. It's another arena in which omni consciousness is off the radar screen—omni consciousness is not out there, it's within.

Yes, it's true that many things we seek for excitement really are exciting and pleasurable. But are they worth the price of addiction and the imprisonment of the self? Once you give over your identity to external events, you are no longer in charge, and events are whipping you around. The conscious presence creates the illusion that you are making a choice and are in control—you are not. The excitement is the center, and you are glued to it. You are out of control and cannot focus energy in ways that are more exhilarating and enduring. You cannot see or feel the power of the higher self.

**Intensity and the Narrowing of the Self**
The narrow centering of the self on a job, politics, sex, money, and so forth serves to feed the illusion of the solid, permanent, and enduring ego. Everything in the vast world around us is constantly changing, casting doubt on the individual ego's importance or durability. All of the choices and possibilities in life become threats to the omnipotence of the ego. Intense focus on a singular activity driven by intense emotions blocks out everything else. We then believe in the super importance of that activity and our ego which "owns" it. Watch people who are so absorbed. They really function as if what they are doing is of cosmic importance. Their one-pointedness and single-mindedness may even be a "high" as it mimics the one-pointedness of meditation that opens awareness of higher consciousness. However, in higher

consciousness you are in the one-pointedness of pure awareness, whereas in the narrow ego one-pointedness you are out of control in the attempt to distort or disguise, if not obliterate, reality. Watch your own behavior when you believe or act as if what you are doing is of immense importance. What would happen if you dropped the intensity? How would you feel? Examine this.

**Quest for Pleasure**
Ask and people will say they want pleasure. But do they? If you say directly to a person, "You don't want pleasure," he or she will dispute you. if not become outright irritated. One person said to me, "What do you mean I don't want pleasure? That's practically all I think about."

In one sense she is correct. Pleasure may be all that she thinks about. But here we have to make the distinction between thinking about pleasure, striving for it, yearning for it, and agonizing over it and actually taking pleasure when it is available. Most people do not take the very pleasures they dream about even when they are easily within reach. What is more remarkable is the mind's ability to support the split and the contradiction. An example will make this clearer.

The same woman who insisted that she thinks only about pleasure complained that she is sexually frustrated. She craves more sex. She was thinking of having an affair: a number of men have come on to her and she's been tempted. Why doesn't she have more sex with her husband? Is he uninterested? Is he repulsive? Does he reject her? Is he impotent? Far from all of these. She even reports, "Oh, he would like to have sex morning, noon, and night. And even though he's in his late forties he gets an erection as quickly as a teenager. In fact, he's angry at me because I won't have sex with him as often as he would like. Maybe we have sex once a month. But I'm not there (psychologically) and hardly feel a thing. I masturbate occasionally to have an orgasm. Why should I give him sex? He doesn't give me what I need. He doesn't make enough money—I make more than him. He doesn't pay attention to my needs. He leaves the room when I try to talk to him about feelings. But he wants to screw. Well, to hell with him. I'm not going to be his sex slave."

She doesn't expect the situation to change, but at the same time she doesn't plan to leave the marriage. "At my age, I'll never find another man. And with AIDS out there, it's a mess. I should have left him ten or fifteen years ago, but now it's too late. I don't want to be alone, and he's good to our two girls. He's also witty and I like his intellectual circle at the university where he teaches." This type of situation is not uncommon. Here is someone who craves the pleasure of sex. By her own admission, she thinks of it all the time. Yet her anger gets in the way. She chooses anger over pleasure. She would vehemently deny this, throwing up a barrage of buts and whys. Her perceptions of the relationship may be accurate, but the bottom line is that she still picks anger over pleasure. What is this anger doing for her? Nothing. She has the possibility of effortlessly satisfying this pleasure right there in front of her but prefers anger. The smoke screen of anger prevents rationality from peeking through. If pushed, the clever mind might come up with, "I don't feel anything with him. It's not pleasure." Maybe, however, if she dropped the anger and placed her priority on pleasure, she would feel something. That would seem better than no pleasure, especially since this has been going on for many years and she foresees and is even committed to the game continuing.

The closer you look at behavior, the more you will see how often pain is chosen over pleasure. Sometimes you have to peel away the rationalizations to see it. What is it about pain that is so vital to our existence that we would choose it over pleasure?

Would you drop *your* anger if you could? People say they would, or yearn for that choice. If you drop your anger, then you don't have to react to it or act on it. Yet the main function of anger (outside of actual self-preservation) is to provide reasons for actions that appear rational. "I am so angry that I am not getting what I need from you that I will demand, retaliate, seek it elsewhere, feel sorry for myself," and so forth. All these feelings and fantasies feed the ego by implying that if you got what you wanted or needed, what an incredible ego that would be. It is the anger (and the greater the anger, the more believable it is to the ego) that justifies the need and the action to get what the anger proves you need. It's a nice, neat package. "Would I be so angry if it weren't justified, if I didn't need?" How will you get rid of these painful feelings? "I must get something, do something, dream about something, or turn them inward, which keeps me in a feeling, yearning state."

Without the intense emotions generated by anger and fear, you just are. But accepting that fact means experiencing a limited ego with no place to go. So we need to get into the anger or fear to trigger the delusions that distort reality and support the feeing that this ego can and needs to be something beyond reality. Whatever is generated from this perspective is doomed to failure because it is based on something that doesn't exist. It is merely a fabrication that only has meaning and validity in an egocentric world. But the broader reality outside the ego distortions is unaffected. Your feelings do not alter true reality. They are just your feelings and delusions. They may work for a period of time if you believe them, others believe them, and you can construct a world that supports and protects them. But ultimately the edifice will collapse because reality is constantly chipping away at the delusions. No matter how big your ego feels, it is a speck and reality is vast.

Unfortunately, there is no easy way to get out of the circularity of the ego's distortions. Trying to reason your way out doesn't work because, like traditional counseling, "reason" enters at the level of the ego. It joins the problem by speaking the same language and logic. Working within the ego's orbit cannot be transformational. It can only move you to different parts of the orbit, which may provide some temporary relief. This relief masquerades as change. But often that's about as much "transformation" as the ego wants or can tolerate. True change means defusing the ego. You must let go of ego consciousness to find yourself in a different place—omni consciousness.

Observe how you use emotions, particularly anger and fear. Where do they take you? How would you function if you didn't experience these at all?

## Pain

Another way of maintaining omni consciousness is to observe how you use pain in the form of needing and yearning to shore up your ego. Suffering and yearning reaffirm the primacy, validity, and reality of the ego. And that's where you want to be when consciousness is wedded to the ego. Pain makes it all seem right. "Would I be suffering if I didn't need something? The fact that I am suffering proves that I need something because when I get what I need, the pain subsides—at least temporarily. Furthermore, the more I suffer, the more convincing I am that I really do need and am deprived." The system is self-validating and self-propelling. Once you are inside the orbit of this logic, there is no escape. It keeps feeding on itself while it dominates your attention.

But what would life be like if you could have what you wanted without the yearning and pain? Chances are, the achieving would not have any meaning for the expansion and fulfillment of the ego; consequently, you would have to want or reach for more in order to get to the point where there was pain so that the ego could get something out of the experience. Emotions experienced as intense feelings are at the core of ego motivation. We need the intense feelings to locate the ego. Then, by resolving or reducing these feelings, we briefly conclude that the ego has grown. This is ego logic. The whole sequence is an imaginary invention of the mind. Nothing has really happened in these dramas. Reality is outside this orbit.

What would life be like if directed by higher consciousness outside the limitations of this emotion-dominated ego? Would people be feelingless and uncaring in some robotized fashion? This is the fear. Actually, in omni consciousness one can see all possibilities. Having and getting may be desirable, but they don't have life-and-death consequences when the self is already complete. It is only an incomplete self that yearns and suffers and needs the triggers to keep it on its desperate course. In higher consciousness, one can see those experiences that produce pain and those that produce pleasure as well as those that enhance oneness with the human community and those that are delusional and destructive. In higher consciousness you can make real choices, and many possibilities are open to you since there are no self-imposed limits or narrowed agendas.

**Internal Dialogue**

Most of us engage in internal debate in an effort to resolve conflicts. We saw how that worked in the discussion of traditional counseling and therapy. Don't confuse internal debate with the use of thinking and reasoning for problem solving. In problem solving, you are applying the cognitive and intellectual powers of mind. Mind and consciousness are unified, not split when applied to problem solving. But when the mind is fragmented into a debating society of selves in an effort to work out conflicts and issues, you surrender to the ego and eventually drown in ego. The split selves involved in the debate are all part of the same mind—the ego has created little satellite egos that will wrestle in hope of a victor. Who are the speakers in your internal debate? Give that some thought. We can invent a long list of "me's." All of these imagined selves can be traced back to a single source in consciousness. They originate in the one consciousness. In that unified omni consciousness, conflict recedes simply because there are no parts to do battle. Only when consciousness is fragmented into separate objects can we project and maintain the illusion of battle or debate. Who will win a battle in which all the participants are one?

You've been debating internally all of your life, so don't expect to be able to drop it all at once. But use the debate as an opportunity to go home to omni consciousness. Witness the debate from a unified posture. If you can't feel the presence of omni consciousness, act as if you were in omni consciousness. At least this acting may get you someplace useful. Sometimes in taking the "as if" attitude, you might be surprised to find an opening. Observe the debate as one consciousness. See the fragments of ego beating up on each other and fighting for supremacy. Note that all these fragments have the same source—they all stand on one pair of legs of consciousness that can lead you home. Recall my earlier example of the two hands fighting. Close up, it looks like two entities in conflict, but when the camera moved back, the fraud was revealed—the two hands were parts of the same single entity. In the same way, your fragmented consciousness and debating society are fraudulently deceiving you. Be one and take charge.

**Word Power**

Watch your language when referring to yourself. Be especially attentive to false definitions of self: "I am angry, I need, I must have, I can't tolerate," and so forth. Stop after every "I am" and see yourself as pure omni consciousness. Then add the word "experiencing" before the anger, need, want, or feeling. Example: "I am (pause) experiencing the need for a new car" or "I am (pause) experiencing the need for a woman to make me feel good." Or "I am (pause) experiencing anger after what he said." This is not just a gimmick or a trivial distinction. The pause and the emphasis on the "I am (without attributes) experiencing something" will emphasize the space between you as pure consciousness (I-am-ness) and the experiential identification to which you attach yourself. In creating that separation and space, you will find that the experiences will lose some of their power to live you. You, not the experience, will be in charge.

## Part 3: Time to Go Home

Physicists say that time is not what we think it is in our everyday usage. In chapter 6 we saw some of the oddities in the experience of time. But tell Christie that time doesn't really exist, or that everyone has access to infinite time given that past, present, and future are all here now, and she's likely to throw something at you. Christie is a single mom with a dizzying balancing act of career, work pressures, two young children to raise, aging parents needing assistance, finances to manage, and a personal need to find time and opportunities for a relationship and a social life. For Christie, like most of us, time is an ever-present and often oppressive tyrant. How could it not be real?

Speaking to the notion that all of reality is illusion or a social construct of mind, philosopher John Searle said that no one walks out of a window on a high floor saying, "Gravity is a social or mental construct. I can do whatever I damn please with it." There's "a brute reality out there," he reminds us, even though there are aspects of reality that are really only mental or social constructs. Similarly, time may not exist in quantum reality, but in our everyday lives it's another brute reality—as it is for Christie. How can the personal reality of feeling pressed for time be reconciled with notions that time doesn't really exist, or that all time is here now?

Revelations from the frontier of scientific discovery informing us about the nature of the universe can't be dismissed; nonetheless, we live in a limited corner of the universe where we are subject primarily to local conditions as well as to some aspects of the bigger reality. These two dimensions are akin to the spiritual and material worlds that define our total reality and must be recognized and reconciled. As the Buddha said, we must accept that we are in the body and the physical world while accessing and celebrating the spiritual, transcendent dimension of higher consciousness. Embracing one and rejecting the other will not work for harmonious living.

Surely there are timeless dimensions to reality. Omni consciousness is timeless and perhaps taps into the timelessness of quantum reality. You can experience that timeless quality in meditation that accesses omni consciousness. Unlike omni consciousness, ego consciousness is time bound and on a perpetual journey of growth and change in quest of the wholeness of the timeless dimension.

To synthesize the time-bound and the timeless dimensions into daily living, you must distinguish between instrumental and psychological time. Instrumental time is functional and practical—it is tied to problem solving. Instrumental time relates to tasks and activities that are measured by clock time. We do things and complete tasks in clock time. Psychological time, on the other hand, is the time of the ego self and ego consciousness. The ego latches on to time to give it its illusory sense of concrete reality—time to achieve its goal of wholeness in the future. As we have seen, time projected into the future supports the grandiose quest of the ego to become. Without time the ego collapses. That's what marks the crisis of aging, spelled out in chapter 6, when the ego perceives the end of time. Psychological time gets us into trouble because it is strictly the ego's time. In omni consciousness, time melts into an eternal "now." Psychological time blocks the path home. Letting go of psychological time opens the realm of "now," which is the home of omni consciousness.

If there is only the "now," does that mean we shouldn't plan for the future? Isn't the future a nonexistent illusion? When tomorrow comes and you find you didn't plan for things, you will lament, "But I was in the 'now' where there is no future, and this sucks because I didn't plan for it."

Yes, you have to plan in the present to lay the foundation for a comfortable and secure physical existence in the present ("now") that will contribute to a succession of presents ("nows") throughout your physical clock-time-bound existence. The "now" encompasses the totality of your existence—including past and future—so that they all form a coherent whole. The present and the future are related in the "now." It's when the "now" is dropped for the future or the past that we lose a grip on the true reality of the total "now." So being fully present and planning ahead are not contradictions.

Awareness of the distinction between ego time and omni consciousness time will help check the distorted use of time. Whenever time is tied to becoming or the conception of self, it is likely being generated by the ego and is not a useful application of time. That time will carry you away from omni consciousness.

The practical application of clock time requires practical solutions. If your instrumental time is cramped—as in the case of Christie—you may have to accept the reality of certain situations; you may have to learn to manage them better, get help, or find other life solutions. In any case, don't trivialize, reject, or escape into "spiritual solutions" denying time. That will make you feel worse. "Time is an illusion—so why am I suffering? I must be off the spiritual mark, or I need to be more spiritual."

## Meditation

At one time, meditation was viewed as one of those far-out, exotic practices. But when you start seeing book titles like *Meditations for Busy People*, *Daily Meditations for Overeaters*, *Meditations for Pregnant Women*, and a host of other designer meditations, you can appreciate that meditation has hit mainstream. Meditation has also received a lot of interest and attention for its purported physical benefits. Dr. Herbert Benson, a physician at Harvard University, popularized the "relaxation response," a brief form of meditation for cardiovascular benefits and general health and well-being. Recently I saw an ad from the Maharishi Enlightenment Centers offering "The Transcendental Meditation Program" to reduce high blood pressure, extend life span, and reduce use of hypertension drugs. Other programs offer similar health payoffs for meditation—even life extension. Meditation has also become a popular adjunct to some behavioral and cognitive therapies. It's introduced as a relaxation technique to clear the mind for enhancing focus on the therapeutic goal of changing behaviors and beliefs.

But meditation is not simple or automatic, as we saw in the brief meditation exercise in chapter 2. Concentration is often undermined by the "monkey mind." In fact, meditation, far from lowering tension and stress, can be agitating and disturbing—at least initially. People with serious emotional problems may find meditation bringing their demons to the surface; if so, they should work with a skilled therapist trained in meditation techniques. Those expecting quick health benefits might be disappointed and quit. Spiritual seekers are more likely to stick with it.

Primarily, meditation is a spiritual practice for connection with a higher consciousness. Concentration, or one-pointed focus of the mind with the goal of transcending mind, is preliminary to relaxation. The deepest state of meditation has different names in spiritual traditions: enlightenment, awakening, Satori, Buddha mind, nirvana, samadhi, dzogchen, and others. For beginners, the task is to calm the mind so that higher consciousness can emerge from the confusion and noise of mind. Relaxation, then, is a means, not an end. It's the first step with no guarantees. Relaxation only provides the platform for meditation to happen. Just as you can't perform the fine brushstrokes of calligraphy while running full speed, you must be still and concentrate. But concentration will not guarantee success in calligraphy or meditation. Like the answer to the proverbial question, "How do you get to Carnegie Hall?" you must practice, practice, practice.

Meditation is an important, if not essential, tool for locating and returning to omni consciousness. In many spiritual traditions, meditation is the royal path to higher consciousness that eventually leads to enlightenment. Simply stated, meditation is observing mind. In the process of being the witness to mind, you are outside of mind where you can become aware of the difference between higher and lower consciousness. The meditative state is an expression of omni consciousness and, therefore, a valuable vehicle for transportation home.

Many instructive books are available that can introduce you to meditation and guide you in practice. *The Meditative Mind,* by psychologist and writer Dan Goleman, gives an excellent survey and review of the popular meditation traditions and techniques. Sharon Salzberg and Joseph Goldstein, authors of *A Step by Step Course on How to Meditate,* are outstanding teachers of mindfulness meditation. Two excellent books for newcomers to meditation are *Mindfulness in Plain English,* by Bonte Gunaratana, and *Meditation for Beginners,* by Jack Kornfield. Then there are extensive offerings of CDs with guided meditations.

You will be surprised to find a dizzying number of techniques of meditation prescribed by various spiritual traditions and spiritual teachers. Some insist that only their technique is the correct and effective one. "Sit this way, not that way; keep your eyes open—no, keep them closed, breathe like this, not like that." One tradition will tell you to meditate by observing your breath, another one says repeat a mantra, and still another instructs you to meditate on a deity or on a light. The visuddhimagga, an authoritative text on Buddhist practices, lists forty meditation subjects for different temperaments, each subject having a presumably specific outcome. Some meditations are guided, with the leader giving various directions, images, mantras, and other supports throughout the meditation. Others give briefer instructions before leaving you on your own.

Individual preferences vary. When I first started meditation, I liked and sought out guided meditation—I also worked with a number of guided meditation CDs. Now I find guided meditation annoying and distracting, preferring to go directly into mindfulness meditation. In mindfulness, you are the witness to mind and just observe. As you get deeper into meditation practice, your preferences may change.

My friend Richard Olson has taught meditation and Eastern philosophy at Adelphi University for many years. Richard practices mindfulness meditation, also called Vipassana meditation, of the Theravada Buddhist tradition common in parts of South Asia. As a young man, he studied and practiced meditation in Thailand and was initiated as a monk. When introducing his young students to meditation, he finds concentration techniques work best initially, with mindfulness brought in later in the meditation sessions. The mind is so conditioned to leaning on or holding on to something that concentrating first on an object makes an easier practice than mindfulness that simply observes and holds on to nothing.

At the same time, Richard points out that mindfulness and concentration are not entirely distinct. Concentration has an element of mindfulness, and mindfulness requires concentration. Concentration can also provide a bridge to mindfulness when the initiate is ready. Olson starts the meditation by instructing the students to focus on counting the breath, as we did in the exercise in chapter 2: 1 for inhalation, 2 for exhalation, to a count of ten, then back to 1. When the mind drifts, the meditator returns to 1 and continues the count to 10. After twenty minutes of this concentration meditation, he moves the students into mindfulness: "Just observe the breath by watching the rise and fall of the diaphragm or the breath passing over the lips. When the mind wanders, note how it is wandering and then return to witnessing the breath."

Olson adds that techniques other than pure witness awareness and observation are props or springboards for entry into the genuine meditative state of being. Techniques are generated by concepts, thoughts, and ideas that are the contents of mind. And mind is all about me—remember Eckhart Tolle's comment that "there is a me in every thought." Holding on to a technique means also holding on to mind. Since mind is the brainchild of ego ("me"), remaining at the level of technique will keep you stuck at the ego level and will be a barrier in your quest for omni consciousness. Yet you have no choice but to start where you are—in mind—with the awareness that techniques will help you to narrow and focus your mind so you can make the mysterious leap to omni consciousness, which is the meditative state of being. Once you are in omni consciousness, techniques fall away.

The Buddha gives the analogy of building a raft to cross a river. When you get to the other side of the river, you leave your raft behind. Every culture, he added, will have a unique technology and design for building rafts. But once on the other side, all the different rafts are all left behind. At the destination, all is one. Looked at this way, techniques are premeditation. Genuine meditation is beyond mind. Buddha mind, for example, is "empty." "Mindfulness" has no shape or form, just pure awareness. Once outside of mind, you are in the timeless, formless realm of omni consciousness.

If you are practicing a particular spiritual tradition, it is a good idea to follow its prescriptions. Otherwise you might find yourself becoming a meditation junkie trying this technique today and another one tomorrow without ever committing to a consistent practice. While there may be nothing essentially wrong with experimentation, overloading your plate runs the risk of focusing on technique, not the inner state of silence. Jumping around will keep you in mind rather than helping you get out of mind. It's like digging many shallow wells in a frenzy of activity and never finding water. Digging one well that goes deeper and deeper is more likely to reach the water.

**Slow or Fast Dance?**
Expecting swift results from meditation is unrealistic. There are legends about instant realizations, awakenings, or enlightenments. But don't count on that. It's rarely a quick leap into nirvana or even steady concentration or mindfulness. For a reality check, keep in mind that the Buddha (Siddhartha) struggled along the path toward enlightenment. Early in his spiritual journey, he studied dharma (teachings and scriptures) and practiced meditation with the renowned master Alara Kalama, revered for his spiritual attainments. Finally Alara Kalama said he had nothing further to teach Siddhartha, who had reached the highest level. Siddhartha was disappointed. He had experienced dispassion, cessation, stilling, and direct knowledge only to find it slip away—he could not hold on to it (a familiar happening for spiritual seekers).

He then asked Alara Kalama: "Can you not teach me the way to get beyond the reach of life and death?" The answer was not what he wanted to hear: "No," said Alara Kalama, "that is a thing I do not know myself, so how can I teach it to you? I do not believe that anybody in the whole world knows that." The Buddha moved on to his next teacher Uddaka, known for great knowledge and spiritual powers. Again he reached the highest level, but Uddaka could not teach him how to overcome birth and death. The Buddha left to pursue his own path, and ultimately achieved permanent enlightenment through mindfulness techniques that he developed and perfected.

While enlightenment may prove temporary or elusive at best, as for the Buddha, a peek into that consciousness can be highly valuable. D. T. Suzuki, the great Japanese Zen master and teacher, said that his first experience of satori (the Zen term for enlightenment) was brief, and he was disappointed that he couldn't hold on to it. But it was an invaluable experience, he said.

It convinced him of the reality of enlightenment and encouraged him to pursue the path. Eventually his determination paid off, and he stabilized in the satori state. Suzuki's experience reminds us of the challenges along the spiritual path. Like Suzuki, until you experience another dimension of consciousness you will have doubts—even a feeling of disillusionment. That's natural, and no amount of intellectual understanding will convince you. But a single experience can. You will justifiably not let go your tight grip on the ego without firm conviction of another ground of being. Then the real work begins. Like the sailor on Columbus's ship in chapter 5, seeing the true shape of the earth from a rocket ship might well dispel the flat-earth anxiety, but the other dangers of the voyage would be far from over—the true vision of the planet could not provide the navigational charts for freely traveling the uncharted waters.

## How to Meditate

My preference is Zen meditation. I find the Zen practice that I do in a group led by Dr. Brenda Shoshanna Lukeman the most comfortable. I value the structure and regularity. Every Monday evening we do three half-hour sittings (zazen) followed by walking meditations. Once a month the group does a full-day intensive and periodically a four-to-five-day intensive. I brought a Chinese Zen group (Chan) into Marymount Manhattan College for Zen mediation every Wednesday evening. Their meditations are very similar to Brenda's. While Zen usually recommends a concentration technique of counting the breath, I prefer mindfulness. At other times I practice meditation at home solo, but I prefer the group setting. Then there are frequent opportunities for meditation at spiritual gatherings that usually begin or end with meditation. Many find that group meditation with a leader generates greater intensity.

There are often opportunities to sit with great spiritual teachers and masters who regularly pass through New York City. This is not the same as jumping around for the "right techniques." In sitting with these teachers, the emphasis is on the power of their presence, not the technique. While I don't favor guided meditations, the ones led by Vasudeva, a highly evolved spiritual teacher based in Trinidad, are particularly powerful because of his extraordinary presence. I don't miss an opportunity to sit with Vasudeva whenever he comes to New York. Loch Kelly, another outstanding spiritual teacher, leads powerful meditations during his frequent satsangs (spiritual gatherings). Yet Loch gives no specific instruction or guidance but rather instructs those present to go into their familiar meditation.

If there is no one-size-fits-all, how do you begin? For those not connected to a spiritual tradition, it's best to find a teacher or a setting that you feel comfortable with. As you proceed, you will know how to continue. There is great wisdom in the spiritual aphorism "When the student is ready, the teacher will appear."

## Luxury of Higher Consciousness

"I'm too busy trying to make ends meet to have time to meditate or explore higher consciousness—poor people don't have the time to do it either." There's an element of truth to this statement. Some degree of affluence or leisure time can make it easier to explore higher consciousness. It's not that higher consciousness and affluence are directly connected, but that people who are struggling just to stay afloat can't see anything beyond their daily pushes, pulls, and anxiety for survival. You have to be able to pause long enough to extricate yourself from lower consciousness and your absorption in the ego. That's why Hindu and other spiritual traditions consider the retirement years the ideal time to get on the spiritual path with serious determination.

But affluence and leisure do not guarantee that you will seek higher consciousness either. On the contrary, affluence often exposes the delusion of the ego ("I made it and still don't feel secure"), which can generate a new mobilization for achievement, sealing you in the prison of the self. On the other side, poverty does not preclude higher consciousness. It just intrudes another obstacle. Enlightened masters of the past were often poor. Others, like the Buddha, walked away from wealth and position to seek enlightenment. There is no one way. We can't predict who will find the path and stick to it until the goal is reached. For some people, it takes a disaster or deep despair to enable them to switch gears and open up to other views of life and self. In some respects, those who have little material goods may feel they have less to lose by making a radical change.

Others may say they are too old. This is only an expression of the ego feeling sorry for itself. Actually, as we noted, midlife, or around age fifty, can be the ideal time to seek a new path or enlightenment. It is at this time that family responsibilities and other entanglements have looser demands so that one can more easily shift attention. Freud missed that point with his pessimism about the prospect for change after age forty. The issue is not change but self-discovery. The highest self—omni consciousness—is within you so you don't have to look very far, and it doesn't age, shrink, or lose its vitality. Anyone in any life situation can find omni consciousness when armed with the courage and determination to pursue it.

**Questions to Pose to Yourself**

There are a number of questions you can ask yourself to help shift the locus of consciousness from ego to omni consciousness.

1. Whose mind is it? Whose thoughts?
2. In your preoccupations, conflicts, and worry, are you living or being lived?
3. Why do you choose intense and painful feelings? Why do you accept delivery?
4. Is the "I" that is observing my conflicts and seeks to escape from conflict the same "I" that is submerged in conflict? Who and where am *I*?
5. When I debate myself, which "I" is questioning and which "I" is being questioned? Who receives the answers? Which "I" takes action? Which "I" benefits?
6. Do you realize that *I am home?*

The time for self-discovery is always now for everyone—young and old. You can go home. But there are formidable obstacles. The next step on this inner journey is unmasking *the near enemies.*

# CHAPTER EIGHT

# The Near Enemies

Just three little words—*I love you*. How much easier they are to say than to truly mean. And how meaningful and welcome they are when they are truly meant—and how pernicious and dangerous they are when they are not. We must always be cautious when we hear the very things that we so much want to hear. This is especially true in the field of spiritual practice, where the path to omni consciousness can easily resemble a minefield. Actions and emotions can seem benign on the surface and then seduce us with the promise of peace, security, and fulfillment while actually carrying us further from home. These treacherous foes of omni consciousness are the *near enemies*.

The spiritual teacher Jack Kornfield popularized the Buddhist term "near enemies" to identify the essence of activities that masquerade as spiritual. Near, because they are deceptively close to genuine spirituality, and enemies because, being false, they will falsify even your best intentions. Every spiritual principle and practice has an ego counterpart that is a "near enemy."

The more distant enemies are easy to spot. Like the seven deadly sins, they are obviously antithetical to spiritual consciousness, so you won't have any difficulty recognizing them. Anger, greed, jealousy, insatiable lust, hatred, violence, restlessness, apathy, laziness, and a host of others clearly miss the mark of spirituality. But that's not true of the *near enemies*. As you read some of the examples of near enemies in this chapter, you may be tempted to dismiss some instances as too obvious, too easy to spot, to lead anyone astray. Yet that's just the point here. The ego is out to protect itself, and it wants very much to believe in the deceptive web that it weaves. From the outside, the contradictions are instantly clear; from the inside, the course of action appears seamless and totally persuasive.

## Love

Good call. Everybody wants love . . . *but*. What appears to be heartfelt love and unwavering dedication for another, like the "I love you," often turns out to be self-serving egoism, attachment, and dependency in disguise. When put to the test, it can unravel; for instance, when love is not returned, anger, even violence, is likely to surface. I recently read a newspaper account of a man stalking and killing his former fiancée who broke off the relationship. It's a familiar story. Sadly, crimes of passion happen all too often when "I love you and can't live without you" becomes "you will not live without me." True love is selfless and unconditional. The moment "love" carries "if" baggage, it becomes a near enemy weighed down by a self-seeking ego—"I will love you only if you return love." Or, "I will love you only if you do what I want you to do." Near-enemy love is absorbed in "my" feelings and "my" needs, not the welfare or celebration of the loved one; "me" is center stage and the main event—perhaps the only event. The near enemy ego has put the "me" cart before the "we" horse.

Others believe they exude love because of their deep feelings of devotion to God, spirit, mankind, or the universe—all in the abstract. Their behavior in daily life, however, paints a very different picture. Once outside the meditation room, ashram, church, synagogue, or mosque, they often can't get along with anyone. Their family and personal relationships are in shambles, and they are dominated by anger and discontent.

Kathy loved everyone at the spiritual retreat—her boundless feeling of love convinced her that her spiritual consciousness was evolving. But outside the retreat she had great difficulties in interpersonal relations. She was short tempered, quick to criticize, and stingy in offering help to others. Kathy had a sharp eye for everyone's flaws. No wonder her relationships with men were always short lived despite her "desperation" for marriage and children. Nevertheless, Kathy felt she exemplified the cosmic love that she experienced solo at retreats and other spiritual settings. On close examination, though, her love was spiritual masturbation and a near enemy of genuine love.

## Compassion

Compassion has many near enemies. Lurking behind what at first blush looks like compassion is often pity or feeling sorry for someone's misfortune. True compassion is the wish for everyone to be free of suffering. It is linked to a sense of connection to all people. Feeling sorry or having pity for others looks good on the surface but often reveals separation—"*your* suffering and misfortune."

The Buddhist teacher Pema Chodron cites another more subtle near enemy of compassion—"idiot compassion"—whereby we are willing to put up with abuse or disdain from others because we don't want to offend them by registering a legitimate protest, in effect equating inaction with acting spiritually.

> This is when we avoid conflict and protect our image by being kind when we should say a definite "no." Compassion doesn't imply only trying to be good. When we find ourselves in an aggressive relationship, we need to set clear boundaries. The kindest thing we can do for everyone concerned is to know when to say "enough." Many people use Buddhist ideals to justify self-debasement. In the name of not shutting our heart, we let people walk over us. It is said that in order not to break our vow of compassion, we have to learn when to stop aggression and draw the line. There are times when the only way to bring down the barriers is to set boundaries.

The compassionate line-setting boundaries and limits can be a compassionate teaching tool.

## Labeling

Naming does not make it so. It's plain bad logic, or outright self-deception, when I define myself as spiritual, then assume that everything I do is automatically spiritual. Now I might genuinely want to be spiritual, but the wanting by itself does not guarantee that I will succeed. Recently, I read an announcement for a conference called "Spiritual Care and the Physiology of Aging." Even though the people initiating the conference may possibly be highly evolved spiritual beings, there was nothing in the conference topics that indicated even a hint of infusing spirituality into the presentations. There is certainly nothing wrong with a sound exposition and advice about health and aging. But if the presentations lack meaningful integration of spirituality with the subject matter, let's not call it spiritual merely because of spiritual intentions or because the organizers are clergy.

A few years ago, my colleague Dr. Marcella Bakur Weiner and I were asked by a division of the American Psychological Association to write guidelines for integrating spirituality into psychotherapy practice. At first I was inclined to turn down the invitation. I wondered at the time if the division was ready for or would accept a genuine integration that recognized and embraced ego consciousness and spiritual consciousness.

Nevertheless, we decided to plow ahead since so many psychologists were flirting with spirituality, often driven by the needs and demands of their clients. Our hard work paid off, we thought, when we devised a list of twelve principles (talking points, if you will) that we believed provided a comfort zone that would allow those in therapy and their counselors to consider spiritual concerns seriously, while allowing for divergences. These general principles are: uncertainty, faith, mystery, meaningfulness, connectedness, higher consciousness, gratitude, compassion, forgiveness, universality, surrender, suffering, and redemption. We purposely outlined these twelve pillars of spirituality in general terms with no references to any particular paths, practices, or rituals. Primarily, we wanted to open the door for psychotherapy to acknowledge and deal with spiritual needs without promoting or precluding any specific approach. Realizing the delicacy of the topic, we trod gingerly and circumspectly, we thought.

We couldn't have been more surprised when our proposal was rejected as "too religious." In our opinion, there was virtually no religion in the twelve principles as we spelled them out. More telling was the confirmation of our suspicions that traditional helping professions persist in their discomfort with spirituality. What the division was really seeking—this came out in further discussion—were some spiritual techniques that could give psychology a spiritual shine. This deception, we assured them, would not go unnoticed. No surprise that the division has still not adopted principles of integration.

This is a near-enemy example of promoting something as genuinely spiritual while all the time just using a cover of superficial techniques that conceals business as usual. It is strongly reminiscent of a story that comedian George Burns was fond of telling, and it serves as a metaphor for many near enemies of spirituality.

In the early part of his career in vaudeville, Burns tried out different comedy routines. He often failed, was booed off the stage, and ultimately fired. So he frequently changed the name of his act to get new jobs. Once he was sitting in a booking office when the agent came out and shouted: "I've got a booking for the act of Valenti and Company." No one responded, and Burns thought, "Maybe I'm Valenti and Company." After all, he had changed the name of his act so many times he couldn't be sure. Finally, as no one answered, he raised his hand and took the booking. It turned out that "Company" was a dog—part of a dog act. Burns, inventive trouper that he was, went on stage with a variation of his usual comedy routine while holding a dog under his arm.

Isn't that precisely what many do with their spiritual representations—the same old act while holding the prop of spirituality under arm in an effort to convince themselves and others that the act is thoroughly spiritual? Spirituality, though, must stand on its own performance.

## Antidotes

How often have you treated spiritual practices as if they were antidotes for nonspiritual behavior—like pigging out on junk food and justifying yourself by finishing up with a raw carrot or a small green salad? Then there are those—I'm sure you've met them too—who hit you over the head with their "spirituality." "I'm a strict vegetarian and don't drink coffee or alcohol"—what about you? Or "I meditate and do chanting every morning and evening. How often do you meditate?" A woman who was caught red-handed shoplifting indignantly said to the security guard: "How can you accuse me of stealing? I go to church every Sunday." Surely spiritual activities and practices are commendable and can be important components of a spiritual lifestyle. But unless infused into all activities and behavior in everyday living rather than self-congratulatory expressions of pride and a "holier-than-thou" attitude, they can become fierce near-enemy props—rituals of self-deception.

## Detachment

Detachment is a state of satisfaction within. It is the self-sufficiency of omni consciousness. All spiritual traditions encourage transcending a strictly material and sensual level of existence. Spirituality says you are more than your mind, body, and possessions. Letting go of these attachments can open awareness of the spiritual dimension. Detachment from desires and obsessive pleasure seeking is, therefore, considered an important spiritual objective. Does that call for shunning and rejecting all forms of materialism and sensuality to achieve spiritual consciousness? An extreme view can make detachment a near enemy; the spiritual task of living in the world, however, is to spiritualize the material—to find the spiritual within the material that elevates the material and transforms it into the spiritual.

Rabbi Simon Jacobson insists that the material world is no less spiritual than what we usually think of as spiritual beyond the material. In elevating the material to the spiritual dimension, we infuse and embrace spirituality in the totality of life. Rejecting the material can be another form of alienation, separation, and a rejection of the relative world—or what spiritual teacher Andrew Cohen calls "the let's-get-the-heck-out-of-here" philosophy that glorifies transcendental reality, the afterlife, and possible future incarnations while rejecting responsibility for infusing this here-and-now, material existence with spirituality—and living it fully.

Uncaring and apathy can sometimes pass for detachment when in fact they are strategies for defending against powerful feelings and avoiding moral imperatives. A refusal to act against correctable injustice, for example, on the grounds that it is only in the material world is neither a moral nor an ethical stance—and it very much impedes the development of true spirituality in the individual. Detachment can become escape, withdrawal, aloofness, disdain, rejection, and even an open battle with the physical and material world. The various forms of obsessive detachment can be as destructive to achieving omni consciousness as obsessive attachment. In omni consciousness, one recognizes and accepts the physical and material but is not ruled or driven by them. We are physical as well as spiritual beings. One of the most difficult tasks is finding the spiritual in the material. Rejecting the material is rejecting the very essence of the creation (no matter how you understand creation) and trivializes human existence. The most extreme form of renunciation and rejection of the material world can have a boomerang effect, producing obsessions with physical and other desires as we unsuccessfully try to exile them from existence. We have seen that all too often with fallen spiritual leaders.

All activities can be spiritual, including sex, eating, work, family life, relations, and almost all other everyday activity. Spirituality is not defined by an activity as much as by your relationship to it. The Buddha called this the middle road:

> Let me tell you about the middle path. Dressing in rough and dirty garments, letting your hair grow matted, abstaining from eating any meat or fish, does not cleanse the one who is deluded. Mortifying the flesh through excessive hardship does not lead to triumph over the senses. All self-inflicted suffering is useless as long as the feeling is dominant. You should lose your involvement with yourself and then eat and drink naturally, according to the needs of your body. Attachment to your appetites—whether you deprive or indulge them—can lead to slavery. But satisfying the needs of daily life is not wrong. Indeed, to keep a body in good health is a duty, for otherwise the mind will not stay strong and clear.

## Self-Sacrifice

What is more spiritual than self-sacrifice? Isn't that what spirituality is all about—transcending the personal self for something higher? Yes, when it's genuine, not when what appears to be sacrificing personal interests turns out to be a near enemy beating the drum of the ego.

Steve was tall and thin, and thought he presented a striking figure as an ascetic. No, he didn't wrap himself in a loincloth or carry a beggar's cup, but he often spoke about how few material goods he needed and how devoted he was to spiritual practices. This sometimes raised eyebrows, as Steve was married to Judy, who came from a well-to-do family and was dedicated to materialism, barely tolerating Steve's spiritual bent. They lived in a very nice house, took frequent, upscale vacations, and dined in the finest restaurants. Steve talked disdainfully about his opulent lifestyle, insisting that he needed nothing and only went along for the materialistic ride in the name of domestic peace with Judy. He wished Judy were more spiritually inclined so that he could expand his practices and participate in more workshops—"I want nothing, seek nothing, and only strive to bathe in transcendence." After five years of their charade, Judy and Steve split up. Big surprise, Steve very promptly hooked up with Ann, who could have been Judy's double. His near enemy of "self-sacrifice" was protected and would live on.

## Living in the "Now"

Being fully present in the here and now is widely considered one of the benchmarks of spiritual consciousness. We have seen that the ego thrives on the past and future with the "now" moment barely touched. You might even say that spiritual consciousness is the "now." Yet even the "now" can be a near enemy when it is not the spiritual "now" but the ego version that distorts its meaning. How can "now" fall into the service of the ego?

When the "now" narrowly focuses on "me" and "my" needs, excluding a bigger picture, it can be strictly self-serving: "I am fully present and want you now." This is a young man speaking to a woman he just met. He has a strong attraction to her and wants to have a sexual relationship with her "now," forgetting his involvement in another long-term relationship. He is convinced that his immediate desire is spiritual because he has the "courage" to feel and act *now*. Similarly, "I want to travel now" or "I want to leave my job now" may convince you that you are exemplifying spirituality by daring impulsive acts in the "now" moment. But a "now" that only serves your impulsive needs and desires and excludes a broader "now" is not the spiritual "now" but the ego version. "Now" is more than your immediate field or momentary personal desires. "Now" is the totality of your existence and should encompass everything and everyone that is part of your universe. "Now" should not selectively include and exclude items solely in the service of the ego. Fully present means fully aware. Narrowly demanding what you want now because you are "fully present" is a self-serving distortion of the spiritual "now"—and a clever near enemy.

## Conceptual Near Enemies

Spiritual concepts like uncertainty, mystery, and surrender can enrich a spiritual philosophy, but they can also be near enemies when they are marshaled to sanction a freewheeling, self-serving ego that celebrates "me": when uncertainty and mystery are used to give license to whatever I feel or think, and when surrender is surrender to "my" notions of what is, without critical evaluation. Applied in that fashion, these spiritual notions can be strictly self-serving—"me" and "my" needs and interests become the center that is camouflaged as the spiritual self by these near enemies.

## Banking on Spirituality

There are those who believe that a variety of activities add points to an account that can be cashed in for spiritual enlightenment. Would that it were true. Bingo!—you're enlightened when you accumulate a sufficient number of points. How often you meditate, do service, or participate in other familiar spiritual practices does not guarantee anything in return—and shouldn't. These practices are ends in themselves. We must diligently ask ourselves: "Am I at one with my practices, or are they rituals for adding to my spiritual bank account?"

## Vegetarianism

Vegetarianism can be a spiritual practice if it is connected to an overall spiritual philosophy that is embraced and followed. But it is not necessarily, in and of itself, a spiritual practice. Many enlightened souls throughout history were not vegetarians. To the best of our knowledge, most biblical giants were not, and the quote above indicates that the Buddha didn't consider vegetarianism essential.

Some people embrace vegetarianism strictly for what they believe are health benefits. Many spiritual aspirants, though, thrust vegetarianism to the forefront as a sign of deep spiritual commitment. We have already seen how some practices can be used to inflate a spiritual bank account that camouflages an ego that still rampages under the radar.

The issue of vegetarianism and spirituality comes up every Saturday when I participate with a group of spiritual devotees, mostly Sai Baba followers, at a lunch service for the needy near the Church of the Nativity on the Bowery in New York City. This dedicated group of people prepares a large amount of the foods in their homes, but bakeries, restaurants, and other establishments also donate some of the food. After the lunch service at the Bowery, the same dedicated group offers feedings on Twenty-eighth Street near Bellevue Hospital and after that in front of a church in midtown. Once a month, other members of the same group help prepare a lunch service at the Cathedral of Saint John the Divine near Columbia University on the fringes of Harlem. There we actually do the cooking as well as the serving. For the past two years, I've been an assistant chef. Sometimes a professional chef shows up as well as young helpers from New York Cares, the Juilliard School's Drama Division, and the American Ballet School.

After that lengthy introduction setting the stage, now to the chase. The food is strictly vegetarian—and these good people will do it no other way. But the needy hungry and homeless who show up at these locations are not happy with the strictly vegetarian menu. Many get downright angry: "Don't you have any chicken or meat?" they ask.

Should spiritual devotees committed to vegetarianism impose it on hungry people they are serving who do not subscribe to or like vegetarianism? Is sticking to your personal practice and philosophy on this issue the right spiritual decision? Keep in mind that many of the clients have poor diets and nutrition and would benefit from the complex proteins of fish and chicken—possibly improving their health. Should serving "me" and "my" beliefs outweigh service to others and their needs and preferences? Is serving the wishes of others in this case a violation of your beliefs—will serving nonvegetarian food knock you off the spiritual altar?

It's a thorny issue that has led to endless discussions. Should service to others be a form of proselytizing? "I'm a vegetarian and I want you to be a vegetarian." Or, "I cannot serve nonvegetarian food—it would be an abdication of my commitment to spirituality."

Here again we may be back to points in the spirituality bank account. Selfless service, I believe, should be just that—serving with "me" out of the picture or, at best, in the background. Imposing views on others is not service and may play the role of a near enemy by promoting or pumping up one's own "deep spirituality."

Then I discovered that when many "vegetarians" are pressed about their eating habits, a number of telltale words surface: *sometimes, occasionally, on rare occasions*, and so forth—referring to slips from the straight and narrow path. Nutritionally, if you have the knowledge and stick-to-itiveness to pursue such a regimen diligently, you certainly can enhance your health. More to the point, with respect to doctrinaire vegetarianism, is the question, can you be nonvegetarian and highly evolved spiritually? Ask the Dalai Lama. He's not a vegetarian. He passes that off quite casually, merely commenting that early in life his physician said he was not suited for a strictly vegetarian diet and that it would impair his health. So taking the Buddhist middle road was no big deal for him.

Obviously overvaluing or rigidly embracing any practice (no matter how beneficial in itself) is likely to create a near enemy that only artificially inflates the spiritual bank account. From the perspective of omni consciousness, finding out who you are is the main event. No particular practice will necessarily get you there, and slippage will not slam the door.

## Spiritual Posturing

Never underestimate the survival capacity of the ego. Some people who seem busily engaged in spiritual activities are actually just protecting their egos. The ego remains untouched and comfortably ensconced while it wallows in supportive, noncompetitive spiritual sentimentality. How can you tell if it's posturing or the real thing? There are signs: the energy and productivity levels are often low as the person retreats, cowering, into meditation or other practices. Missing is the opening up, the freeing of energy, and the expanding of abilities, talents, and interests. Nonattachment and nonseeking do not usher in a spiritual sense of identification with a higher consciousness, but rather seek to maintain fantasies of grandiosity, protecting the ego from being tested. "I don't have time for responsibilities or commitments; I'm too busy getting enlightened." Energy is still locked in the battle for ego dominance while the surface exudes nonstop spiritual posturing. The self-indulgent piety makes this near enemy difficult to expose.

Spiritual teacher Loch Kelly stresses the importance of what he calls "waking down." Everyone, he says, wants to wake up (get enlightened), but fewer want to wake down. Waking down, Kelly goes on to explain, is integrating spiritual gains into everyday life and behavior. It's exactly what is absent in the near enemy described above.

Waking down is as important as waking up, insists Kelly. Postponing waking down to a distant future or time when you will be enlightened almost assures that many will never complete the journey and perhaps don't want to—if getting there means waking down and then feeling obligated to live a full life with an enlightened perspective: giving, sharing, making commitments, taking on responsibilities, developing unconditional loving relationships, and more. Fear of waking down and keeping it at a safe distance preserves the spiritual ego—a near enemy with the fiercest resistance to uprooting. If you seriously want to prevent this near enemy from sprouting, waking down should be an integral part your journey all along the path—not just postponed for the end game.

The more I think about it, the clearer it becomes that Loch Kelly's notion of waking down demands as much attention as waking up.

## The Right Practice and the Right Teacher

Another spiritual seeker, my friend Richard Schiffman, lived in India for a number of years at the Ashram of his teacher, Jillellamudi Mother. He wrote a biography about this great sage, called *Mother of All*. Richard tells of "Mother's" answer to the frequent question posed by devotees: What is the best spiritual practice? Her answer: "The one you actually do." Many of us, particularly at the beginning of our search, jump from teacher to teacher, guru to guru, in search of the master or practice that will magically transmit enlightenment. In jumping around you may look and feel like a devoted spiritual seeker with a passion for spirituality. The absence of commitment to a teacher or a practice, however, can be just another ego deception that keeps you at the level of mind embedded in yearning for ego completion and ego transcendence. Settling down to a regular practice can expose the ego's fear of facing its sense of incompletion. On the other hand, being in the presence of evolved or enlightened teachers can inspire and infuse energy into your practice. How to differentiate sincerity from escapism requires honest assessment of your motives and, often, the helpful input of a knowledgeable friend or teacher. This near enemy is not easy to unmask.

## Spiritual Seeking

Adyashanti, one of the leading American spiritual teachers, describes a subtle near enemy that seems almost contradictory. Isn't spiritual seeking the most prominent marker of spiritual commitment to spiritual attainment— the trajectory that will lead ultimately to awakening or enlightenment? Yet Adyashanti says the impulse to be free or realized comes from outside the mind and that makes the mind feel insecure. He adds, "Most spiritual seekers move away from this insecurity by seeking and striving for a distant spiritual goal that avoids facing the unknown. In creating the seeker, the ego, he says, distances itself from the unknown. In a flip-flop, seeking reinforces the separate self: "The seeker who is separate from the sought is purely a creation of mind. You are not the seeker, you are the sought."

Restated, you are omni consciousness; there is no literal journey, only self-discovery within. So jumping aboard the spiritual-seeking bandwagon should raise the near enemy flag to remind you of who you are.

## Turning to God

The crisis of aging, which we have redefined as the ego up against the ropes of time, will lead many to grasp solutions that seem to recapture the ego's need for power. With life time shrinking as birthdays advance, the ego's playground for becoming—the future—is lost. A feeling wells up, "There's not enough time left for me to become the person I want to be, to reach the achievement I yearned for, to attain the enlightenment I was seeking, or ____ ____ ____ ____" (you fill in the blanks). Some, as we have seen, turn to the past to recapture a feeling of wholeness. Others may fall into despair. More fortunate ones will shift gears to look within and find the spiritual self—omni consciousness—that restores wholeness and integrity here and now. Still others will turn to religion and God. Sometimes, though, embracing religion is not as much a spiritual quest as a near enemy of spirituality. Some will say that religion has always been prone to being a near enemy of spirituality—a most seductive near enemy because it looks so persuasively like the genuine article. We have already seen that some use religion as an antidote—"I go to church, respect the Sabbath, celebrate holidays," and so forth, while demonstrating little spirituality in day-to-day conduct.

Gerontologists have noted a resurgence of interest in religion among the elderly. Many become more active participants in their religious institutions, attending services and activities. All well and good. But the "yearning for God" in many instances may be driven more by the fear of death, loneliness, dependency, and helplessness than love of God or transcendence. "Here am I, limited, vulnerable, facing the realization that I am not enduring or omnipotent, regardless of what I have accomplished in life. So I will now turn to the ultimate power—God—for forgiveness, reassurance, protection, restoration of personal power, and, hopefully, salvation. God has these things in his power and can give them to me." Religion used in this fashion is a near enemy at any age because it becomes a stand-in for the ego—the I/me/ego can feel on top again with a powerful ally in its corner. That's not spiritual consciousness replacing the ego, it's the ego dressed up in religion and spirituality.

Presbyterian minister Don Sandin is very much aware of these self-deceptions. Nevertheless, he sees the fact of older people—or anyone of any age—showing up in his church as a challenge, and an opportunity, for him to unmask the near enemies and transform them into genuine spirituality. "What brings you to the oasis is less important then the fact that you are there," says Reverend Sandin. His insight is true for all of us faced with our own self-deceptions and near enemies. Showing up is the first step toward success. Then sincerity, honesty, awareness, self-examination, and determination are the tools we must apply diligently and ceaselessly in order to unmask and defeat our near enemies.

# CHAPTER NINE

# Affirmations of Omni Consciousness

I don't think I ever read an affirmation that I didn't like. Affirmations are seductively inspirational. How taunting their alluring but often seemingly unreachable truths. When hearing an inspiring affirmation, don't you long to assimilate it into the core of your being so that you can rise to its transcendent realm, forever freeing you from the ego-bound, mundane state of existence? "Love yourself, appreciate yourself, be nice to yourself, be content, find happiness and joy in the mere awareness of existence, celebrate life, give up material preoccupations, feel whole and complete, find divinity within, I will live in the present moment and let the future take care of itself, I will reject fear, I have within me everything I need, I will love and accept myself just as I am, I have the power to create the life I desire, I will let go of desire and trust the universe to fulfill my needs, I do not need power and control—my strength comes from within," and the list goes on and on. Oh, if only by the simple act of nodding agreement we could merge with an affirmation, transformation would be so easy. Why can't we live affirmations that we deeply and genuinely feel tap the truth of a higher dimension?

The obstacle we face is that same nagging one that impedes all efforts to leap to higher ground. The problem is not in the message or the messenger but the "I" that is receiving the message. In chapter 5, we learned that efforts at change dialogues with the limited projected self, the very ego self that defines itself through its problems and conflicts. The near enemies that we just explored showed how tenaciously the ego will defend its self-conception with an endless bag of deceptive tricks to pretend that it yearns for change. So don't expect the ego object to act like a subject or willingly yield to the sub-jective source—omni consciousness. Yes, the ego loves those affirmations. The problem is, they implore the ego to stop being the ego. Fat chance. As long as the locus of consciousness is the ego rather than omni consciousness, spiritual messages will get short-circuited. The inspirational aphorisms will register as appealing sentiments. But as much as you might think you believe and embrace them, they will not go to your subjective core where real change can take place. We have a dilemma. How to begin?

Given the limited choices, sentiment may not be a bad place to start. At least it will keep you focused and point in the right direction. However, it is essential to know where *you* are and to constantly work on shifting the locus of the self. The self-deceptions that you will invent will be ingenious. The near enemies will trip you up at every turn. So you must constantly question and be aware. Remember, the fact that you like or believe an affirmation is no indication that it is registering in a way that can foster change. Change is not the issue. Locating and lodging yourself in omni consciousness is the is-sue. In fact, once you are lodged in omni consciousness, affirmations will not be needed. You will not have to say them to know them. Omni conscious-ness will automatically register the messages. They are expressions of omni consciousness and you are omni consciousness.

The sage Nisargadatta Maharaj, cited earlier, kept hammering away at that point: You don't have to affirm that which you deeply know beyond just superficial intellectual knowing, he said. Affirmations are appealing—and necessary—only when you don't really know.

Then it's not necessary to repeat or convince yourself "I am a man" or "I am a woman"; Nisargadatta Maharaj's seemingly silly example now may make sense—"I'm not the dish" (he was holding up), "I am a man." You would look askance at anyone who was unsure and needed to be convinced or reminded of those affirmations stating who and what they were and weren't—you would wonder what strange world they were living in if they weren't sure and needed to convince themselves. Similarly, perhaps we can now understand Nisargadatta's puzzlement that the seekers who questioned him didn't know absolutely and deeply that they were not the body and were not the mind but just I-am-ness consciousness—and needed affirmations to remind them when it was so clear and obvious to Nisargadatta.

Despite the difficulties in making affirmations a living part of your con-sciousness, affirmations of omni consciousness are useful for helping refocus attention on the genuine self that Nisargadatta persistently pointed to. Affir-mations of omni consciousness will not lead you directly to omni conscious-ness if the ego is your operating system of choice. So much conditioning goes into diverting attention from omni consciousness in favor of a projected, limited self that persistent concentration on wrenching attention from the limited self to omni consciousness is necessary. The affirmations will help.

There are endless possibilities for affirmations, as many of the books on affirmations will illustrate. There are volumes that are divided by subjects. Some writers offer an affirmation for each day. They typically cover a wide range of spiritual ideas and sentiments. One outstanding book of inspirational sayings is Gary Fenchick's *Timeless Wisdom*.

In contrast, the following affirmations of omni consciousness are exclusively focused on one central issue: the locus of consciousness. That's the frontier where the battle to escape the prison of the self must begin and end. Each of the affirmations challenges the ego's posturing and calls attention to omni consciousness. The affirmations strive to chip away at the ego's fierce grip on consciousness. Through the process of working with these affirmations (and you might want to add some of your own), the balance will eventually shift and omni consciousness will begin to feel like your natural home.

## How to Work With the Affirmations

Read each affirmation and note the ones you are comfortable with and the ones that jar you. Pay close attention to your bodily and emotional reactions to each affirmation. It is important to be honest with yourself if you are to make progress. An intellectual acceptance is no proof that you own an affirmation. So watch out for the tricks of the ego's ingenious disguises.

In reading these and other affirmations, avoid the ego trap of getting caught up in the idea of the power of omni consciousness. Many fool themselves into believing they are embracing an affirmation when, in fact, all they want is the power that's implied to expand the limited self. It will not work. The limited self is limited and cannot truly expand. The power of omni consciousness is that omni consciousness is subjective power. Omni consciousness does not have to do or get anything to know its strength. Power for the sake of power is the ego's game.

After observing your reactions to the affirmations, start with the affirmations that seem to generate the least resistance. Work with only one affirmation in a session. You might want to combine it with meditation, or just prior to meditation—if that's comfortable for you. Remember, you don't have to get anywhere. Speed is not the goal. Any progress or breakthrough will shift the balance toward omni consciousness and thereby make the overall task easier. Effort and struggle run counter to omni consciousness. Therefore, the very manner in which you work is as important as the affirmations.

## Affirmation 1: I Am Complete—There Is No More of Me to Be Found or Created

This is an important affirmation because it challenges the basic assumption of the ego that the self is incomplete and must "become." It is this assumption that leads us to the never-ending path of needing and wanting. Omni consciousness is complete and does not have to become. Growing through synchronicity and the outflow of creative energy is different from the ego's frantic effort to become. As I have repeatedly shown, "becoming" is an end in itself and therefore has no end except frustration and the perpetuation of becoming more and more. Eventually you implode from this process and never feel gratified or fulfilled for long.

If you find yourself resisting this affirmation ("But I need . . . , then I will be complete"), look squarely at the things that you think make you incomplete. Try to stay with a sense of completeness and see "the thing" as something external, as desirable as it may be. See that your core self is the same with or without that thing. If you can feel this, you will have a new sense of inner strength and power.

## Affirmation 2: I Am Enough and Have Enough to Be Fulfilled and Content Here and Now

This is very much related to the previous affirmation, but it more specifically focuses on the here and now. If you are content in this very moment, which is the only reality (past and future are only mental concepts), then you need very little if anything now to be content. It is only when you recall all the things you have attached to your self-concept that you feel discontent. Try to feel and see the self without its baggage in this very moment. That is the self that is free and unencumbered. Get familiar with this pure self and try to go to it when you are discontented. See the space between the self and its "needed" baggage. We tend to think that the contented self can only be self-content with all its external fixes glued to it. But this is a dependent and chronically unhappy self. The truly powerful self is the one that is free from externals and can stand on its own foundation of contentment within.

## Affirmation 3: I Want, but I Do Not Need

The distinction between wanting and needing is another assault on the ego's identification with its attachments. The genuine self does not need. It may want certain things that will enhance its functioning and comfort in the relative world, but it does not *need*. The self is complete. Grasping the difference between needing and wanting will affirm the completeness of the genuine self—omni consciousness.

## Affirmation 4: I Will Not Be Lived by My Emotions

In chapter 3, I detailed how the limited, projected self is defined by its emotions and, therefore, can't let go of them. The key to gaining freedom from the tyranny of emotions is the ability to see the *space* between you and your emotional experiences. If you have the strong conviction that you are not your emotions, then you are ready to *not accept delivery*. Once you know that you are not your emotions, then you can let go of them and not pay attention to them. It is only because you take possession of emotions and believe that you can't let them go that they have power over you. You want to own them and reject them at the same time. That can only produce the frozen stalemate of hitting the accelerator and the brake at the same time. Emotions lose their power when you stop paying attention to them and stop taking them seriously. Then you don't need either the accelerator or the brake. What a relief! And by standing back from your emotions, you weaken the entire fabric of the ego.

If you accept this affirmation, then try the following experiment. When you experience a negative emotion like anger, let it go. Keep in mind that it is something that you are experiencing but that you are separate from it. Refuse to let the emotion live you. You will find yourself fighting this with a barrage of arguments: "I can't let him/her get away with that" or "If I let the anger go, she/he will get the wrong idea." There is no end to this kind of thinking. Dropping anger doesn't mean you should be passive and not respond to situations. Just respond without the anger, or promptly acknowledge it and let it go; then craft a goal. Often we are so caught up in getting our anger out that we wind up with little or no advantage and no change in the anger-producing situation. Anger can do irreparable damage to a relationship, raise your blood pressure, compromise your immune system, and generally place you in an agitated state that interferes with other productive work. But we might feel good that we got the anger out and defended our ego. Does that make sense?

Neurophysiologist Dr. Robert Sapolsky in his book *Why Zebras Don't Get Ulcers* provides convincing evidence that stress, and the anger and agitation associated with it, releases hormones called glucocorticoids that destroy brain cells. I actually saw a speeded-up video of this happening when glucocorticoids were injected into animal brain cells. Since viewing that, every time I'm inclined to get really angry, I remember those brain cells dissolving.

The old-time comedian Jack Benny, in his classic skit, had a hard decision, and hesitated, when facing a holdup man who said: "Your money or your life?" How about the choice between your ego or your brains? I'll take my brains, thank you very much.

## More on Anger

Anger is one of the main driving forces behind the ego. Defuse anger and you will make great strides in disabling the ego's game plan. The ego uses anger to obliterate reality so that its strivings can have the illusion of rationality. Without anger, how could the ego justify its intensity to become? "I need and want and have to have" is the credo of the ego. What is the proof and validation of these demands? "Look how frustrated and *angry* I am. Would I be this angry if I didn't need so desperately?" Without anger or the intensity of other emotions, reality peeks through making it clear that nothing is really happening to you and that your strivings are self-created. When blaming the world is taken away from us, we are stuck with the responsibility for ourselves. Anger gets rid of all that and opens the door to dreamland. Giving up anger is an important and essential step in letting go of the ego and finding omni consciousness.

If all this hasn't convinced you that you should work diligently at separating from destructive emotions, you might want to try it anyway—as an experiment, one that can change your life and free you from the imprisonment of your emotions. If it doesn't work, you can always go back to sloshing around in the quagmire of emotions. After all, you've been doing that all your life. But if you are successful even once in letting go of a negative emotion and shifting to a positive state of mind, that can accomplish more than intense emotions ever delivered—and will convince you that you and your emotions are not the same. You will know that there is a space between you and your emotions and that *you can be in charge.* Then when you are in an emotional state you can focus on the safe space between and be liberated.

But what about loss and grief? They are real and can't be ignored or trivialized. Pain is real and can't be avoided—and shouldn't. The Zen master D. T. Suzuki was asked why he was mourning the death of his wife, Beatrice. The questioner misunderstood Zen practice and philosophy, expecting Suzuki to be the detached master of his emotions. But Zen practice accepts and experiences everything. Suzuki responded: "Yes, I am grieving, but it has no roots."

## Affirmation 5: I Accept My Attributes, but They Are Not Me

This affirmation calls attention to the relationship between omni consciousness and your limited self that has evolved from your personal experience.

When you fully perceive the relationship between omni consciousness and the experiential self, you have achieved *conservation of the self*. Now you can see that your particular attributes are you but are not you. You are more than these attributes, and you—omni consciousness—are the creator of attributes.

## Affirmation 6: I Can Be Many Things, for Omni Consciousness Is the Creator of Attributes and Omni Consciousness Is Me

Knowing that you are complete and whole and having the conviction that you are in charge, you can be, or try out, whatever you choose to focus your energy on. That's different than the ego's struggle to become. Roles are like containers. You can fill the container of your choice, or you can withdraw the energy from one container and shift to another one, giving you a different role. When identified with the energy, or omni consciousness, the role is always you. The container does not define you, so you can shift without the anxiety of feeling alienated. When you are identified with the container you may experience "this new container doesn't feel like me. I'm lost and shaky. Let me get back to the other container where I can feel safe." Can you now see that these emotional reactions are fueled by the locus of consciousness? In omni consciousness, you are no-thing, or every thing. Identified with one thing, you are limited and stuck, driving you to seek freedom while committed to your single container. The ego is ruled by the anxiety of deficit. Knowing who you really are and that you are in charge takes the drivenness out of your functioning. You don't *have to* become.

Also, the fact that you can be whatever you want to be does not mean that you should abandon your identity and what you are currently doing. It does not mandate that you radically uproot your life circumstances (career, relationships, etc.) to pursue grandiose goals or running in many directions. That would be using the understanding of omni consciousness in the service of the ego—the ego would then still be in charge with the cloak of omni consciousness concealing old ego tricks and games of "become something." In fully grasping the meaning of this affirmation, you will be freed from the feeling of being a limited projection. At the same time, it will make it easier to try new roles or take risks that make sense.

Ultimately, all projections are limited. However, since everyone has to be somewhere, where you are may be fine. It may be easier and more economical to be where you are while redirecting the locus of the self in omni consciousness. It may be a waste of energy to devote yourself to creating a new limited projection. If you do that, it will only prove to be a deception, an effort to seek liberation through your shadow. Every manifestation is just a small piece of the vast whole. So relax. Omni consciousness is the whole, and you are omni consciousness.

At the same time, does this mean that we should just accept all circumstance and strive to make no changes in our lives? No! There is one principle that governs changes. It's the principle of *synchronicity*. According to this application of synchronicity, when energy flows freely it finds its own natural paths. When it is encumbered by limiting or diverting concepts, we are out of sync. For example, a person who is talented in and who loves music might choose some other career outside of music. This choice could be motivated by many factors governing the limited self. There can be fears, anxieties, negative self-perceptions, and other individual psychological factors cemented into the limited self that lives you. Change may then be in order to restore synchronicity. But you don't have to change yourself to accomplish this. You only have to become yourself. Similarly, there is no virtue in struggling. The modern world has provided many comforts. If you are aware that you can have them, why not? As long as you are not identified with them, comforts will enhance the flow of energy and give you greater opportunities to be yourself.

## Affirmation 7: I Am Responsible for My Feelings—Nobody Can Make Me Feel Anything

If you have an undesirable feeling, it is because you allow that feeling to own you. Either you want the feeling or you feel you have no choice and believe you are that feeling. Since you are not any particular feeling, the feeling can only affect you if you accept delivery. It is your unwillingness to refuse delivery that makes the feeling seem inevitable. Since you believe the feeling is part of you, something essential for your self-definition, you can't let it go. The tug of war in which you believe you are fighting the feeling, trying to get rid of it, is illusory. It's like having your foot on the accelerator and slamming the brake periodically, to use a variation on an earlier analogy. The car keeps moving while you insist you are desperately trying to stop it. You block out the part that is pressing down on the accelerator and won't let go. When consciousness is unified in omni consciousness, such a split can't occur. The split state is the common state of existence that allows the ego to play its games and live us while our conscious presence makes us think we are striving for something else. We are locked into a narrow, no-win situation that doesn't permit us to be ourselves. We are too busy inventing dragons to battle. But there is only one consciousness. It cannot be divided. It only appears to be divided by the tricks we play. All the energy is generated from the same source. When you grasp this and restore omni consciousness as the center of action, your existence will be unified and conflict will begin to recede. You then will not allow your right hand to battle your left hand. You will see that *all is one*.

## Affirmation 8: The World Is Neutral—It Just Is; Therefore, Nothing Out There Can Disturb Me

The ego is constantly at war with the world. It feels good when it deludes itself into believing it is winning the war, or on the road to victory. By separating itself from the world and perceiving its insignificance, the ego has no other posturing than the constant defensive stance. It must keep moving or feel overwhelmed and passive. Yet often little is really happening in the world outside of the ego's personalization of experience and its combative posturing. "I am" is at one with the world. When you get to awareness beyond the mind's personal interpretations and "becomings," there is only silence. When you find that silence, the world becomes neutral and a friend.

## Affirmation 9: I Am Free and Liberated—I Just Didn't Know It

In its constant movement to get somewhere to fill the holes in its self-perceived deficiencies, the ego never feels free. It is always getting out from under. But in omni consciousness, the self is whole. It needs nothing and is therefore free and liberated. So freedom is part of the natural self. It is only a matter of uncovering that self. You are already liberated but just don't know it.

Liberation is inherent in omni consciousness. Since you are omni consciousness, you merely have to go home or, stated otherwise, let go of your mistaken identification with the projected, limited self. Consequently, the task of life is not to seek liberation but to act as the liberated person that you are. Just go to omni consciousness. Liberation is your natural self. Just focus on the "I" who is seeking and lodge yourself there. That "I" is the you that is already liberated—it is omni consciousness. Just stay with it. You need not search any further. Look inward rather than outward.

## Affirmation 10: Struggle Is Unnecessary and Does Not Accomplish Anything Useful

Struggle is a reflection of the limited, projected self. It expresses the desperate effort to pump life into the lifeless projection we call the ego self. It screams out the ego's need to get somewhere or become something. As I have shown over and over, these efforts are futile and will ultimately lead to dissatisfaction and frustration. For even if the immediate goal is achieved ("I desperately need that and now I have it"), a new need will replace it because the real need is the need to remain in a state of need so the illusion that the lifeless projection can become alive and a subject can be maintained. Success will only reveal the emptiness of the quest. At that point, you have three choices: You can redouble your efforts in new quests that will live you and thrust you back in your dreamlike world of illusions and delusions. You can fall into despair because "I now have everything I've wanted and I still feel empty inside" and you don't know where to turn. Or you can rethink the whole nature of your self and its quests and find a new locus of the self. I have recommended the latter and have tried to show where that self is and how to begin getting back to it. It is probably no coincidence that the path to personal transformation often begins after a person has achieved great success. It is at that point that the illusions are revealed for what they are and a search for genuinely new answers and directions can begin.

For those still intensely involved in their personal quests, the grip of emotions and illusions is too strong. The belief in the expansion of their projected selves through the ultimate success of their quests cannot be seen as the empty mental concept that it is. Only failure or success can get them on neutral ground where they have a shot at seeing more clearly. But then the pulls to get you back into the dream state are very strong. It is a rare person who can truly shift directions on his or her own. But a guide can show you the way. If you can nurture a strong conviction that there is another you and another dimension on which you can live more peacefully and take charge of your life, you can find your way back to that home.

## Affirmation 11: There Is No Place to Go

Most of us are constantly searching for a safe haven, a place to go, where some plateau of achievement will once and for all shield us from our fears and anxieties. We are constantly looking and searching. When we stop the search and turn inward to discover our true selves—omni consciousness—the search is over. There is the sudden realization that what we are searching for cannot be found in running away from ourselves toward some invented projection where we then lodge ourselves. There is no place to go to find the whole, secure self.

The problem of accepting this affirmation is the problem of bridging the gap back to omni consciousness. We are so identified with the projected self and its support systems—struggling, needing, wanting, expanding, and so forth—that life without these intense feelings seems untenable and empty. "If I am not seeking more, what would I be doing? Would I just sit around in some passive, blissful state?" Such statements show how far we have abandoned our original nature. "No struggle and no place to go" does not mean lifeless or no energy. On the contrary, struggle is truly lifeless because it strives to make an object—a shadow of our selves—alive and vital. Omni consciousness functioning according to synchronicity is life and energy, but without struggle or overarching purpose to become.

There are numerous situations and behaviors that provide an opportunity for getting a close-up view of omni consciousness. While omni consciousness is always present and easily accessible, our addiction to the experiential self draws us away from it. But once you have the conviction that you are omni consciousness, you will be better able to see it.

## Control Mechanism

Moments when we are "out of control" provide a good opportunity for accessing omni consciousness. This seems contradictory since *out of control* suggests the opposite of omni consciousness. Yet when we are "out of control," there is more control present than we think. It is like looking at the half-empty glass rather than the half-full glass. There must be a control mechanism that has a consciousness that is in charge, otherwise human existence wouldn't work. Think of the times when you have said, "I am out of control." You may feel that you are out of control with, let's say, eating, anger, or sex. However, close examination will reveal that you are very much in control. Control enters when you go beyond a certain point—call it your set point. We keep the control mechanism disguised so we can play the games of dreamland—being in the dream and then pulling back. This sustains the ego by allowing its delusions, but not letting the delusions go too far. The out-of-control eater fights the same twenty-five pounds for a lifetime. When the twenty-five-pound limit is reached, then the dieting and deprivation begins so that the "out of control" can start all over again.

There are people who do get totally out of control, but that is relatively rare and very self-destructive. One of the dangers of modern society may be that the limits of all forms of "out of control" seem to be widening. Sometimes one does go too far and can't return, as in the case of a narcotic overdose. But more typically, omni consciousness, the supreme consciousness, is in the background and is brought in when loss of control gets to its prescribed limit. If we could only see through this game and shift the balance so that omni consciousness was in total charge. Then there would be no conflicts. But we are afraid of letting go of the ego with its dream logic that permits delusions. We call on omni consciousness for emergency work—damage control—but resist lodging ourselves there. We prefer the dream of life. Contrary to what traditional psychologists say, the real nature of being out of control is handing over control to the ego.

To focus on omni consciousness, pay attention to those moments when you take charge and shift gears after being "out of control." How did that happen? What did you do? What is different from when you are "out of control"? Expand the self that is in control and see that it is you—omni consciousness.

## The Space between Subject and Object

Here is an elaboration of an experiment that was touched on in chapter 2. When you wake up in the morning, remain in the pure state of being and awareness. Resist the pull to enter your object-self identity. It will likely be very difficult. There are so many things to pull you: reports due, jobs to be done, chores to perform, worries, and so forth. You might find yourself saying something like, "I can't fool around with this, I have too many things to do." Aside from the fact that you do have many things to do, you are in this dialogue endorsing the object self as the real and only you. The other thing is just a play thing. This is why omni consciousness is so difficult to capture. So resist arguments and temptations and stay in awareness. The object self can wait this one time.

Now focus on the space between your awareness self and the object self that you are resisting in this moment. Where is the object self when you are in the state of pure awareness? Now enter the space and feel its presence. From the space, you can more clearly experience the separation of awareness self and object self. Observe yourself entering the object self and taking on its identity. Experience it as a willful act.

Repeat this experience for at least two weeks. As you become more skilled in moving from awareness to space and then to object identity, you will increase awareness of omni consciousness. As you move back and forth across the space, you will see that there is a choice of where to be. Where do you prefer to be? Can you see that your object self is just one possible object, that omni consciousness as subject can project many different objects, if it chooses? Can you affirm that you are not stuck in your object identity? Can you see that you have a home—and it is you?

# CHAPTER TEN

# Talking Back to Omni Consciousness

"I live on the planet earth. I have to get up every day and go to work." This is Kelly, a forty-two-year-old real estate broker, in a shaky marriage with two school-age children, questioning the need for a new dimension or shift in consciousness. She goes on to elaborate, "There are many responsibilities that I have to concentrate my energies on—family, money, relationships, and my future. I'm constantly fighting against time—there just doesn't seem to be enough time to do all the things I have to do. Why should I be interested in another dimension when my problems and demands are in this dimension that I exist in every day? Wouldn't it be enough to make peace with a workable balance where I am?"

Kelly is not alone. She speaks for legions of stressed-out people who are managing delicate balancing acts of demands on many fronts. Kelly wants relief from her pressure-cooker life and bristles at the suggestion that she consider a new way of looking at self and reality.

Kelly's challenge is just one of the themes that reverberate through the provocative questions that I've assembled from my presentations and seminars on omni consciousness. Some are the word-for-word questions that were posed. Others are montages that I put together to focus more pointedly and thoroughly on key issues. The questions give me an opportunity to expand on subjects that are in this book but beg further elaboration. At the same time, I didn't shy away from thorny questions that put me on the spot. Mea culpa. I don't always have complete or totally satisfying answers. More work needs to be done—the final word is not in. Hopefully others will join me in developing omni psychology.

The questions also serve another useful function. Because of the difficulties of holding on to omni consciousness, or even recognizing it (as the questions will reveal), it's necessary to approach it from many different angles. If you persist, eventually omni consciousness will take root and you will begin to develop a firm conviction that is real, is yours, and is you—not only your birthright but your birth identity.

At first, there is great resistance to "seeing." The barrier is the paradox we have hit up against throughout this book, that the mind must enlist the mind to get outside itself—in a sense, give itself up. The very process of questioning and seeking is embedded in the constricted thought process that comprises the prison of the self. But in sleuthing out omni consciousness, there's a difference. Unlike analysis and other psychological strategies that are committed to the stuck level, in seeking omni consciousness we grope, hoping to stumble onto a key that will enable a leap to another dimension—or at least a peek into it. This is by no means an exact process. Some are better than others in finding the key. Perhaps they are more evolved or possess greater spiritual intelligence. Most of us just have to stay the course and be ready to make the plunge into the void and then beyond. This may sound very mystical, but it's not. The problem of getting outside our familiar dimension to a different one that is right there within us is just more slippery than logic dictates. Perhaps as more attention is given to this problem and psychology applies its tools and methods, hopefully better or more efficient methods of locating omni consciousness may emerge. For the moment, though, we must walk the murky path with determination while never losing sight of the goal. Persistent questioning can help maintain attention and resolve.

As stated at the outset of this book, if there is a locus of consciousness called omni consciousness and it is the conflict-free, truly subjective creator of mind, why would anyone choose to remain a shadow of that light rather than the source? If gold is there for the picking right before your eyes—and free—why not reach for it? Just let go and be omni consciousness? Not so fast! The questions posed about omni consciousness speak to the obstacles.

First, let's return to the dialogue with Kelly about the planet earth and the value of pursuing a new dimension.

RESPONSE: There's a short answer and a long answer to your question. First the short answer. Yes, a new dimension—omni consciousness—could do a lot for you. If you were living in omni consciousness, perhaps you would have different priorities and would have organized your life in such a way that you wouldn't be in your current stressful situation. But given where you are at now, pursuing a new dimension will not magically extricate you from your pressure-cooker life. It's not a quick fix. It can be a lengthy process of recognizing and getting untangled from a lifetime that worked diligently on building up ego attachments that you now may want to break down.

The famous educator John Dewey said, "You have to begin where the student is at." You want immediate relief, as indeed you should. So that's where you have to begin. That's similar to what I say to people with intense emotional conflicts and psychological suffering: see a therapist and get a better grip on your emotional life, starting where you are before working intensively on leaping to another consciousness—that may be escapism. An "energy" therapist I met recently who does body work insists that her clients be simultaneously in psychotherapy to insure that they are not just expecting magic that they believe will enable them to leap over and not face their demons and everyday practical issues. Even with trying out meditation, it's useful to get professional supervision to provide knowledgeable guidance and to monitor the sincerity of motivation.

So, Kelly, what makes most sense for you now is to first find practical solutions that can make your life more manageable. For that, it's probably best for you to seek guidance from a therapist, counselor, financial advisor, and others to sort things out objectively. At the same time, you might want to explore omni consciousness, but not with a quick-fix expectation.

QUESTION (CONTINUED): I've been thinking about getting help. But still, what would a new dimension or omni consciousness eventually do for me?

RESPONSE: That's the long answer. What if I told you that you had another arm or leg that you were unaware of and that I could help you locate and learn to use? Or that you were only using a fraction of your brain and that I could show you how to use much more—or all of your brain? Would these possibilities have any appealing bearing on your existence? Would they taunt or tempt you to seek them? I think so. Yet another comprehensive dimension of consciousness is far more significant than those additions.

Also, keep in mind that the course of our development is the progressive unfolding of new dimensions. Each of these dimensions represents a monumental leap forward. For example, the newborn infant is largely limited to reflexes. While these reflexes provide the basis for survival (the infant can suck to take in nourishment, can cry to get needs met, etc.), they are only minimally adaptive. The infant is enormously dependent for survival. As the infant gains more and more skills and understanding of the world, the developing child becomes increasingly self-sufficient and widens his or her scope of activities. When symbolic thinking enters his or her repertoire, the infant is no longer tied to immediate sensory experiences but can now represent the world and carry it around in his or her mind. This again vastly widens the infant's scope of possibilities. Later, imagination and abstract thinking will enable the child to invent worlds, further expanding his or her horizons. So in principle, new dimensions are clearly pluses. Lower dimensions are always more rigid and inflexible compared with higher dimensions. For example, reflexes are a mere backdrop of the abstract thinker. But for the infant, reflexes are the main and only event—and they are rigid and inflexible until the ability to modify them is acquired.

Why would you choose a lower level rather than a higher one?

QUESTION (CONTINUED): I get the point, but that's very abstract. I still don't see how another dimension of higher consciousness is going to directly help me.

RESPONSE (CONTINUED): Let's look at the issue this way. We live in a three-dimensional world. Perhaps there are more dimensions, as physicists tell us, but most of us recognize and live in a three-dimensional world. We can perceive width, length, and height. What if you could only perceive two dimensions: length and width. How would that impact your existence? First, those who could perceive the third dimension, height, would really seem strange to you, maybe even mystical. They would be able to do things you couldn't. For you, protruding objects would appear flat, like dots on the surface. You would continuously bump into these objects since you could not see that they protrude up from the surface. You would marvel at three-dimensional people navigating effortlessly. Your inability to see the third dimension would limit your functioning and movements. You might confine yourself to a small geographical area and move out only cautiously. Your field of play and activities would be constricted.

Now envision someone arriving who tells you about the third dimension, and adds that you too have the ability to see it. He proposes to show you the path to retrieving *your* third dimension. And what is your response? "Why should I bother with that? I have my problems in this little, narrow area that I live in, which is all that I know. Why should I venture out of it for this other dimension that I only have a vague sense about (although I know that others have it) when my problems are here? Leave me alone." Or, "Just show me how to deal more effectively with my two-dimensional world—that's the one I have do deal with every day." Can you see the absurdity of that reaction?

QUESTION: I know what you say about personal problems makes sense and is true. But I just can't let go of my problems. For example, there's someone at work who always puts me down, often in subtle ways. When a compliment is there, the back of the hand is sure to follow. Sometimes that gets me in a bad mood for hours.

RESPONSE: It's good to start looking at the self in what appears to be small matters that may be a little less threatening to deal with. Ultimately, it doesn't matter where you start because recognizing the problem and breaking through to omni consciousness will shift the balance and make it easier and easier to lodge your self there. Sometimes we fight fiercely in small matters because on some level we know that if we crack or repudiate the ego, the game is over and the system won't work as smoothly. That's why I pointed out that sudden, huge success is often catastrophic. It denies the ego its springboard of needing, wanting, yearning, and mobilizing against the "not-me" world. When success is less drastic, we have time to weave new delusions or rationalizations to cancel out, minimize, or ignore success.

But let's get back to you and your hostile coworker. Now I won't get into the question of how much you might be distorting or contributing to the situation you describe. One conventional approach would examine the possibility that you may be instigating or inviting the response and then playing the helpless victim. Since there is so much happening in a relationship, we can always find elements that would support that view, or a number of other interpretations. But to go down that road is to join the problem and lock in at the level of the ego. That's what happens in most counseling, or when we think traditionally about our problems. People spend years on such issues and believe they are actually getting somewhere through their obsessive analysis.

What I want to stress is that the problem can't exist without a "me" that is hurt and angry. It doesn't matter whether you participated in setting up the situation so you could be hurt and angry to give life to your ego, or whether the other person solely and without provocation is on the attack. Without a "me" to self-reference the event, it can't register. And if there is clearly no "me" there to register the event, chances are the other person wouldn't do what he or she does. Egos are like sonar devices. They can zero in on exactly what they need—the ego knows how to press the right buttons to get responses that it feeds off. When the response isn't in their game plan, they move on.

The trick is, when you are in such a situation and sense yourself reacting, stop the reacting and become aware of omni consciousness. Say to yourself, "I am pure consciousness, I am omni consciousness. 'Me' is just one form of omni consciousness." If you firmly believe in omni consciousness, the "me" will lose some of its power to pull you into it. Try to take the posture of the observer looking at a play. "Hmm, isn't it interesting that she's trying to suck me into her dreamland?"

QUESTION (CONTINUED): But isn't that like denying who you are and playing another kind of pretend game or, worse, fooling yourself?

RESPONSE (CONTINUED): Not at all. You can only say that when you believe that "me" is a real entity and the only you. This is what is so difficult to grasp. You are omni consciousness, pure energy. "Me" is only a shadow, a particular transient manifestation of this energy. It is not you. The problem is knowing this but still not being willing to let go of the shadow. Out of frustration, on this very question the Indian sage Nisargadatta Maharaj held up a dish and said, "You know that this is not you."

I keep coming back to this example because it's so powerful if you grasp the insight. You firmly know you are not any object I might show you, like the cup I am now holding. The cup is not you. You don't have to repeat the negating mantra "I'm not the cup." Do you doubt that? Do we have to discuss it any further, or introduce proof? There is no confusion on this point. Yet "me" is also just an object, a conceptualization and contraction of consciousness based on certain experiences. It is not you any more than the cup is you. It is just more difficult to see because it bears some closer relationship to who you really are. It is an object created by consciousness that we have identified with and allowed to live us, and we are stuck and can't let go of it. But if you could see "me" for what it is, you wouldn't identify with it any more than you would identify with the cup. You would use it when it served you and would ignore it when it didn't.

QUESTION (CONTINUED): But isn't that denial?

RESPONSE (CONTINUED): As far as denial goes, I am not suggesting that you shouldn't experience "me." I'm not telling you to abandon or destroy it. Feel and experience "me" as much as you want. In fact, it's useful to experience "me" to the fullest so you can clearly know *who you are not in essence.* You see, we generally try to experience the "me" in all its forms and struggles throughout its history to find out who we are. We go back into our pasts to uncover every minute detail and potential trauma and influence. Sometimes we can't even remember the events. We rely on others—parents, siblings, friends—to supply the gaps and cherish every detail for the construction of a richer object that only exists conceptually, if it ever existed at all. In omni consciousness psychology, we experience the "me" to discover what you misidentified with as your totality. You may still love and cherish the object, use it to navigate the physical world, and be curious or bemused by it, but you know what it is. This is a totally different perspective on experience, personal narratives, and "our stories." Denial is not good because you can't disidentify from something you are protecting through denial. The disturbed person who denies all feelings or emotions and then commits some horrible crime does so because the feelings and emotions explode from the pressure-cooker effect. They build up autonomously to a peak and break through while the denial is maintained (e.g., "I'm not feeling angry—I've never been angry in my life"). So feel and experience everything, but know who you really are. And more importantly, make sure your action springs from that source, not an inert object.

QUESTION: I can't imagine how I would function if I were not a person as a personality, or the unique me that I have known since childhood.

RESPONSE: Everybody has to be somewhere. Unless you are planning to live in a monastery or cave, your consciousness has to be channeled into a particular form that can function in the everyday, ordinary world you live, work, and play in. The most convenient form is the experiential person that you are that you identify as "me." There's nothing wrong with that. What is limiting is not that you are a particular person or limited object, but that you totally identify with that object person and believe it is the whole of you. It's not that you as a person or personality is an illusion or nonexistent. It's just a temporary form of the manifestation of omni consciousness. There's nothing wrong with a personality. Even great sages have distinct personalities. Being in a body means having predispositions and unique characteristics. Passing through the stages of child development and your personal experiences compel you to develop a distinct "me" personality. It's not possible to be in the world without a personality. But for the sage, the personality is a style of functioning, not something directed and controlled by a conceptual ego core. Consciousness remains lodged in omni consciousness. It seems like your personality is the only possible you because you protect and keep it that way by not allowing anything else in; that makes it a self-fulfilling prophecy. As long as you believe it is the only you, you will protect it and give it primacy. See through the charade. When you deeply perceive the relationship of the object "me" to its source in consciousness, the limited identity is no longer a threat or a limitation. You are lodged in omni consciousness. Rather than defending the object and feeling trapped in it, you can use it to express omni consciousness. Therefore, no radical transformation of self is necessary. You don't have to *become*; you *are*. The locus of consciousness is in omni consciousness. The experiential self now becomes useful and a friend. It is the vehicle for omni consciousness to function in the relative, experiential world. But remember that you have a bigger home to return to. You are not stuck in experience; you create experience. You do not fight experience; you own it.

QUESTION: You say that identification with experience from the moment of birth is the culprit. But if those experiences are necessary for acquiring the skills the child will need, is there any way of avoiding identification? Would a different kind of child rearing make a difference? Let me put it this way: how should I raise my children to avoid the pitfalls of attachment?

RESPONSE: That's an excellent but difficult question—one that I've given a lot of thought to. Unfortunately, I don't have a good answer. We don't know enough about methods of child rearing that can counter the pull of experience without impeding or damaging the positive side of experience in childhood. For the child, developing cognitive and social skills are so important that I'm hesitant to flippantly dismiss them. The great sage Nisargadatta Maharaj, whose entire teaching focused on detaching from the personal self, was once asked if we should teach young children detachment. Much to my surprise Maharaj promptly replied, "No, that would destroy their ambition to grow." Unfortunately, Nisargadatta didn't elaborate further, and the questioner did not pursue the issue. We need to study and learn more about childhood and spiritual consciousness. At the same time, we should heed the sage's warning and proceed with caution. Interestingly, Nisargadatta was married and had children and grandchildren. I don't think that celibate monks meditating in caves are going to help us out on this issue. But Western psychology has the methods and tools to add an important dimension to spirituality—child development.

Thus far, psychology has placed so much emphasis on acquiring, exploring, changing, and adjusting to personal experience that little attention has been given to the value of rejecting, bypassing, and transcending personal experience to locate a higher self. The focus on infant and early childhood experiences in relation to levels of consciousness is new. Spiritual traditions have neglected childhood, treating it as one big, insignificant glob. Western psychology since the late nineteenth century has scrutinized the nuances of child development but has not integrated this knowledge with spirituality; psychology until recently was determined to distance itself from spirituality. And spiritual traditions have lacked psychologies of childhood and have not integrated Western findings. Perhaps in the present more friendly and receptive environment, the two approaches can join forces for a richer and deeper understanding of the evolution of consciousness.

One thing we can say is that children model themselves after their parents and other significant caretakers. Since almost everyone is immersed in the experiential self, there is no reason for the child to question or doubt the exclusive reality of the ego self. Children see people all around them in perpetual motion—seeking, acquiring, and trying to get somewhere. If parents and society presented an alternative model and different messages, it might make a big difference. This is something we will have to observe as more and more people move into omni consciousness and develop a spiritual perspective on life.

QUESTION: If a child is loved and shielded from intense disabling emotions like rage, wouldn't that be enough to lay the groundwork for omni consciousness to emerge? If omni consciousness is in everyone, then why wouldn't the happy, content child see it or act through it?

RESPONSE: You're right. It would seem that omni consciousness should shine through, but it doesn't. Remember what we just spoke about. The child from the moment of birth is a slave to the body and personal experiences. The child is compelled to attend to experiences and react to them in building a self-system based—it's a tactic of the separate speck self confronting the overwhelming "out there" world. There is a constant undercurrent of friction between self and world. Then there are all those messages from the people around the child constantly reinforcing a limited identity. "You are Johnny and you're afraid of the dark" or "you're good at math but you can't fix things." You might be told repeatedly, "Fight back, defend yourself." By the time we reach middle childhood, we have a fixed identity and all the acquired armor to defend it. Reactions are stored in memory, ready to explode at the least provocation. We are totally trapped in mind and can no longer see omni consciousness—the creator of mind.

While a loving childhood environment keeps delusion within a less intense orbit, you are still within the constricted world of the ego and mind. Only through the knowledge of who you really are can you begin to loosen the grip of mind and ego to uncover the layers and allow omni consciousness to shine through. As many of the Eastern philosophies say, you are already realized; you just don't know it. In Buddhism, for example, it is said that the goal is not to become a Buddha (you are already a Buddha), but to act like a Buddha. Similarly, you are already omni consciousness; the task is to act through omni consciousness.

QUESTION: Can you really be in a state of awareness that does not react to experiences? Isn't that a kind of zombified existence?

RESPONSE: Reacting to experience is always a past reaction retrieved from memory. In other words, we really don't let experiences happen or let them run to completion. If we did not react, we could then let the complete experience happen and see it for what it is. By reacting from memory, we are acting in a robotized fashion. You think you are responding appropriately and immediately because of your conscious presence. But your reaction is a past reaction, a conditioned reaction. That's what is robotized. By not reacting, you are aware here and now of the actual reality. That is fresh and real, not robotized. We have been so conditioned by experience that we have turned things topsy-turvy. If you would let an experience run to completion, you would often find that no reaction is necessary, and there are no residuals to be stored to mechanically bring on for the next related experiences.

Let's look at an example. Let's say you are anxious about your performance on the job. The moment the anxiety appears, you react. You have all kinds of thoughts that generate other thoughts that then invoke your whole defensive armor. "I'll lose my job. What will happen to me then?" and so forth. Eventually the anxiety subsides, and you believe it subsided because of your reaction—so the reaction pattern is strengthened. But if you just did your work and let the anxiety run its course and you observed but did not react, it would also end—and would leave no defensive memory patterns. Also, by observing and letting it happen, you will weaken it. The anxiety is strengthened and intensified by your very reactions. The reactions confirm the danger and threat. The defensive reactions trigger more anxiety because they say there is a great danger present. So reactions feed on themselves and then tend to be mechanically repeated. Now let's talk about zombies.

QUESTION (CONTINUED): How is that different from cognitive behavior therapy in which you work on changing your beliefs?

RESPONSE (CONTINUED): In shifting to omni consciousness, we are not challenging or changing anything; we just observe and know that we are not our experience and that nothing needs to be changed. There is no entity to change. It is the constant quest for change that distorts thinking and turns us away from omni consciousness. We are always looking for ourselves out there, or when time feels like it is running out, we to try to find ourselves in the past. The consciousness that is doing all this looking and seeking is here and now and needs no other support—certainly not imaginary supports in a nonexistent past or future.

QUESTION: Why do experiences have such a fierce hold on us? Why can't I just make a decision to let go?

RESPONSE: In my elaboration of psychological birth (chapter 4), I go to great lengths spelling out the incredibly persistent sensory and experiential conditioning that goes on starting at birth. We get seduced by the senses and have very little awareness of what is happening to us—so we have little say in the matter. Then the process of emotional bonding and attachment locks in the focus on "out there."

The conscious presence of observing these happenings gives the illusion that we are generating them and controlling them when, in fact, we are merely witnessing them. For example, as an infant you may have pleasurable experiences. You then take ownership of the experiences and the pleasure. Then when the pleasure is over or withdrawn, you miss what you have come to believe is yours and react. You need, want, and must have what is "yours." When you are having an unpleasant, undesirable, or even neutral experience (perhaps even a state of quiescence), the mind reminds you of the pleasure and you want that experience rather than the present experience. You are hooked and will forever be imprisoned and lived by your identifications as you reach into the past and project those memories into the future, bypassing the present.

What would happen if omni consciousness were brought into the picture? How would you respond differently to experiences? The self (as omni consciousness) would be seen apart from experience. Since there would be no sense of consciousness being enhanced or diminished by experiences, there would be no marriage of the two. There would be no emotional intensity as an aftermath of experience, nor would the self be whipped and controlled by experience. Omni consciousness would remain in charge.

Obviously, this awareness is not present in infancy. On the contrary, ordinary experience sucks the self into identification with experience, leading to ignorance about the genuine self. That's why I said that normal psychological development is a double-edged sword. For the rest of our lives, we live the legacy of this period's inability to know its true self. We then seek the self in the nonself of experience. But now you have the knowledge of omni consciousness. You can reclaim your true identity—or at least experience it to know there is another locus of consciousness that is on firmer ground. Will you do it, or will you continue to be lived by your experiences and the contraction of consciousness into a limited self?

Ultimately, the answer that makes sense to the question, "Why can't we let go?" is that we don't want to let go. Only by lodging in omni consciousness can the standoff charade end.

QUESTION: The principle of omni consciousness seems so simple and clear. Why is it so difficult to hold on to and live through?

RESPONSE: You're right. It does seem puzzling. Who wouldn't want to live in a higher state rather than a lower one? Who wouldn't want to be free and in charge of their mind and emotions, rather than being imprisoned and lived through them? It all comes back to the power of the ego. In tracing human psychological development from the moment of birth, I have attempted to show how we are flooded with experiences that weld us to the ego and experience. Very early on, when we identify the separate "me," we are made anxious by the "me against the world" feeling. The "me" then desperately seeks a concrete foundation to rest upon. It wants something to hold on to for what it perceives as its life-and-death struggle. For that quest we turn to mind and experience: mind for the thoughts that we believe represent real things that will give us the security we so desperately feel we need, and experience for the fulfillment of those thoughts and beliefs. We are not about to give up this delusional system when it is the only one we know or believe is necessary for our survival.

Many people sense the truth and reality of omni consciousness and would like to repudiate the conceptual ego self that is living them. But they are in the grips of fear. They will not let go. Many people fool themselves by believing in omni consciousness but actually are looking for peak experiences of a mystical or "spiritual" nature to bring back to their egos where they are still firmly lodged. They have not really let go to allow themselves to be planted in omni consciousness. The locus of consciousness is everything. To use the analogy of floating on water, there is no experience that can be brought to you that will convince you that if let go, you will float. You must give up the thrashing and fighting to experience floating. There is no substitute for making the leap. You must at some point take a chance. Letting go is even more difficult to accomplish for the clinging ego. The ego is very deceptive and can throw up smoke screens and tricks to believe it is letting go when, in fact, it is still in a life-and-death mode. That's why so many people keep shopping around for more and more transformational experiences. They get attached to one guru for a period of time and then move on looking for new and better experiences. The ego must keep in motion to maintain its sense of concrete reality. It needs to be busy and move on. Resting in one place will eventually expose its delusions. So in the quest for "higher consciousness," to move on means new gurus, new techniques, new revelations, and new affirmations that the self has been transcended. Actually very little has often taken place. Only new thoughts have been added to mind that simulate higher consciousness. It is all happening in the realm of thought and mind. Omni consciousness has not been revealed. So when you find yourself endlessly shopping for the peak experiences, take stock of what is happening. Who is shopping and who is going to benefit from the new experiences? Contemplate where your *locus of consciousness* is lodged. Remember omni consciousness just is. *I am* is the supreme principle.

QUESTION: If needing and wanting are unnecessary and part of the ego self, why would someone do anything in this omni consciousness state that you describe as beyond desire? What is the motivation to be alive in the state of omni consciousness?

RESPONSE: Consciousness is a vast energy system. It is the same energy that is running the ego, but in a narrow, constricted form. When this energy is freed from the ego, it is still energy and still moves toward expression. It can now navigate more freely to be synchronous with creative forces that are unencumbered by defense. The main function of the ego is to channel energy for defense and delusion—to make the ego feel secure and more than it is. Once liberated, that energy is free to do more, not less.

QUESTION: If you don't *need*, why would you have any relationships? Would omni consciousness people get married and have children?

RESPONSE: We are so used to seeing relationships in terms of needs that we can't imagine another force or motive behind relationships. It is doubtful that a relationship based on need is genuine or truly loving. When a relationship is driven by need, it is really saying, "I will love you and have this relationship as long as you satisfy my needs. When you don't, then I will be angry and will reject you or will control you in some fashion to get you to give me what I need." This is near-enemy love masquerading as genuine love. You read about extreme cases of "love" turning into hate, even murder, when love in the desired form isn't returned. A genuine loving relationship is not conditional or dependent. You *demand* nothing. The problem with relationships is that most are not genuine. At the least provocation or denial of a want or need, the anger explodes, causing conflict. When genuine, *selfless* feelings are behind a relationship, there is a natural tendency to relate or create children and give to children. It is all part of the natural state. Many people are in relationships or have children not because they want to give but because it's the only way they can get what they think they need—a comfortable home, regular safe sex, avoidance of loneliness, looking good in the business world, a family, and so forth. Sometimes when these needs fade, the relationships fall apart because there is nothing genuine beyond personal needs. So relationship and need are not part of an exclusive package. In fact, it is a rather fragile package. There is a better ground for relationships when you transcend personal needs.

QUESTION: Isn't it unreasonable to expect people to meditate or engage in other practices for long periods of time? I'm busy and have so much to do. Wouldn't it be better if I did something constructive?

RESPONSE: The thought of meditating or quieting the mind for thirty minutes or an hour a day seems quite abnormal. Statistically it surely is abnormal since relatively few do it. Longer periods would seem even more deviant from the norm. Yet statistics also say (Nielsen survey) that Americans watch on average more than four hours a day of television, adding up to about twenty-eight hours per week and two months of continuous television viewing per year. More alarming, over a seventy-seven-year life span—the average today in the United States—that translates into a whopping twelve years of nonstop boob tube watching.

Now that's truly strange, if not bizarre. Yet we think it's normal since so many are doing it. We even minimize and trivialize the behavior with the amusing name "couch potato." These couch potatoes are in a numbed trance state in which little of value is going on most of the time. How does television stack up against meditation? In contrast, sit in meditation and you can transcend mind and find a higher, liberating inner power that can energize and free you from suffering and conflict, bringing you in touch with reality for, perhaps, the first time in your life. That we call meditation strange and our daily mesmerized state normal is a serious problem. Reflect on that carefully and ask yourself, "Whose mind is it?" Am I living or being lived?

QUESTION: You say that needing and wanting are bad. Isn't that elitist? What about poor people who have nothing?

RESPONSE: When I talk about needing and wanting, I am not referring to the basic necessities of life. As I have repeatedly pointed out, needing and wanting are addictions that can be experienced as desperate and have little relationship to real needs that are useful and necessary. The very nature of the ego is needing and wanting since it is founded on a perception of deficit and the principle of becoming. Both deficit and the need to become will enslave you to needing and wanting while concealing the unceasing drivenness and insatiability of your quest. Just look at the corporate crimes of the super wealthy who have destroyed their lives driven by needing and wanting more.

QUESTION: How would the state of omni consciousness help someone who is being tortured by a totalitarian government, or someone who was a hostage, or in a concentration camp? Similarly, how would achieving this state of conflict-free contentment help with the massive problems that confront us on this planet like the destruction of the ozone layer and the rain forests, famine, civil wars, and the like?

RESPONSE: What you are really saying with your question is, "Shouldn't we be more socially minded and address the problems of the world rather than go within to find personal peace or enlightenment, which looks narcissistic and self-serving?" Addressing social problems and finding a higher self are not mutually exclusive. As a matter of fact, as one attains higher self-awareness and is freed from ego-self identification, there is greater sensitivity to world problems. This is a natural unfoldment because the higher self does not feel the separateness of the ego. There is a sense of at-one-ness with the world and other people. The same consciousness is seen in all so that race, ethnicity, and nationality are transcended. When all is one, your suffering is my suffering, making me and you more sensitive to each other. The isolated "me" in a perceived dog-eat-dog world is the barrier to seeing one world. The individual ego separates and alienates. Many of the global problems exist because there are so many individual egos centered on personal needs and strivings. Six billon separate "me's" do not easily translate into peace and harmony. Even the commonality of the belief in one God does not bring people of different religions to celebrate their similarities rather than superficial differences. If the God principle can't bring people together, what hope is there for achieving peace and harmony with six billion individual egos focused on "me-ness"?

When we cease to struggle for personal psychological survival, we are more sensitive to and at one with our surroundings. As more people live in omni consciousness, there will be a natural shift in the priorities of world problems. But don't hold your breath. Sages have been preaching spirituality and peace for many millennia. Divisiveness is so widespread and massive that world problems will not be resolved by a magic stroke. Yet true enlightenment, which erases differences between you and me, yours and mine, my beliefs and your beliefs, or your God and my God, is the only way that peace can ultimately be attained. It starts with individuals. As a critical mass comes into being, change will occur. Individuals can make a difference. The bigger question is, will this happen in time to save us from self-destruction?

QUESTION: You say that omni consciousness is whole and complete and that it is the ego that feels incomplete and therefore strives to become. You then add that becoming is a lifelong futile struggle. But if I don't become, how will I be anything or achieve anything in life?

RESPONSE: The problem with becoming is that it is based on the deficit feelings of the ego—"I am incomplete and need more." Because the deficit is a defining principle of the ego, "more" and becoming are never satisfying for long. Becoming is an endless drivenness. So even when people achieve, they can rarely remain peaceful and fulfilled by their success. The ego must move on to fill the bottomless pit. That terror of "what will happen to me if I don't become?" is the fuel that keeps the ego on its upward and onward course. In omni consciousness, one achieves as a natural expression of creative energy. But it is not fueled by "making it" or "getting somewhere." When achievement is not driven or self-conscious, it has a totally different quality. It may seem peculiar at first because we are so used to doing for the sake of something else, rather than just as an expression of our creative force. Achievement becomes very natural, although there may not be the pride of achieving or becoming.

QUESTION: What's wrong with having the best time possible, lots of fun and exciting things, or even lots of sex? Omni consciousness seems to be against having a great time. If feelings and emotions don't count, how can you have pleasure or a good time? What is life all about?

RESPONSE: It's not that emotions, feelings, and good times don't count or should be avoided. The point is that in the usual course of psychological development, we get identified with these experiences and become addicted to them. And it's not strictly the pleasure that's addictive; it's what the pleasure means to the ego. Addiction, while providing its ups when you get your fix, eventually leads to the depths on the other side. It also leaves you in a never-ending cycle of ups and downs. In omni consciousness, pleasurable experiences can be lived without the addiction and craving. Since they do not define the self, save the self, or transform the self, they do not leave addictive residues of craving. The pure self generally feels good and does not need intense experiences to affirm itself from that locus of consciousness—pleasure is natural and not addictive.

QUESTION: What do you mean, don't react to experiences and they will have no effect? How is that possible? If I am afraid or anxious, isn't a reaction normal and necessary? Wouldn't I be a zombie if I didn't react?

RESPONSE: We're back to the zombie. You very clearly state the problem. Not reacting is inconceivable and has gone unquestioned until I made the outrageous statement, "Don't react." It is not fear or anxiety that is the problem but the process that these set off. If we merely experience anxiety with no thought, interpretation, or reaction, it would run its brief course and not own, direct, or imprison us. Many of these anxieties and fears would instantly disappear if we did not extend and preserve their life through reaction. But how is it possible not to react? you say. Isn't that pathological, unfeeling, or zombielike? It would certainly seem so since everyone reacts. Statistically, not reacting (like meditating) would be abnormal. It is because we have no models of not reacting that we have not seriously considered it. Nor are we aware that there is a choice—it is possible not to react.

Let's take a closer look at an actual situation to see how reaction works to imprison us. The mother leaves the room and the three-year-old is afraid. The anxiety then sets off anger. "I want mommy so these feelings will go away." The anger intensifies the anxiety because they become mutually justifying and dependent. The greater the anxiety, the more justified the anger, and the greater the anger, the more justified the anxiety. Further reactions might generate other frightening ideas of abandonment and betrayal that in turn lead to other ideas of retaliation or defense. Once in motion, the reactions produce more reaction energized by the intensifying emotions. All of these reactions then become incorporated into a conceptual self-system that gets stored in memory. Whenever any of the components occur in the future, the reaction pattern is triggered. The child's initial reaction of fear when the mother left the room is already set off by stored memories of earlier reactions. Actually, very little happened. All of the happenings are in the reactions and the reactions to the reactions. Mommy leaves the room and the child is anxious. If there were no reaction to the anxiety but the awareness "I am anxious" with no interpretations or reactions, the feeling would dissipate and attention would turn elsewhere. That is not to say that it is not more pleasant to have mommy there—it surely feels warmer and cozier. But that's different from the reaction of anger, which generates a self structure around the incident to be replayed in the future. Of course the child can't do that. All pulls are toward reacting from the center of "me." Also, the child has no perspective for knowing that there is another center of consciousness.

Now let's look at the situation from the perspective of you as an adult. You are anxious about _____ (you fill in the blank). The anxiety produces your familiar chain of reactions. These reactions produce other reactions and emotions each playing off the other. Guiding all of this are thoughts and conclusions about the self. The whole package is stored in memory and retrieved each time you are anxious. It's not just that you are anxious. That would just run its course, or you would note it and move on to something else. But you get stuck with the anxiety. Everything comes to a halt as the self reaches into memory for the interpretations, conclusions, and reactions. So it is not anxiety that is the problem but thought and memory. Furthermore, all of your reactions are based on the past—concepts from the past reactions and interpretations that are stored and then retrieved. Both the past and the concepts are not real. They are dead and without substance. Reacting and being lived by the dead past to my mind is being zombified. If you would not react from memory and could transcend thought, awareness would be tuned in to the present moment and what is real. Out of this nonconceptual awareness, you could then act appropriately, freshly, and creatively. Reaction from thought and memory can only repeat the past.

QUESTION: Why is anger never justified? Life is frustrating and competitive. How can you get anything or protect your interests if you don't get angry? Won't people take advantage of you and step all over you if you aren't assertive and don't get angry?

RESPONSE: Is it really anger that gets you things? When we get angry, we are usually either defending ourselves or retaliating. It is strictly ego motivated, rarely goal oriented. It might temporarily make you feel better if you believe it's good for you—"I got that off my chest—I defended myself—I didn't let her get away with that." But anger may actually weaken you—you have allowed a person or event to hijack your feelings and impose negativity that may absorb you for days, months, years, or a lifetime in the belief that it has empowered you. But actually you've been taken. If it's results that you want, there are better ways than anger. Anger also pumps chemicals into your system that throw you off balance, compromise the immune system, distort reality, and may even destroy brain cells.

Let's say someone is cheating you. When you get angry, it is usually motivated by thoughts like "He thinks he can do that to me—does he think I'm stupid?" or "I'll show him I can't be pushed around." These and similar responses are the ego speaking; they have nothing to do with goals. If you focus on the goal, you will find that there are many courses of action you can take to get results without the debilitating introduction of anger.

QUESTION: How can you be in control of your thoughts and mind all the time? Isn't that like forcing the mind to do something unnatural? Isn't it interfering and controlling a natural process? Isn't that what obsessive-compulsive people do—constantly trying to control and contain themselves? Shouldn't a normal person just be able to flow naturally without being self-destructive? To you, all mind seems to be bad.

RESPONSE: We have had many glimpses into the "natural mind" and have seen that reverence for the word "natural" is not always warranted. Volcanoes, earthquakes, tsunamis, and hurricanes are also natural, but I doubt that you would want to be in the center of one of those natural phenomena. The "natural mind" is very much like these cataclysmic events in that *your* mind whips you around based on past conditioning, creating all kinds of devastations. Yet to take charge of this out-of-control mind is still widely perceived as unnatural or, worse, pathological. It is these very notions that will keep you imprisoned in a narrow dream world. It is the ego's tactic to keep you asleep while pretending to be in charge. But now you know the truth; it's your choice.

QUESTION: You say to be the witness to mind, and when you enter your personality or have to function in the relative world, be like an actor entering a role. Yet you also say that the prison of the self is like an actor trapped in a role. Isn't that a contradiction?

RESPONSE: The difference between believing that you are the role that you are playing versus taking the posturing of an actor is a crucial difference. When you are fully identified with your role, it is no longer a role; it is you and the only you that you know. Your center of existence is in that role. You try to grow, develop, and change from within the role rather than from the force that produced the role. It is the shadow seeking to be the subjective source of light. Taking the posturing of the actor places you in the consciousness that creates the roles. From that locus, you are not stuck. You can move in and out. You are in charge. It is your role and your shadow. It is you and it is not you (conservation of the self). You can be in a particular role but not limited by that role. You know you are the source and the power. You can relax and enjoy the role. You do not have to be liberated from it. You are liberated by the fact that your locus of consciousness is omni consciousness.

QUESTION: I always thought a strong ego is good. Yet you keep talking about letting go of the ego. What is wrong with a strong ego that is not all self-centered and that acts to get you a secure place in life? Frankly, I love my ego—it's what gets me what I want.

RESPONSE: It's true that modern psychology emphasizes a strong ego as the benchmark of mental health. "Ego strength" is one of the most important measures of adjustment in psychiatric and psychological evaluations. Early in my career as a psychologist, when I worked in child and adolescent psychiatry at Downstate Medical Center in New York City and as a school psychologist before that, all case conferences focused on ego strength as the end of the royal road to successful psychological adjustment and mental health. Generations of counselors and therapists are trained in this philosophy. Any wonder that it is so difficult to give up the ego?

Yet, within their own systems, they are not entirely wrong. If the alternative to ego strength is dissolution of the ego and a reversion to acting on primitive uncontrolled impulses (what Freud called the "id"), then indeed ego strength is better. But these professionals leave out another alternative: omni consciousness or the state of pure consciousness of which the ego is a manifestation.

Although the ego can adapt much better than primitive, impulsive functioning, it has some serious handicaps. The ego is in a constant state of stress because of its need to defend itself. Freud spelled this out with his graphic description of the relentless tug-of-war between the instant gratification striving of the id and the restraining pull of the superego. The ego's job, according to Freud, is to find a workable balance that sustains these opposing forces in dynamic tension while allowing a modicum of effective functioning in the world. At best, in this view, psychological balance is a stress-laden compromise that is in constant danger of upset.

Then add to this that in placing psychological existence on the same plane as physical existence, we seek the same security psychologically that has been programmed for physical existence. We take this concept we have projected mentally, called the self or "me," and now treat it like a real, physical entity. We want it to have concreteness and continuity like a physical entity. But it is only built on memory and is not real. To feed this illusion, we strive to keep the self constant—it must remain same self through time. This is a catch-22—we want to change and stay the same. How is that possible?

Then we take the autonomic nervous system responses intended for biological survival and apply them to this conceptual entity. This adds to our conflicts by making all of our psychological life a struggle to survive. Now all threats to this nonsubstantial, conceptual entity will be met with the same ferocious protection and defenses as the physical self under assault. The major difference here is that in the psychological realm, nothing is really happening. The assaults are interpretations and projections of the same mind that is now calling on the biological mechanisms for a life-and-death defense. When someone yells "Fire!" or you see someone coming at you with a knife, these are real dangers that threaten your existence. Defensive actions are appropriate. When I am anxious about a relationship ("she doesn't really love me") and go through all the usual maneuvers to protect the self, there are no real dangers, only the imagined ones that the mind produced through its interpretations and reactions from the past experiences stored in memory. While the rejection may be painful, it is not life threatening. This can all be seen in omni consciousness that transcends thought.

In omni consciousness, there is no concrete self, and therefore there is nothing to defend. This awareness, when applied to life situations, produces truly appropriate, fresh, new responses to situations without all the baggage from the past. This is true freedom. So yes, your ego may get you lots of things—but at a price. We want the ego more than the achievement. The same achievements can be attained without ego, but we are stuck on feeling that ego is the center of doing—"my" ego. The ego self is a prison. You have a choice. Where do you choose to be?

QUESTION: I accept a lot of what you are saying. Intellectually, it seems to make sense. But I still can't imagine just letting go of my ego. I can't feel that there is anything else there as solid as my ego for me to hold on to. I'm not even sure I really understand what it means not to have an ego or not to be me. It seems very free-floating and dreamlike.

RESPONSE: It would be nice if you could pay a visit to omni consciousness or get a three-dimensional guided tour so you could go back to your more familiar self and then decide where you want to live. But it doesn't work that way. Some people can grasp the notion of the narrowing of consciousness in the creation of an ego self. They can even sense that the ego is not real but conceptual. You may even suspect that the entire edifice of needs, emotions, and becoming is an artificial structure to support an illusory system that by its very nature cannot offer peace or contentment. You may also yearn for the true subjective state of consciousness—after all, an object cannot exist without a subject behind it. Fine, but now the problem: you must let go and surrender to consciousness to experience the state of omni consciousness. Like my example of learning to float on water, you can imagine what it is like, desire it, and observe others doing it. However, you can't experience it directly if you insist on fighting and thrashing furiously while also insisting that you really want to experience it—and then demand that the experience of floating be delivered to you while you are fighting and thrashing so you can't decide whether or not to give up the resistance and surrender.

A lifetime in the dream world of the ego has turned you into an addict. You can feel your dreams, but not reality. You understand but do not trust that there is a reality out there beyond the void. Surprisingly, if you stick to the path, you will find out that there really is no void and nothing to cross.

The terror of the void is the ultimate trick of the ego to hold on to its world. Like generating emotions to keep the ego in its mode, the terror of the void will keep omni consciousness at a safe, unreachable distance.

Few are willing to change. Most are willing to make modifications, but not real change. We confuse ideas with change: "I will get a new idea or new concept and that will change me." This is change within the world of the ego. It is changing one inert concept for another, one conceptual identity for another. But the change or liberation we are talking about is beyond thought and concepts. It is lodged in consciousness itself—omni consciousness.

QUESTION: You said that psychotherapy doesn't work very effectively because the therapist joins the problems and functions at the level of the problem. Are you then saying that psychotherapy and counseling are worthless?

RESPONSE: Psychotherapy and counseling are not at all worthless. Many people who seek help with their problems and anxieties do find relief in psychotherapy and counseling. Also, there are people in acute states of crisis who need guidance and the soothing support of a skilled therapist to stabilize them. In some cases, there are physical factors such as hormonal imbalances that can be helped with medication. Sometimes, though, medication is overused as a quick fix and a way of avoiding looking within or facing oneself. As for therapy and counseling, there are many gifted and sensitive therapists who are very effective in helping people. While the therapy may not be transformational, it can bring a person to his or her attainable set point level of adjustment. Not everybody is seeking, or is ready for, real transformation. Some people just want relief or help with an immediate crisis—dealing with a divorce, workplace issues, interpersonal conflicts, and a host of others. Those problems need to be initially addressed on their own level—that's what the patients are seeking and paying for. We live in two worlds—the material and the spiritual. Both are real. At the same time, a therapist schooled in Eastern traditions and aware of omni consciousness or a similar higher consciousness can work toward introducing that dimension at the right time—selecting the right time being an art form.

The belief and confidence in the therapist or counselor often allows people to let go of their tensions temporarily. The therapist becomes the ego's ally to fight the undesirable parts of the ego. There is relief in this shift of attention. However, there cannot be any real resolution or transformation since the work is all at the ego level, and it is the ego itself that is the problem. As I indicated in chapter 5, sometimes the calming effect of treatment is meditative, providing an opening for omni consciousness to enter awareness. This may have little to do with the particular school of therapy or analysis. It may have more to do with the charisma or personal power of the therapist and the person's readiness or willingness to "see." That may explain why all the therapies have instances of successful outcomes. Also, for many people, therapy and counseling may be a first step on a journey of self-discovery.

QUESTION: Is analysis of a problem or conflict ever useful or effective? Can't understanding help?

RESPONSE: Understanding in the sense of analysis means producing a thought to counteract the existing thought that is the problem. The "new" thought is merely a reaction to the old thought and thereby continues the conflict, or perhaps shifts it. Let's look at an example. Ellie was put down and criticized by her parents throughout childhood as far back as she can remember. As a result, Ellie has a low estimate of herself. In John Bradshaw's terms, she has a hurt child guiding her behavior. That hurt child, however, is a *thought*. Mind interpreted those childhood experiences and concluded, "I am an inadequate person." These interpretations were then stored in mind. Now in analysis we are going to do battle with this stored thought process by introducing challenging, soothing, or other thoughts. This very process is additional conflict. But the more important observation is that all of these thoughts, although experienced as different selves, are part of the same consciousness. The conflict cannot be resolved by producing conceptual, lifeless entities as new players in the drama of fragmented parts of consciousness fighting each other.

If the child had the capacity for not accepting delivery of those early messages, or not reaching conclusions from the experiences about the self, or not storing them as reference points for the self, the conflict wouldn't exist. But that's not how we are taught to think about ourselves. Psychological development takes a wrong turn when we personalize all experiences and relate them to the self. When consciousness is contracted into these interpretations and conclusions, the wholeness and independence of consciousness is lost. *What needs to be reclaimed is not the hurt child but consciousness itself.* In omni consciousness, the fragmentation dissolves, and experiences are seen for what they are—occurrences that have no bearing on the subjective self (omni consciousness). With this understanding, conflicts can be resolved. It is different from understanding "causes" in experience.

QUESTION: But don't you have to experience your problems to get rid of them? How do you know they are there otherwise?

RESPONSE: That's exactly the point. If they are not there, they are not problems. Holding on to them, giving them a location, and then looking for them maintains and gives them a home. Let's look at this another way. "I want to experience my problems in order not to experience them." That's in effect what you are saying. How can you resolve conflict in that manner? Every time you want to not experience your conflict, you have to experience it, which throws you right into the throes of conflict. What if you had a mechanism whereby you could disidentify from your experiences, that is, not feel them as part of your self (in fact, they aren't)? The self that you carry around is a conceptual entity based on your interpretation of experiences and your identification with them. If you saw those experiences happening to someone else, you wouldn't identify with them or use them to define yourself. So you say, how can I know that they are mine? Yes, but what has the "mine" done for you? You can't erase problems from memory. They are there. They really happened to you and were painful and hurtful. But going back to them restores them and puts you back in the vortex of pain and suffering. By dredging up the past, you re-create and validate it, saying, "Yes, that's me." Then you set out to defeat that "me"—that's a case of the self fighting the self. If you are not those experiences, why fight them? If you could let go of them, you would be free and the self would be whole and lodged in the vastness of consciousness. But you refuse to do it or try it because of your reverence for personal experience. Is that reverence justified? Will you gain or lose by giving it up? Would you give it up if you could? If your answer to the last question is no, then you will have to accept that you love your conflicts and really don't want to get beyond them. Getting beyond them means giving up your experience (by whatever means that is accomplished). There is no other way. You can't resolve conflicts by "working them out" but still being identified with them. And if you are not identified with them, you have let them go and they are no longer "your" problems.

QUESTION (CONTINUED): Are you saying it's futile to work out your problems?

RESPONSE: Yes, if "working out" means resolving them and making them disappear through analysis, dialogue, or some other form of figuring out their *cause* in experiences. All of that is what validates and keeps problems and conflict alive. Remember the person I described who awakens to find himself a character in a play. Then, believing he is that character and only that character, he feels limited and tries to get outside the character through the character. That's like working out your problems. The belief and acceptance of the reality of the character is the problem. The same is true for all of your psychological problems and conflicts.

Imagine the character in the play now being told that the experience was induced by a drug and that he was not that character, that it was a case of mistaken identity. He is then taken off the drug and soon realizes that he, indeed, is not the character in the play. Would he continue to work on the problems and conflicts of that character? Would you encourage him to do so? Not likely. If you were that person and realized that you were not that character, wouldn't you just drop it? I think you would want to concentrate your energies on the real you that you had just remembered. That doesn't mean that you do not have some feelings of attachment or connection to the character in the play—perhaps even affection for the character you played for a period of time. But it is not you. So why work anything out? Just let it go.

Similarly, the personality that you identify with is also a character in a play—the play of consciousness. But it's no small task to get outside your character. The forces from psychological birth onward drove you ever deeper into your mistaken identity. There were many "drugs" to keep you in this character: powerful emotions, needs, your belief in the character, the messages of those around you constantly injecting the character with reinforcements, and the powerful feeling that you needed this character and could only survive through it.

But now the drugs have been temporarily withdrawn and you have a glimpse of your true self, omni consciousness, the subjective source of consciousness and the projector of characters. Once you know omni consciousness, how can you get caught up in working out your mistaken identity? You can't effectively fight or work out what you own. You must disown it and let go. As long as you own the character, you are stuck. If you return to the play and the limited character, you will do it with omni consciousness. Where are the problems and conflicts now? Can they be taken seriously? Do they need to be "worked out"? You are home. Are you ready to embrace omni consciousness?

QUESTION: My suffering is real. I had a horrible childhood. There was much abuse—I won't go into the details. You say to drop your experience and that you are not your experience. But my experience is real: it really happened and it hurt me and continues to hurt. I don't want to just forget it. I want to honor it, remember it, soothe it, and heal it. How can you just dismiss it? That feels hurtful and rejecting.

RESPONSE: You're right. Your painful experiences really happened and they can't and shouldn't be dismissed. You should honor them and be aware of how they hijacked your sense of being and kept you riveted to those awful experiences because they were so overwhelming—especially for a child who feels helpless and without an ally. That's especially true if the parent is the abuser. It would be cruel and insensitive to dismiss or trivialize what happened to you. But the question for here and now is, can that suffering be ended? Do you want to end the suffering? And if so, how?

Omni psychology poses the question, Did those horrible experiences happen to you or are those experiences you? If they happened to you, then there is a you—a consciousness of self—prior to those experiences. In recognizing the separation of you and your experiences, you can begin to see how your experiences beat you into accepting them as the definition of you that set the template for self-condemnation and your self-concept as a helpless victim that must suffer forever. Since they are now experienced as an appendage— a part of you—you want to surgically remove them by remembering them, analyzing them, beating up on them, soothing them, and a host of other strategies that engage and resurrect them. But how can you surgically remove what you believe is a part of you without feeling that you are damaging yourself—fighting and cutting away a piece of yourself? It's a real bind. At the same time, you don't actually want to cut these pieces of your self away because, as painful as they are, you revere them as a part of yourself—because they were so painful and damaging. So you keep visiting them with the intention of "working out" the pain, but in fact what you do is constantly return to experience the pain and thereby repeatedly validate it. But if there is a whole, complete, wise you that preceded these experiences, from the vantage point of that consciousness—omni consciousness—you can witness what happened to you, experience the pain, and honor the pain but at the same time know that it is not you. When you know who you really are, the pull of the pain has a chance of receding—again, that does not mean dishonoring it, or that it's going to go away in a flash. But you do not have to be in the throes of suffering to recall and honor what happened to you. And you do not have to surrender your being to experiences that happened to you and are not the essence of your being. In honoring your history, you might even want to dedicate yourself to helping others who have suffered as you have—that would honor without remaining a victim.

QUESTION: I'm seventy-one years old and I consider myself a pretty lively and active person. I don't feel old, and I don't think I act old. Yet when I go into stores and other situations I often feel I'm being ignored. How can omni consciousness help me?

RESPONSE: Omni consciousness, unfortunately, won't help you change others who are prejudiced against older adults. We live in a very ageist society. Our youth-oriented society doesn't like old people. I think that deep down, older people are threats because they confront younger people with mortality and undermine their delusional ideas about the invulnerability of the ego. This is especially true for adults age forty-plus who are grappling with the crisis of aging. Young people like to distance themselves from the full impact of the aging process by treating the elderly as a different species rather than "me," a me separated by a few breaths of time.

At the epicenter of the aging crisis is the collapse of time. The ego needs time to get whole. Without time, the ego becomes devalued. Our evaluation of the worth of life is based on time. So it's our concept of time that accounts for much of the prejudice against older people—ignoring them, rejecting them, and making them invisible. They don't count because they don't have time. From the ego perspective, if you don't have time, your life is meaningless; you're nothing without time—you don't count—you can't become complete. That's why psychologists have seized on reminiscence to create meaning for the ego. In the ego conception, the past exists and will endure while the future will disappear.

It's curious that many indigenous cultures that we call primitive have a spiritualized view of existence including an expansive notion of time or timelessness. In spiritual cultures, time is not confined to material existence. Could that explain why older people are respected and have meaningful roles, often leadership positions, in indigenous cultures? I think so. Supporting this, I've noticed that in all of the spiritual groups that I have attended, there is less emphasis on age in social and other interactions. There is greater interest in the age of the soul—that is, how evolved a person is spiritually rather than their physical age. If we can transcend our limited notion of time, I think a lot of the ageism in our society will vanish. If we focus on the "now" moment, which is the only reality, all existence in the "now" is equal because nothing else counts but the "now." It is "else" that devalues existence in the here and now and supports ageism.

If you were more focused on the "now" and the timelessness of omni consciousness, I think you might be less reactive to the responses or views of others. You can't change other people; you can only change yourself—and change in this instance means shifting your locus of consciousness.

QUESTION: You make childhood sound like a tragedy. The child never recovers from separation and individuation and is always looking for something unreal to restore the earlier bliss. Where is the joy of childhood?

RESPONSE: It's not that there is no joy. Infants and children experience lots of joy because the slowly developing cognitive functions protect them from the full impact of the dark side of psychological birth. Eventually though, the full picture will be grasped, and that's when joy becomes much restricted and gets attached to unrealistic strivings. Joy is often also short lived because the ego doesn't permit the joy of pure existence. The delusions constantly get in the way. In fact, don't we often question the struggles throughout the life cycle and ask, what happened to the playfulness and joy of childhood? So I'm not the only one to pose that question. But I do offer an answer: the ego taking over.

But joy can be recaptured. Everyone right from the moment of psychological birth falls through the *trapdoor of experience*. That is when we experience ourselves as separate and the template for trouble ahead is set. The self from the moment of psychological birth wants experiences to provide the ultimate feeling of security remembered from the earlier symbiotic state. Experience, though, can't deliver. Only when we stop seeking salvation "out there" and turn back to pure consciousness can the enduring joy of the self be recaptured. Existence is joy, but we abandon it right from the start while thinking we are seeking it. We are chasing shadows that keep moving away from us as we try to get closer to them.

QUESTION: What do you mean when you say that we are attached to thoughts, not reality?

RESPONSE: In response to anxiety, fear, insecurity, and so forth we discover that thoughts can quiet us: "I will be strong, I will get even, I will find the right relationship that will bring me happiness, I will get, get, get to become secure and kill the fear and anxiety or deprivation." These thoughts are projected into the future when *in time* we will achieve the imagined, wished-for security. Desires and "more" therefore exist as thoughts. So we become attached to these thoughts because they make us feel good. They give us the feeling that we will be secure when they are achieved. But these thoughts are not real. The security that the thoughts represent are projected into an amorphous future. We feel good because we believe we will be secure when the thoughts become reality. However, the security that we seek does not exist in the physical world. The world is temporal, transient, and unstable, and we want something that is permanently secure to possess forever. That's why when we achieve our pleasures and goals we are ultimately disappointed. There is a feeling of loss or being cheated. We then miss our thoughts because they gave us better feelings and more hope than reality. We therefore reach back into thought for our security and the quest in the future. We are addicted to these illusory thoughts that we confuse with security. We will not let them go. Yet there can be no ultimate security in thoughts, and the secure reality we seek does not exist in the realm where we are looking for it. We are trapped in our own minds and the mind's illusory world of conceptualizations drawn from the past and projected into the future. It is a pure dream world of existence.

Only "I am" beyond time and space is the ultimate reality of existence. It is unconditioned and free. It needs and seeks nothing. It is all of consciousness. But it is not identified with experiences. Omni consciousness knows that all the contents of mind are passing images not to be taken seriously. The moment you are identified with passing images, you are trapped in illusion. Yet they are *your thoughts* in *your mind*, a reflection of *your consciousness*. You will try to escape from some of your thoughts ("I am afraid, I will attack, I will run, I will protect myself, I will collapse, I will demand"), but remember, you created them as a life-and-death defense and identified with them. Now another fragmented part of you will get rid of them? How? You must go to the "I-am-ness" of omni consciousness to see the play and the dream. When you wake from a dream, the dream simply does not exist or is not taken seriously. If you dreamed you were running from a dragon you would not organize your life around running from dragons. Yet we organize our lives around our waking dreams. "She rejected me and I'm anxious." Fear is my dragon and I will fight it (control people, depend on them, make demands, etc.) to quiet the dragon. Like a dream, nothing really happened. An event occurred that you took delivery of personally. You felt anxious and insecure and reacted with thought. Now you will react to the reaction and continue to live the dream. In "I am," you can see that nothing happened. There was an event and there was an experience. But *I am* and those things are not me. I can see the passing images and let them go. If you don't attach to them, they go away and consciousness remains as the eternal, infinite ground.

QUESTION: How can I experience the universal consciousness or connectedness that you talk about? I am conscious of myself and feel myself as a separate person. I don't reject other people and I feel a responsibility to the entire human race as a family, but the sense of oneness eludes me. It seems more like a poetic idea than a reality. I am me and you are you.

RESPONSE: Getting beyond self-consciousness is one of the most difficult challenges for the reason you express. We can feel ourselves but experience others apart from us. How can you and I be one? Yet, oneness or interconnectedness is not only a spiritual notion. Physicists tell us that everything in the universe is literally related. For example, it's been found that particles at hugely separate distances seem to communicate with each other instantaneously. But if they were communicating, because of their great distances that instantaneous communication would require speeds greater than the speed of light, which presumably is not possible according to physicists. One explanation is that the two entities that are communicating although distant are not really communicating but are parts of one organic entity—that what is perceived as particle A communicating with particle B is actually a singular event. It's like holding my hands as far apart as possible and snapping a finger on each hand at the same time. In one view, it would look like the fingers are communicating their snaps with no time lapse in the communication. But in fact the two snappings are one event of a single organism.

Another analogy for getting a handle on how self-consciousness impedes awareness of universal consciousness and interconnectedness is the example I like to use of the individual blood cell and self-consciousness (chapter 3). But you're right, it's an extremely difficult and challenging notion to hang on to. Speaking for myself and other spiritual seekers, it's experienced from time to time but slips away.

QUESTION: I believe in science. And why shouldn't I? Science has given us so much. It works and it has proofs. So why do I need spirituality for answers when spirituality is vague, cannot be seen, and demands faith rather than predictable proof?

RESPONSE: It's perfectly true that science has changed our world, giving us innovations that have made life easier and safer with advances in medicine and health that have extended life and enhanced the potential for healthy, long lives. It also has given us many conveniences. So it certainly works in those respects. Of course, it has also introduced great dangers and threats including the potential for destroying all life and even the planet. But for the moment we won't go into that. Let's stick to the contributions.

From the spiritual perspective, it's not whether science is good or bad, works or doesn't work. It shouldn't be a contest between spirituality and science with the aim of deciding on a victor. Both have a place and both have contributions and limitations when thought of as separate from each other.

But let's go back to the beginning of your question. I'm pleased that you opened with "I believe in science," because belief is very much the basis for most people embracing science—particularly since the emergence of the new science when relativity theory and quantum physics entered the picture. Speak to almost any normal human being—and by that I mean someone who is not a trained scientist—and you will find that they know very little factually or conceptually about science. Most accept science on faith—faith that science is the truth, and they trust (surrender to?) scientists to tell them the truth. These same people might be surprised to learn that scientists themselves are not sure of many things and rely on faith as well. I was amused at a report in the New York Times a few years ago about a vote taken at a high-level meeting of physicists working at the cutting edge of cosmology: Do you believe in dark energy—the hypothesized energy that no one has seen or measured that might explain why gravity is not pulling back the universe toward eventual collapse?

The dilemma is that we can't escape from belief—there are just too many unknowns. If we didn't function by belief, we would most likely be paralyzed to act on many fronts.

Also, many scientists will acknowledge that even if science could answer all the current unanswered questions, we would still be left with the nagging question of the beginning. Where did anything come from? Why does anything exist? And more puzzling, where did life come from and why is there life? How did the explosion of a small super-compressed mass (the big bang theory) that unleashed subatomic particles and a few elemental substances and waves banging into each other or interacting in random fashion form the vast, infinite universe? More baffling, how did the random actions of inorganic material produce globs of meat (organisms, animals, and so forth) that eventually started thinking and talking—a question posed by philosopher of science Colin McGinn? If there ever was a miracle, that story beats anything miraculous and supernatural cited in any bible or scriptures. Jesus walking on water is a vaudeville stunt compared to the big bang. Yet we call one natural and the other unnatural or supernatural. It could easily go the other way and make more sense.

QUESTION: But still, science deals with real things that you can see and touch, while spirituality and religion deal with all sorts of invisible things. And science deals with natural explanations and spirituality goes off into the supernatural.

RESPONSE: To answer the first part of your question, at one time that was true, or we believed that science and spirituality were separated by a great divide—and science had the "facts" to support that view. But now those facts have changed, or more accurately, we have a bigger, broader, more inclusive picture of reality provided by science itself. At the surface level, reality seems to consist of solid objects that are extended in space. But at the most fundamental subatomic level, particles making up those solid objects of our perception often alternate between waves and particles. Put another way, they fluctuate between existence and nonexistence. Science always assumed that the ultimate nature of reality was material so that studying the material level would lead to the material absolute substructure. But if the ultimate nature of reality is not material—if the material can morph into the nonmaterial and vice versa—then what does that do to the great divide, the separate realms of spirituality and materialism? If being and nonbeing, reality and what we used to call unreality (the nonmaterial) are all part of the same continuum moving in either direction, then spirituality can no longer be considered a pariah separate from science. At the same time, erasing the divide doesn't mean that all spiritual notions are valid, nor does it open the door for a laissez-faire spirituality—"whatever I believe is as valid as what you scientists say." Whether we are talking about the material world or the spiritual world, we must still adhere to rules of evidence and what makes sense. At the same time, there must be a respect for other ways of knowing, not only the traditional experimental methods for investigating the material world.

Science always placed great faith in observation, particularly consensual observation that has been the bedrock of scientific method. According to that view, if most people share the same observation—perception—then it is accepted as fact or real. But then Einstein came along with relativity theory and upset that fundamental principle of science when he proclaimed that all perception is relative to local conditions, particularly the speed that you are traveling at. At earth speed, we all are traveling at more or less the same rate, so we all for the most part see the same things and then call that reality or the truth. But at speeds approaching the speed of light, we would see those same phenomena differently. It's not that there would be anything wrong with our perception—it would be perfectly accurate—but the phenomenon would be different. For example, clocks slow down the faster you travel. Someone traveling in a spaceship for a year at a speed close to the speed of light, when returned to earth, would find that many years had passed on earth. If you were an identical twin and returned to earth, you would find your sibling had aged much more than you—more time had passed on earth at earth speed.

So what is the ultimate nature of reality? The short answer is we don't know based on observation. In fact, scientists now say that what we refer to as the infinite known universe represents only a small percentage of what actually exists—the rest is in a form totally unknown to scientists. So where does that leave science? If perception will not lead us to ultimate reality, what will? Is it possible that other ways of knowing can? It certainly humbles the arrogance that only science can lead to the truth. It can't—and scientific discoveries have made that point!

QUESTION: Can an intellectual understanding of omni consciousness get me there? Do I have to go through practices and work at it or can I just keep thinking about it, study it, explain it to myself, read your book, read other books, and go to talks about it?

RESPONSE: There is no one answer to that question. It may come fast or slow. Perhaps some have greater "spiritual intelligence" that makes the trip easier and quicker. For others it may require much inquiry and "work." I've met people who have had (or claim to have had) instant enlightenment experiences. Others, including myself, continue to work at it, slip back, but keep moving forward. Ultimately, how you do it, or how fast, doesn't really matter. The more crucial question is whether or not you grasp the presence of omni consciousness. If you do, can there be any question of what direction you must move in? Knowing that is enough!

# References

Adler, Alfred. *The Practice and Theory of Individual Psychology*. Paterson, N.J.: Littlefield, Adams, 1959.

Adyashanti. *The Impact of Awakening*. Los Gatos, Calif.: Open Gate, 2000.

Atchley, Robert. *Social Forces in Aging: An Introduction to Social Gerontology*. 6th ed. Belmont, Calif.: Wadsworth, 1991.

Baba, Sathya Sai. *A Recapitulation of Satya Sai Baba's Divine Teachings*. 1982.

Balsekar, Ramesh S. *Pointers from Nisargadatta Maharaj*. Durham, N.C.: Acorn Press.

Barbour, Julian. *The End of Time: The Next Revolution in Physics*. New York: Oxford University Press, 1999.

Beck, Aaron. *Cognitive Therapy and Emotional Disorders*. New York: International Universities Press, 1976.

Benson, Herbert. *The Relaxation Response*. New York: William Morrow, 1976.

Bowlby, John. *Attachment*. New York: Basic Books, 1969.

Bowlby, John. *Attachment and Loss*. New York: Basic Books, 1980.

Bradshaw, John. *Homecoming: Reclaiming Your Inner Child*. New York: Bantam, 1990.

Buddha, Shakyammuni. History of Spiritual Quest. www.sibv.org/bv10.htm www.accesstoinsight.org/ptf/buddha.html#bodhi

Buddha, Shakyamuni. *The Teachings of the Buddha*. Tokyo: Bukkyo Dendo Kyokai, 1984.

Chodron, Pema. Idiot Compassion. www.shambhala.org/teachers/pema/qa5.php

Chopra, Deepak. *Ageless Body, Timeless Mind*. New York: Harmony Books, 1993.

Clarke, J. J. *In Search of Jung*. London: Routledge, 1992.

Cohen, Andrew. *Embracing Heaven and Earth*. Mississauga, Ontario: Moksha, 2002.

Cumming, E., and W. E. Henry. *Growing Old: The Process of Disengagement*. New York: Basic Books, 1961.

deMasue, Lloyd, ed. *History of Childhood*. New York: Psychohistory Press, 1974.

Downs, Hugh. *Fifty to Forever*. Nashville, Tenn.: Thomas Nelson, 1994.

Dunn, Jean. *Consciousness and the Absolute: The Final Talks of Sri Nisargadatta Maharaj*. Durham, N.C.: Acorn Press, 1994.

Dunn, Jean. *Seeds of Consciousness: The Wisdom of Sri Nisargadatta Maharaj*. Durham, N.C.: Acorn Press, 1995.

Dychtwald, Kenneth. *Age Power: How the 21st Century Will Be Ruled by the New Old*. New York: Tarcher, 2000.

Dychtwald, Kenneth, and Joe Flower. *The Age Wave: How the Most Important Trend of Our Time Will Change Our Future*. New York: Bantam Dell, 1995.

Elizabeth, L. *Food for Thought: Daily Meditations for Overeaters*. New York: HarperCollins.

Ellis, Albert. *How to Stubbornly Refuse to Make Yourself Miserable About Anything: Yes Anything*. Secaucus, N.J.: Lyle Stuart, 1988.

Ellis, Albert, and Raymond Yeager. *Why Some Therapies Work: The Dangers of Transpersonal Psychology*. Buffalo, N.Y.: Prometheus Books, 1989.

Epstein, Mark. *Thoughts Without a Thinker*. New York: Basic Books, 1995.

Erikson, Erik H. *Childhood and Society*. New York: Norton, 1963.

Erikson, Erik H. *Identity and the Life Cycle*. New York: Norton, 1980.

Erikson, Erik H. *The Life Cycle Completed: A Review*. New York: Norton, 1982.

Erikson, Erik H., Joan M. Erikson, and Helen Q. Kivnick. *Vital Involvement in Old Age*. New York: Norton, 1986.

Ferraro, Kenneth F., ed. *Gerontology: Perspectives and Issues*. Springer, 1997.

Frankl, Victor E. *Man's Search for Meaning*. New York: Washington Square Press, 1964.

Freud, Sigmund. *Collected Papers*. New York: Basic Books, 1959.

Freud, Sigmund. *New Introductory Lectures on Psychoanalysis*. New York: Norton, 1965.

Friedman, Howard S., and Miriam W. Schustack. *Personality*. New York: Allyn and Bacon, 2003.

Fromm, Erich. *Escape from Freedom*. New York: Holt, Rinehart and Winston, 1941.

Fromm, Erich. *Psychoanalysis and Religion*. New Haven, Conn.: Yale University Press, 1967.

Fromm, Erich. *To Have or To Be?* New York: Harper and Row, 1976.

Fromm, Erich, D. T. Suzuki, and Richard De Martino. *Zen Buddhism and Psychoanalysis*.

Galileo, Galilei. *Dialogues Concerning Two New Sciences*. Ed. Stephen Hawking.

Gist, Richard. *Response to Disaster: Psychological, Community and Ecological Approaches*. New York: Taylor and Francis, 1999.

Goodman, David, ed. *Be As You Are: The Teachings of Sri Ramana Maharshi*. New York: Arkana / Penguin, 1985.

Greenspan, Stanley I. *The Development of the Ego*. Madison, Conn.: International Universities Press, 1989.

Gunaratana, Bante Henepola. *Mindfulness in Plain English.* Wisdom Publications, 2002.

Hampsch, John. *One-Minute Meditations for Busy People.* Ann Arbor, Mich.: Servant Press, 1996.

Hawking, Stephen. *A Brief History of Time.* New York: Bantam, 1990.

Hewlett, Sylvia. *Creating a Life: Professional Women and the Quest for Children.* New York: Miramax Books, 2002.

Hillman, James. *The Soul's Code.* New York: Random House, 1966.

*The Holy Bible: Old and New Testaments* (Authorized King James Version). Thomas Nelson.

Horney, Karen. *Neurosis and Human Growth: The Struggle Toward Self Realization.* New York: Norton, 1970.

Horney, Karen. *The Neurotic Personality of Our Times.* New York: Norton, 1937.

Jinananda. *The Middle Way: The Story of Buddhism* (CD). Naxos Audio Books.

Johnson, Colleen L., and Barbara M. Barer. *Life Beyond 85 Years.* New York: Springer, 1997.

Jung, C. G. *Modern Man in Search of a Soul.* New York: Harcourt Brace Jovanovich, 1933.

Kerouac, Jack. *The Dharma Bums.* New York: Viking Press, 1958.

Kinsey, Alfred. *Sexual Behavior in the Human Female.* Philadelphia: Saunders, 1953.

Kinsey, Alfred, Wardell B. Pomeroy, and Clyde E. Martin. *Sexual Behavior in the Human Male.* Philadelphia: Saunders, 1948.

Kornfield, Jack. "The Buddhist Path and Social Responsibility." *ReVision* 16, no. 2 (Fall 1993): 83–86.

Kornfield, Jack. *Meditation for Beginners: Six Guided Meditations.* Boulder, Colo.: Sounds True Publications, 2004.

Krishnamurti, J., and David Bohm. *The Ending of Time.* San Francisco: Harper and Row, 1985.

Krystal, Phyllis. *Sai Baba: The Ultimate Experience.* Newburyport, Mass.: Weiser, 1994.

Levinson, Daniel. *The Seasons of a Woman's Life.* New York: Knopf, 1996.

Levinson, Daniel. *The Seasons of a Man's Life.* New York: Ballantine, 1979.

Llewellyn, Vaughan-Lee. Rockport, Mass.: Element Books, 1990.

Maharaj, Nisargadatta. *The Experience of Nothingness: Sri Nisargadatta Maharaj's Talks on Realizing the Infinite.* San Diego: Blue Dove Press, 2001.

Maharaj, Nisargadatta. *I Am That.* Durham, N.C.: Acorn Press, 1973, 1978.

Mahler, Margaret S., Fred Pine, and Anni Bergman. *Psychological Birth of the Human Infant: Symbiosis and Individuation.* New York: Basic Books, 1975.

Marvick. "Nature vs. Naure: Patterns and Trends in 17th Century French Child Rearing." In *History of Childhood*, ed. Lloyd deMasue. New York: Psychohistory Press, 1974.

Marvick, Elizabeth Worth. *The Making of a King.* New Haven, Conn.: Yale University Press, 1986.

Maslow, Abraham. *Psychology of Science: A Reconnaissance.* Washington, D.C.: Regnery, 1969.

Maslow, Abraham, and Bela Mittlemann. *Principles of Abnormal Psychology.* New York: Harper and Brothers, 1941.

McGinn, Colin. *The Mysterious Flame: Conscious Minds in a Material World.* New York: Basic Books, 1999.

Mehta, Rohit. *J. Krishnamurti and the Nameless Experience.* New York: Samuel Weiser, 1973.

Menaker, Esther, and William Menaker. *Ego in Evolution.* New York: Grove Press, 1965.

Moody, Harry R. *The Five Stages of the Soul.* New York: Anchor Books, 1997.

Muktananda, Swami. *In the Company of a Siddha.* New York: Syda Foundation, 1978.

Muktananda, Swami. *Play of Consciousness.* New York: Syda Foundation, 1987.

Muktananda, Swami. *Satsang with Baba.* Genespuri, India, 1978.

Neugarten, Bernice, ed. *Midde Age and Aging: A Reader in Social Psychology.* Chicago: University of Chicago Press, 1968.

O'Leary, Brian. *The Second Coming of Science.*

Oneill, Michelle Leclaire. *Meditations for Pregnancy: 36 Weekly Practices for Bonding with Your Unborn Baby.* Kansas City, Mo.: Andrews McMeel, 2004.

Osbourne, Arthur. *Ramana Maharshi and the Path of Self-Knowledge.* Tiruvannamalai, India, 1997.

Ouspensky, P. D. *The Fourth Way.* New York: Vintage, 1971.

Papalia, Diane E., et al. *Adult Development and Aging.* New York: McGraw-Hill, 2002.

Peck, Robert. "Psychological Development in the Second Half of Life." In *Psychological Aspects of Aging,* ed. J. E. Anderson. Washington, D.C.: American Psychological Association, 1954.

Peck, Robert. "Psychological Developments in the Second Half of Life." In *Middle Age and Aging: A Reader in Social Psychology,* ed. B. L. Neugarten. Chicago: University of Chicago Press, 1968.

Perls, Thomas T., and Margery Hunter Silver. *Living to 100.* New York: Basic Books, 1999.

Prabhavananda, Swami, and Christopher Isherwood. *How to Know God: The Yoga Aphorisms of Pantanjali.* New York: Harper, 1953.

Rama, Swami. *How to Know God.* New York: New America Library, 1953.

Ram Dass. *Still Here.* New York: Riverhead Books, 2000.

Rimpoche, Sogyal. *The Tibetan Book of Living and Dying.* San Francisco: Harper San Francisco, 1992.

Rowe, John W., and Robert L. Kahn. New York: Random House, 1998.

Salzberg, Sharon, and Joseph Goldstein. *A Step by Step Course on How to Meditate.*

Sandweiss, Samuel H. *Sai Baba: The Holy Man and the Psychiatrist.* San Diego: Birth Day, 1975.

Sandweiss, Samuel H. *Spirit and the Mind.* San Diego: Birth Day, 1985.

Sandweiss, Samuel H. *With Love Man Is God.* San Diego: Birth Day, 2004.

Sapolsky, Robert. *Zebras Don't Get Ulcers*. New York: W. H. Freeman, 1994.

Satel, Sally L. "An Overabundance of Counseling." Op-ed, *New York Times*, April 23, 1999.

Schachter-Shalomi, Zalman. *From Aging to Saging*. New York: Warner Books, 1995.

Schaie, K. Warner, and Jon Hendrics, eds. *The Evolution of the Aging Self*. New York: Springer, 200.

Searle, John R. *Mind: A Brief Introduction*. New York: Oxford University Press, 2004.

Searle, John R. *The Philosophy of Mind*. Course Number 424—12 Lectures. The Teaching Company.

Seligman, Martin E. P. *Authentic Happiness*. New York: Free Press, 2002.

Skinner, B. F. *About Behaviorism*. New York: Knopf, 1974.

Skinner, B. F. *Beyond Freedom and Dignity*. New York: Knopf, 1971.

Slater, Lauren. "Repress Yourself." *New York Times*, February 23, 2003.

Smyer, Michael, ed. *Mental Health and Aging*. New York: Springer, 1993.

Starr, Bernard D., and Marcella Bakur Weiner. *The Starr-Weiner Report on Sex and Sexuality in the Mature Years*. New York: McGraw-Hill, 1982.

Stern, Daniel. *The Interpersonal World of the Infant: A View from Psychoanalysis and Developmental Psychology*. New York: Basic Books, 1985.

Stewart, Thomas. "How to Think With Your Gut." *Business 2.0*.

Sullivan, Harry Stack. *The Interpersonal Theory of Psychiatry*. New York: Norton, 1953.

Suzuki, Daisets Teitaro. *The Essentials of Zen Buddhism*. New York: Dutton, 1962.

Suzuki, Daisets Teitaro. *The Awakening of Zen*. Boston: Shambhala, 2000.

Suzuki, Shunryu. *Zen Mind, Beginners Mind*. Berkeley, Calif.: Shambhala, 1973.

Tillich, Paul. *The Courage to Be*. New Haven, Conn.: Yale University Press, 1952.

Tobin, Sheldon S. *Preservation of the Self in the Oldest Years*. New York: Springer, 1999.

Tornstam, Lars. *Gerotranscendence*. New York: Springer, 2005.

Tornstam, Lars. "Late-Life Transcendence: A New Developmental Perspective." In *Religion, Belief, and Spirituality in Late Life*, ed. Eugene L. Thomas and Susan A. Eisenhandler. New York: Springer, 1999.

Tulku, Tarthong. *Love of Knowledge*. Emoryville, Calif.: Dharma Publishing, 1987.

Tulku, Tarthong. *Time, Space, and Knowledge*. Emoryville, Calif.: Dharma Publishing.

Vasudeva, Sri. *In the Spirit You Are Free*. Trinidad: Blue Star, 1999.

Watson, John B. *Behaviorism*. New York: Norton, 1924.

Watson, John B. *Psychological Care of Infant and Child*. New York: Norton, 1928.

Watts, Alan. *Buddhism, the Religion of No Religion: The Edited Transcripts*. Boston: C. E. Tuttle, 1996.

Watts, Alan. *The Essential Alan Watts*. Berkeley, Calif.: Celestial Arts, 1977.

White, Marjorie T., and Marcella Bakur Weiner. *The Theory and Practice of Self Psychology*. New York: Burner / Mazel, 1987.

Winicott, D. W. "Transitional Objects and Transitional Phenomena." *International Journal of Psycho-Analysis* 34 (1953): 89–97.

Yogananda, Paramahansa. *Autobiography of a Yogi*. Los Angeles: Self-realization Fellowship.

# Index

Adler, Alfred: Freud *v.*, 99; Horney *v.*, 99; psychology of, 99

Adyashanti: on spiritual seekers, 201–2

affirmations: advice for, 207; books of, 207; ego *v.*, 205–7; ego *v.* omni consciousness and, 207–8; emotions and, 209; needs *v.* wants, 208–9; obstacles with, 205–7; omni consciousness and, 206–7; omni consciousness *v.* personal experience and, 210–11; seeking and, 214–15; self contentment and, 208; self-definition and, 212–13; struggle and, 213–14

aging: acceptance of death and, 147–48; baby boomers and, 134–35, 143–44; centenarians and, 148–49; childhood and, 125–26; combating, 134–35, 148–49; crisis of, 128–29, 136, 151; death and, 154–55; denial and, 154–55; depression and, 144–45; disengagement and, 138–39; ego and, 125–26, 128–30, 132–34, 137, 140–41, 145, 149; Erikson and, 139–41; Ethel and, 146–47; integrity

*v.* despair, 140; Katz and, 145–46; later years of, 129–30, 137–38; life expectancy and, 129, 137–38; menopause and, 135; omni consciousness and, 153, 155, 241–42; perception of, 133–34; reminiscence and life review in, 141–42; sex and, 126–27; spirituality and, 124, 128–29; spirituality *v.* Freud and, 136; stages of, 151–53; stereotypes of, 126–27, 138–39; success and, 149, 153–54; time and, 132–33

Atchley, Robert: on aging, 139

attachment behavior: ego and, 61–62; prison and, 63; psychological birth and, 61; security from, 61–62; spirituality *v.*, 62

Barbour, Julian: on time, 131

Barer, Barbara: on aging, 148

Beck, Aaron: cognitive therapy and, 101

becoming: delusions of, 168–70; ego and, 169, 172, 231; ego *v.* omni consciousness and, 208